Hikes, Walks and Rambles in Western Crete

A GUIDE

Angelos Assariotakis
Yannis Kornaros

This book was printed on FSC
(Forest Stewardship Council)
certified paper

Angelos Assariotakis, Yannis Kornaros
Hikes, Walks and Rambles in Western Crete

Translation: Aristos Grigoriadis
Editing: Chris Stokes
Layout: ScriptSoft
Correction: Elena Tsoukala
Illustrations: Antonis Papadis

© **2009, Kritiki Publishing SA**
75, Patission Str. 104 34 Athens, Greece
Tel.: (+30) 210 8211811, Fax: (+30) 210 8211026
Bookstore: 3 Guilfordou Str. 104 34 Athens, Greece
Tel.: (+30) 210 8211470
e-mail: biblia@kritiki.gr
www.kritiki.gr

ISBN: 978-960-218-644-2

About the authors

Angelos Assariotakis is a mountaineer since 1984, and has climbed a lot of mountains in Greece and abroad. He is a founding member of the Hellenic Rescue Team of Attica. He professionally organizes outdoor activities since 1995, and is an amateur photographer, having won two photography awards. He has published many articles on outdoor issues in different magazines.

Yannis Kornaros is an active mountaineer for the last 25 years. He is a member of EOS Acharnon, a mountaineering club, and has done hundreds of climbs and treks in Greece and abroad. He works as a leader/guide of foreign groups in the Greek mountains (Crete, Epirus, Pindus). He has published a lot of travel and mountaineering articles and trek descriptions in Greek magazines.

TABLE OF CONTENTS

Table of Contents

INTRODUCTION

If we were to let the numbers speak about Crete, they would tell us that it is the southernmost Greek island covering 8,259 km^2, that it has about 600,000 inhabitants, and a history of five thousand years. What the numbers are unable to tell us is the warmth felt by each and every traveler who visits the island, a warmth that is not only a consequence of the dazzling sunshine, but also of its friendly inhabitants, and even of its landscapes, sometimes wild and sometimes docile.

What is happening in Crete is strange. Even though over the past few years the island has become flooded with tourists, even though its small villages are slowly becoming deserted as their last inhabitants leave or die, there still is the feeling of hospitality in the air, the feeling of love…

Certainly much of Crete is almost sinking under the weight of its large tourist industry, but there are many places that resist the pressure. There are still villages where the people will smile at you, they will offer you something to eat or drink, or they will open their houses to you just because they like you. Even though thousands of miles of new roads have ripped through the mountains, roads financed by the E.U. (the same E.U. that gives large amounts of money to maintain the hiking trails), one can still find hundreds of spots of unique natural beauty.

Crete was and always will be an island of contrasts. It's as though the island's destiny, due to its position in the Aegean Sea, is to attract people with different interests and objectives. One thing is certain, the visitor who can feel its pulse, if only for a little while, will never forget the experience.

Even though the island is mainly mountainous, this fact is not always acknowledged, perhaps because the sea always seems to have more fans, but also because visitors cannot easily find information about Crete's mountains. It is this void that we hope to start filling. We want to be an inspiration for visitors who would like to go to these places, and so decided to write a book about what we have learnt about the island we love.

We know Crete as visitors, but also as residents. We have walked its trails. We have climbed the Madares Mountains as inquisitive hikers, but also as mountain guides. Certainly everything we saw we understood in our own terms. We saw beauty, but we also saw ugliness. We lived unforgettable moments, but we were also sometimes disappointed. Up to now, though, the balance is definitely weighing on the positive side.

Even if you don't want to hike on rough and difficult mountains to search for the different Crete, just leave the stylish resorts and the real Crete will find you. Of course, each and every one of us sees and understands things in their unique way....

In this guide we have tried to give a detailed description of some walks that we, as well as others, consider to be interesting. Fundamentally, we think that the beauty of a place lies in the trail which leads us to it and the effort we make to reach our destination.

For every walk we describe, we will give you as much useful information as possible. Most descriptions are accompanied by an appendix that has information less practical, but will provide insights that put the finishing touch to the Cretan mosaic.

The content has been gathered by travelling to these places over several years, and therefore some of the information may not be fully up-to-date, since new gravel roads appear all the time, shepherds put up new fences wherever they want to, and change is constant. Although we have tried hard to include all these changes, we apologize in advance, if you encounter any problems, and ask you to let us know about any difficulties you meet. You are welcome to contact us at *angelobike@yahoo.com* or at *ikornaros@hotmail.com*.

Finally, we hope you enjoy hiking, walking and rambling in the Cretan outdoors as much as we have done, experience many unforgettable moments, and come back to this island many times, always feeling at home.

• A map of Western Crete and a Summary
with details about the routes
(difficulty, duration, elevation change etc)
is available at pp. 214–219

• A key to maps' symbols is available at p. 221

CRETE – A QUICK GLANCE

The place

It is very difficult to describe an island like Crete in a few paragraphs. Covering 8,286 km², Crete is the largest Greek island and is also the fifth largest island in the Mediterranean Sea, following Sicily, Sardinia, Cyprus, and Corsica. It lies in the most southern part of Europe (the island of Gavdos is the southern extremity of Europe), at a latitude equivalent to Africa's northern shore (in fact, the Tunisian coast is more to the North than Crete).

All its big cities are on the northern coast, where the terrain is flatter. The four largest cities which act as administrative centres for the Prefectures are Chania, Rethymnon, Heraclion, and Agios Nikolaos. The southern side of the island is mostly steep and rugged, except at the eastern tip. Even today, there are places in the South that can only be accessed on foot or by boat. Western Crete, the area we describe in this book, has the most inaccessible sites.

The high mountains dominate the island and divide it into its four geographical regions that almost coincide with its four Prefectures. Cretans call this high, rocky, barren mountain range, the Madares. The island's three highest mountains are the Lefka Ori (White Mountains, 2,452 m) at the western side, Psiloritis or Ida (High Mountain, 2,456 m – Crete's highest mountain) in the middle, and Dikti or Lasithiotika (2,148 m) at the eastern part. But besides these, there are a lot of other mountains lower than 2,000 m, like Asterousia (1,231 m) which is translated as the "starry mountain", Kedros (1,777 m), Angathes (1,511 m), Thryptis (1,476 m), plus some more. Those mountains are framed by numerous high plateaus, some of them inhabited, others deserted. Of these the most renowned is the Omalos plateau at an altitude of roughly 1,100 m. on the Lefka Ori Mountains; the Nida plateau at 1,350 m. on Psiloritis Mountain; and the Lasithi plateau –the largest one– at an altitude of 850 m on the mountain of Dikti.

Due to the nature of its rocks (porous limestone) and to intense geological movements in the past, there are hundreds of gorges, large and small, usually dry although some of them have seasonal flows. The most famous is the Samaria Gorge, the largest in Europe, 18 km long and just 3m wide at its narrowest point. Smaller but equally beautiful are the gorges of Imbros, Asfendou, Kourtalitiko (or Prevelis), and Aradena among others.

Crete has no large rivers, only small seasonal ones that are usually dry in the summer. The biggest river in Crete is the Anapodiaris River that flows on the plain of Messara. For the same reasons, one can only find one lake in Crete, the Kournas Lake in the northern part of the Chania region.

The mountainous terrain leaves little space for plains, and the ones that do exist are small but very fertile. The largest is Messara in the southern part of the Heraclion Prefecture. It is actually the only flat region that can properly be called a plain, having a length of 35–40 km and a width of about 10 km.

If there is a potholers' heaven, Crete is probably it. There are more than 3,000 caves, most of them unexplored. Some of them were known in ancient times, such as the caves of Dikti and Idea, which were used for religious ceremonies connected with Zeus' birth and upbringing.

Geology

Crete's geological history is strongly connected with the tectonic plates of the wider Aegean Sea and with the collisions of the lithospheric plates. A large sea completely covered the area where Crete – and the whole of the Eastern Mediterranean Sea together with the southern parts of Europe and Asia – lies now.

About 23 million years ago, in the beginning of the Miocene period, the intense geological movements and the underwater plate collisions caused a rise of the sea bottom, thus forming – after thousands of years – a piece of dry land covering the whole area covered today be the Aegean and Libyan Sea and the Eastern Mediterranean Sea. This piece of dry land, called Aegis, connected Greece with Turkey, Peloponnese, and the islands of the Aegean Sea in the form of land "strips". In this way, all these different parts were connected, a fact that helped the spreading and cross breeding of plants, as well as the migration of animals (man had not appeared yet).

During the Miocene period, the area covered by Aegis increased and diminished many times. This was because the seas that divided the strips of dry land froze and melted frequently due to climate and temperature changes.

By the end of the Miocene period, about 10 million years ago, the sea started covering Aegis again; many creases and cracks started forming on the dry land's surface, and parts of land that would later become Crete (of course in a different shape than the one we know today) started to part from the mainland. These small pieces of land were islands that correspond with the Cretan mountains of today. The sea continued to rise, so more and more mountains ceased to exist; until, 8 million years ago, only three of them remained. During the Pliocene period, about 3 million years ago, parts of land rose while others sank, forming new creases and cracks that altered the shape of the island.

Finally, 1 million years ago, Crete assumed the shape and the form we know today. Geological phenomena did not stop completely though; changes and movements were just milder. Many climatic changes occurred, with frequently changing icy and dry periods, and many rises and falls of the sea level that, during the ice age, reached 300 m.

Subsequently, Crete's size increased and decreased accordingly. At the same time, the collision between the geological plate of Europe with the geological plate of Africa in the Eastern Mediterranean Sea – almost directly under the island of Crete – resulted in the rise of the European plate and the subduction of the African plate, causing intense tectonic action and earthquakes, and forming volcanoes in the neighboring area (at the islands of Santorini and Nisyros). This collision caused the rise of the western part of Crete and the subduction of the eastern part. Thus, from the Minoan times until today, that is in 4,000 years time, the western shore has risen about 8 m (evident if one studies the shape of the coastal rock formations), while the eastern shore has fallen 4 m lower (so if you have any long-term investment plans, buy land on the western shore). Crete's mountains continue to rise about 1 mm per year (thus in 2.5 million years the Lefka Ori Mountain will be Europe's highest mountain, so you can delay your summit attempt), while every year Crete moves 4 cm closer to Peloponnese (the speed is not satisfactory, so it might be wiser to take the boat to Gythio or Piraeus).

All those geological restructuring defined the nature of the rocks and minerals of Crete, almost all of them being sedimentary and metamorphic. Limestone prevails, in all its different forms and colors (depending on the oxides it contains), frequently mixed with dolomite (a rock containing calcium carbonate and magnesium), thus forming harder rocks. In smaller percentages, one can find silicates, sandstone on the coasts and in coastal caves – though heavily corroded by the sea and the winds, and –frequently near metamorphic limestone (calcite)– gneiss and gabbros. Of course, one can also find bauxite; in fact in some regions clay prevails.

The rock colors are defined by the different oxides that the rock contains in smaller or larger quantities; magnesium oxide gives a gray or almost black color, ferrous oxide gives pink or light red, copper oxide gives a green or blue-green color, sulphur oxide or even pure sulphur gives a yellow color, and so forth. In many places, the rocks – due to mechanical (wind or water) or chemical corrosion – have assumed strange shapes forming eerie sceneries (route to Gingilos, Amoutsera high plateau, Lefka Ori Mountain peaks, the cape near Chania). Crete is poor on minerals; it produces only marble, clay, and good quality building stones.

Climate

Crete's climate is heavily affected by the sea surrounding the island. Due to its many high mountains, the inland climate is a little more northern. Cretan weather generally is mild, warm and dry. Winters are not very cold with fairly high rainfall, but there are also many sunny days. Spring and autumn are pleasantly cool with short showers, mainly on the mountains. These are the best hiking seasons on Crete. Summers are hot, dry, and always sunny.

The northern regions are slightly cooler than the southern (especially in the summer), while the West gets more rain than the East. The southeastern parts of the Lasithi Prefecture are the hottest and sunniest parts of Greece, with a yearly average temperature of 25^0 C, an average rainfall of only 200 mm, and more than 3,000 hours of sunshine. In Chania, the annual rainfall reaches 700 mm (1,400 mm on Lefka Ori Mountain), whilst in Heraclion it is 500 mm.

In the plains, the average yearly temperature is 18^0 C. In the summer it sometimes reaches 40^0 C, while in the wintertime it drops a little below 10^0 C, but never below 0^0 C (except on the mountains). Intense sunshine makes summer days almost unbearable, but the nights are cool and pleasant, due to sea breezes.

The sea temperature is over 20^0 C almost all year long. The southern seas in summer reach 28^0 C, and even in deep winter they are still warm at $17–18^0$ C.

The prevailing winds are northerly and northeasterly. Every summer the seasonal Meltemia winds from the Northeast keep the high summer temperatures lower but also, due to their strength, they often create problems on the beaches, making big waves, blowing up the sand, and carrying away sun umbrellas and anything else they find in their way. Beware – on many occasions, ships are not even allowed to leave the harbour! In the spring and in autumn, a southerly wind usually blows from Africa, raising the temperature quite significantly, even at night.

Snowfall is very rare on the plains, but the high mountains get snow from the end of December until the end of March, and often even up until May in certain places. But, except for the highest peaks, conditions are good for hiking and walking even in the winter.

Plants and Trees

As soon as you reach the island, especially in the summertime, the last thing that will get your attention is vegetation. Its mountain slopes will seem bald and barren. Nevertheless, this seemingly barren landscape hides a totally different reality.

Did you know that Crete has 1,624 different higher plant species, of which 161 are indigenous, the same number of plants as in the UK, which is 15 times larger?

A short walk around the large markets of Chania and Heraclion will show you that Crete is a small botanical paradise. You will be surprised by the variety and the quantities of fruit and vegetables which are produced on the island. The surprise will be even bigger if you think that most Cretan vegetables never reach Cretan markets, because they are shipped directly to the rest of Greece and also to other countries.

If we add olive oil, herbs and aromatic plants, our image of Crete's plant wealth is enhanced, but still not complete. Have you, by any chance, heard that in Crete we grow four kinds of wild tulips, two of which are indigenous? The catalogue of Crete's flowers is really long.

25 million years ago, Crete was not an island. At that time, vast forests covered the area, and animals like dwarf hippos, elephants and deer grazed the grass that had just appeared. About 12 million years later, the Mediterranean sank and became a sea. Crete was cut off permanently from the land around it, and its plants were also cut off from their related species. Then came the

glaciers which made many species extinct in Europe, although some survived in Crete.

Until the appearance of man on the island, at around 9,000 B.C., few things changed in its vegetation. Men's need to survive drove them to clear the land to make fields and to cut trees to make firewood, while their domestic animals overgrazed land, thereby destroying the cypress and oak forests that existed there before. On the other hand, however, they imported new plant species such as the tulip, which after many years became part of the local flora.

On the high mountains and in the gorges, man did not intervene, at least until the 19th Century. As a result, the vegetation in the alpine zone and in some rugged places did not change at all for millions of years. This is the reason that one can find species like the beautiful indigenous flower Petromaroulo (rock lettuce) which has no relatives anywhere in the world. The steep gorge slopes became a shelter for many plants, because nothing could harm them there, not men nor animals nor even competing species.

An important factor for Cretan flora is the Cretan climate, itself based on the island's geographical position. As we mentioned, Crete lies further south than some places in Africa. The latitude of Palaiohora (a Cretan village) is 35°, whereas Tunis in Africa lies at 36°50'!

Therefore, it is natural that the climate is dry and that summer rainfalls are really rare. Furthermore, although in the limestone of the Cretan terrain there is plenty of subterranean water, there is not enough water on the surface. So, from very early in the summer, most plants have fruited and will remain dry over ground, but underground, their deep roots are ready to make them green again when the first rains fall.

Plants which typically grow in dry areas are the ones with fleecy, small, or hard leaves (sclerophyllous plants), i.e. plants with minimum loss of moisture. Many of them, for reasons unknown, produce essential oils, mainly during the summer months, releasing very pleasant scents. Also typical is the existence of thorns on many of the plants, as a means of defence against animals.

Forests

After 9,000 years of human presence, intensive logging, clearings, farming and overgrazing, the great forests that existed before the Neolithic period do not exist anymore. The pine and cypress forests prevailed over the oak and other trees. In their relatively poor undergrowth, one can often find different kinds of orchids. Other trees that make up the Cretan forests are varieties of sclerophyllous trees, like Maples, Kermes oaks, Holm oaks (Quercus Ilex, an evergreen oak), Locust trees, and, in some mountain slopes facing north, one can find the indigenous tree Abelitsia (Zelkova Abelicea).

Maquis

This term refers to shrubby areas across the Mediterranean. The tree that dominates the Cretan maquis vegetation is the Kermes oak (Quercus Coccifera). Maquis vegetation is essentially a degraded forest. The omnivorous goats, their numbers increased due to E.U. subsidies, eat everything that looks green. Therefore Kermes oaks never grow higher than 2 m and look like small green thorny balls. If one of them manages to grow a bit higher than a goat-reachable height, it becomes a proper tree. Near the creeks, one can also find Ligaria, the chastity tree, as well as Oleanders. In the maquis undergrowth, especially in Western Crete, you can find two exquisite orchids, Dactylorhiza Romana and Orchis Provincialis. (Wild orchids are widespread in early spring).

Phrygana and Garrigue

If maquis vegetation indicates a degraded forest, phrygana indicate a degraded maquis. Here you can find many plants the goats do not like, such as greenwood (Genista Acanthoclada), thorny burnet (Sarcopoterium Spinosum) and asphodelus (Asphodelus Aestivus), that grow and blossom during the winter, whereas in the summer look completely dry and dead. Here one can also find a plant which makes a very tasty salad, with the local name of stamnagathi (Cichorium Spinosum, a kind of chicory).

Alpine Zone

In the mountains of Crete, there are no forests higher than 1,500 – 1,700m. Above that, the most interesting species of Cretan flora grow because, as we mentioned earlier, the plants there are unique remnants from a previous era. At these altitudes you will find quite a few interesting indigenous species, such as the very beautiful small wildflower Anchusa Cespitosa, or the amazing "glory-of-the-snow" (Scilla Nana) that grows in the melting snow. Some of these highly indigenous species have only been observed in one and only spot!

Chasmophytes (crack-plants)

In the humid environment of the rock-cracks, away from competing species and protected from enemies, some species have survived millions of years, though they are extinct all over the rest of the world, such as the unique Petromaroulo (rock lettuce).

Cultivated Species

The olive tree has been cultivated since Minoan times, producing olive oil of the finest quality. During the last few years, olive tree cultivation has spread even in places where just a few years back there were only vines. Economies of scale, as well as international competition, favour single crop farming, and so many other species that grew in the fields along with the main crops are next to extinct, like the very rare Leontice Leontopetalum.

Today, thousands of tons of vegetables, like tomatoes, are produced in greenhouses in Messara and Ierapetra, which are something like a Cretan Eldorado.

The People and their Work

Nobody knows exactly how the first inhabitants arrived on this isolated island, but we can be sure that the need to find new, more fertile and safer locations led them to the Cretan land, which of course was not yet named Crete. Since then, many people have arrived on the island, but no one wanted to leave.

Although modern Cretans' occupations have changed, you will still find people proud of their ancestry, people who are friendly and hospitable, but still ready to defend their own code of honour if needed. The only problem is that the modern Cretans, especially the younger ones, having no enemies threatening their fatherland, have slightly misunderstood the concept of the Cretan manliness.

In the old days, for example, it was customary to offer stolen sheep at a wedding. Stealing a few sheep from the rich Venetian families of the island was certainly a manly deed. Today though, when there are no Venetians or Ottomans, the "manly" guys who make entire flocks of sheep disappear have significantly increased.

There are many guns in the hands of Cretan folk. As long as they are used only to practise on road signs they come across (you will see many such signs), it's not that bad. Things get worse though when they are used to shoot "balothies" (something like joy shootings) at weddings and other festivals, especially when the gunslinger has drunk a bit and his aim is not the best possible.

Even today, many of the locals are ready to open their homes to strangers and offer whatever they have. The unassuming joy of giving and the endless reasons for celebrations and other social events are typical of Cretans. They know how to live and enjoy their work, their family warmth, the joy of company, but they are also reconciled with sadness and death.

Family is the basic link in Cretan society. This hasn't changed for thousands of years. Cretan people still follow their ancestors' example, and keep having a lot of children. Not as many as in the old days, but they are the 2nd highest region in Greece in terms of population growth.

The only thing that can change these ancestral customs is tourism. The lucky ones who owned pieces of land in areas that were developed for tourism sold them, unexpectedly making a lot of money. Some of them used this money to invest in businesses in these areas to make even more money. When these shops opened, the Greek government was on a very long lunch break, so Crete, without any planning whatsoever, was filled with "Rooms-to-let" and "Happy Hour" bars. There was no room left for hospitality, honour, and all that jazz!

Fortunately, in the last few years, things have started changing. After a dramatic drop in tourism, people have started to understand that in order to take, you must also give. So the quality of service offered to tourists has started to improve in many places.

Crete, with three million tourists per year, is one of Greece's favourite destinations. Crete gets 25% of the total foreigner overnight stays of Greece, with 21 overnight stays per inhabitant. More than a quarter of its workforce is directly or indirectly occupied in the tourist industry. Even in the Rethymnon Prefecture, that used to have the lowest tourism, the proportion of farmers and stock-farmers relative to people directly involved in the tourist industry has radically changed. Now, 18% of the Prefecture's income comes from tourism. Let's just hope that the new generation of tourists will not destroy all the beautiful things that remain on the island.

WELFARE INDEXES	CRETE	GREEK AVERAGE	RANK IN GREECE (13 regions)
Per Capital GDP, 2001	11,600 €	11,900 €	6
Natural Population Growth	1.25	0.25	2
Unemployment Rate	6.7	10.5	12
Contribution to the Country's GDP	5.3%		7

Source: National Statistical Office

	AGRICULTURE	MANUFACTURING	MINING	GOODS PROCESSING	ENERGY	CONSTRUCTION	SERVICE	TOURISM
GDP percentage (1998)	12	10.4	0.1	2.9	2	5.1	57.6	19.4

Source: NSO

Agricultural production has increased, even though the number of farmers has decreased. What Cretans have done for thousands of years is to cultivate this difficult terrain and produce everything they needed and more. The main produce from the land has always been grapes and olives.

Today, the Arhanes, Peza, and Sitia regions produce excellent wines registered as having an "origin of superior quality". Large quantities of grapes are packed in the local co-operatives and exported directly to the markets of Europe. Wine varieties such as the Malvazia are really hard to find.

The olives that are cultivated in Crete are the "lianes" (thin) variety which produces the high quality virgin olive oil, as well as the "fat" olives that are mainly edible. Crete is responsible for 35% of the total Greek olive oil production, making the island the country's biggest olive oil producer. Olive oil is the key ingredient in Cretan cuisine, and, besides its great taste, it is also very healthy.

In the South you will see many greenhouses which are ugly, but responsible for a large proportion of the Cretan economy. Crete is also famous for its oranges and its potatoes.

Goats and sheep are the most common mammals on the island. Their population must currently be over 1.5 million, although no one knows for sure because stock-farmers sometimes register them twice to get more EU subsidy! There are very few properly organized large breeding farms. Sheep and goats graze free, a good thing on one hand because they produce very good quality milk, but this uncontrolled grazing has downgraded the environment to a large extent. If you get a chance to taste free-range goat, don't miss it. These goats are called fouriarika by the locals. Their shepherds cannot catch them; they have to shoot them like hunters!

Small local cheese dairies produce the very tasty "myzythra" cheese, the "anthotyro" cheese with low or no fat, and the very tasty "graviera".

All these cheeses blend perfectly with the very tasty honey produced on the island. Honey production, especially coniferous tree honey, has increased over the past years.

So this is an overview of Crete's agriculture. On an island of 600,000 inhabitants and 3,000,000 visitors, it is more than natural that most of its inhabitants work in the tourist industry.

PREFECTURES	Area in km^2	Population/ km^2	Population (1991 census) Total	Population (2001 census) Total	Change percentage 91–01 Total
CHANIA	2,379	62	133,774	14,863	10.8%
RETHYMNON	1,396	56	70,095	8,181	16.7%
LASITHI	1,828	42	7,179	7,503	6.5%
HERACLION	2,656	111	26,406	29,512	11.5%
CRETE'S TOTAL	8,259	73	54,054	60,159	11.3%
					Source: National Statistical Office

Cretan Mythology

To outline Crete's mythical heritage, we will focus on the most common versions, as recorded mostly by the Athenians, picking some figures whose existence marked the beginning of Cretan history.

Elements central to Crete's mythology were the tradition of star-worship and King Minos' centralized authority.

Myths coming from the East, like the ones about Phoenicia (a name indicating the red sun) and Sidon inspired Cretan people, who combined the foreign elements with local ones, forming new deities, like Asterios Zeus (asterios meaning "from the stars").

Cretan religious life was filled with rituals connected with the seasons: the rain, the dry periods, the harvest, the most famous of all being the "tavrokathapsia" (bull-leaping) feast.

At the same time, local heroes like Sarpedon and Idomeneas highlighted Cretan power, creating the necessary sense of security and justice which, in its turn, supported a central authority connecting the mythology of the island with that of the rest of Ancient Greece.

Let's try to unravel the mythical web, starting with the father of Gods!

Zeus was the only surviving child of Cronus and Rea. This was because an oracle had once warned Cronus, a Titan, that he would lose his power to the hands of one of his children. To exterminate all possible contenders, Cronus ate his children.

But Rea, wanting to save at least one of her children, gave Cronus a stone covered in nappies to eat and gave birth to Zeus in a cave on Dikti Mountain, called Dikteon Andron (meaning "cave of Dikti"). The child was then raised by Amalthea, a nymph who fed him goat's milk. In some versions, Amalthea was the goat itself. From then on, the horn of the goat who fed Zeus would be a symbol of abundance, known as "Amalthea's horn".

Zeus would also visit another important mountain, Idi. There, on Ideon Andron (cave of Idi), he would lay down laws to King Minos every 9 years, but let's not get carried away. Let's start at the beginning!

Europe was the daughter of Agenor and Tilephassa (the one who came from far away) from Phoenicia, whose name was to be tied to Crete and to Europe.

Zeus' eyes, always keen to spot a beautiful woman, stared at her while she was playing with her friends on the Phoenician coast. Wanting to lure her away, he transformed himself into a magnificent white bull smelling of saffron and approached her. She was dazzled by his grace, stopped playing and, since he looked harmless, climbed on his back as the tavrokathapsia athletes would do later.

The bull flew into the air, took the young woman with him to Gortys, made love to her, and produced three children who would become

Crete's main heroes, Minos, Rhodamanthys, and Sarpedon. He also gave her some very useful tools to protect both her and Crete, like the bronze giant Talos, a golden dog, and a spear that never missed its target!

Asterion became Europe's partner. He raised the three children as his own and had a reputation for being honest, as his adopted sons would also be! But when he died, his three heirs naturally fought for the throne.

Minos, in order to claim the kingdom, said that he could prove his divine ancestry. So he spread the word that all his wishes were met. He then asked his father Zeus to send him a white bull to sacrifice in his honour. **Poseidon**, ordered by the father of the Gods, sent a white bull rising up from the sea. The animal was very beautiful, with a moon adoring his great horns. In fact he was so beautiful that Minos could not sacrifice him, and thus broke his promise.

He could not have imagined his punishment. A little while later, his wife **Pasiphae** (meaning "she who is visible to all"), a woman of great ancestry, sister of **Circe** the witch and aunt of **Medea**, fell in love with the bull. Wanting to mate with him, she asked for the help of **Daedalus,** who at that time was living in Crete (in exile from Athens). Daedalus built a wooden cow with wheels and covered it with cow skin in order to trick the unsuspecting bull!

This mating was intolerable because it showed hubris towards the gods. As a result, the abominable Minotaur was born, half man, half bull. The irony is that his name means "Minos' bull". Daedalus, who had abetted this evil deed, was then asked by Minos to build a dark prison where the monster would have to spend his life. This is how the Labyrinth was built, a building with a visible entrance but with no visible exit. Whoever entered it could never get out.

So the years passed, and Minos had many legitimate and illegitimate children. He had four boys and four girls with Pasiphae. Among them was **Androgeus**, an exceptional athlete honoured many times. In fact he was so good that if he lived now, he would be an Olympic gold medalist. When he took part in a competition in Athens, along with all the medals, he won the envy of his Athenian competitors who set an ambush and killed him.

As punishment for this huge insult, Athens was forced to pay blood tax to Crete, so the Athenians each year had to send seven girls and seven boys to Crete in order to feed the Minotaur. This lasted for many years, until **Theseus**, son of **Aegeus**, King of Athens, decided to try and kill him to end the terrible obligation. He sailed to Crete with his comrades and reached Knossos, where he met one of Minos' daughters and sister of Androgeus, **Ariadne**.

Ariadne fell in love with Theseus and wanted to save him from the monster. She persuaded Daedalus, the builder of the Labyrinth, to help him find the exit and provide the know-how. It was a ball of string, one end of which Theseus tied to the entrance and unrolled as he walked. So, to find the exit, all he had to do was to follow it back. Love once more defeated death, but Ariadne's treason to her family forced her to leave her homeland. Following Theseus to Athens, she found herself in Naxos, where he abandoned her, probably afraid of Minos' wrath. Let's not forget that in ancient Greece, kidnapping a woman could lead to war (viz. Troy)!

It seems that Theseus was right to be afraid, if you consider that Crete was protected by **Talos**, the bronze giant who could run from one end of the island to the other. He had been Zeus' gift made by Hephaestus. Invincible, he threw rocks at the enemy ships that approached the coast and, with his long strides, could run round the island three times in a day.

But Medea, being a witch, knew where his only vulnerable point was, a bronze nail closing the vein behind his knee. She removed it with an arrow she shot from the Argonauts' ship that had brought her back from Colchis. She thus managed to kill him and remove Crete's best defence.

As an epilogue, we should mention Minos' two most famous brothers, **Rhodamanthys** and **Sarpedon**, who had of course been exiled after he took office.

Rhodamanthys, famed as an honest man, wandered for a time in the Aegean Sea and along the Ionian coast, and after his death became a judge of people's souls in Hades, where he finally met Minos again.

Sarpedon ended up in Miletus, where he reigned as King until his death, thus linking Crete once again with its neighbours through ties of blood!

History

The following sketch is not intended to cover or analyze each and every historical event. It is a simple summary of historical events to inform you of what happened in Crete in the distant and not-so-distant past.

We apologise in advance for any omissions.

Cretan Civilisation

✓ 33000–8000: Homo Sapiens makes the first stone tools.

✓ 7000–2800: **Neolithic Age** – Man produces his food ⇨ tames animals ⇨ settles permanently ⇨ starts cultivating land and making utensils.

✓ 6000: 1st documented Cretan settlements (Knossos, Phaistos, Katsampas, Agia Fotia).

✓ 3800: Neolithic settlements in other places in Crete.

✓ 3500: **Late Neolithic Age** – Extensive population spread all over Crete. Total population 1,000–2,000.

✓ 2800: **Bronze Age**.

✓ 2000: **Early Palatial Age** – Building of the first palaces in Knossos, Phaistos, Zakros and Malia. Common elements: Sea access, no fortifications, Minoans exercise control over the plains, and meet agricultural and commercial needs.
Organised writing system: Linear A as an evolution of hieroglyphs. Crete-Cyclades relations.

✓ 2000: Piracy spreads all over the Mediterranean Sea. Use of the pottery wheel.

✓ 1700: **Late Palatial Age** – Palace rebuilding starts (this time with wall-paintings) ⇨ the most brilliant phase – age of great Minoan brilliance ⇨ Pax Minoica. Pottery flourishes ("floral" and "sea" style).

✓ 1700: Phaistos disc.

✓ 1450: Linear B writing. The first confirmed Greek writing! This writing is used in the Minoan palaces. Final palace destruction in Malia, Zakros and Phaistos.

Achaeans conquer Crete.

✓ 1380: Complete destruction of Knossos Palace.

✓ 1200: Dorians appear in Crete. The Palace institution is replaced by the City State. Minoans take refuge on the mountain tops.

✓ 1100–900: **Late Minoan Age** — Settlements on mountainous areas like Karfi, Lasithi, Vrokastro and in other places. Ancient sources report the existence of 150 towns and cities in Crete. According to Homer, (Heliad, B649) the cities were 100. In Odyssey (T173), the poet says there were 90.

Social facts:

The system of government was aristocratic, while the **parliament,** the **lords** (nobility) and the **assembly** (all the citizens) had the power. The social classes were formed after the arrival of the Dorians, according to the resistance which the citizens had showed against the invaders. The classes were the **Perfects** (including horsemen) and the **Subordinates**. The Subordinates were divided into **Freepeople**, **Bondsmen** and **Slaves**. The economy was based on livestock breeding and not on commercial activities, due to the self-sufficiency of the island. The laws resembled those of Sparta, and it is said that Lycurgus used elements of Gortyns' Laws.

✓ **Beginning of 5th Century:** Gortyn' Laws. It is the most ancient Greek, therefore the first European, written state and family law.

Crete does not take part in the Persian Wars, mostly due to its geographical position, and also because of internal warfare.

✓ 330: **Hellenistic Age** — Destructive city-v-city wars and wider alliances with the Greek kingdoms in the East and Egypt. Cretans become famous mercenaries.

✓ 69: The last area in Greece to be conquered by the Romans after three years of fighting. This occupation will last until 395 A.D., when Crete will become a province of the Byzantine Empire. Gortyn becomes the capital of the island (See Roman ruins in the area).

✓ 1 A.D. Christian dating begins, designed by a monk named Dionysious of the Rocks.

✓ 59: Paul the Apostle and Titus organise the church.

✓ 248–251: Christians are persecuted. The martyrdom of the "Ten Saints".

✓ 395: Crete becomes part of the Eastern Roman Empire, with a local commander appointed from Constantinople.

✓ 623: Slavs raid the island.

✓ 828–961: Arab occupation.

✓ 910: The Byzantines try to recapture the island.

✓ 961: N. Fokas arrives at Handakas with 3,300 ships, and conquers it, eliminating the Arab population. Because the population is now very small, he orders some of his troops to settle there, founding villages that have the names of the first settlers up to this day.

✓ 1204: The Venetians buy Crete from Bonifacius Momferaticus to exploit it as a commercial trading station.

✓ 1210: Venetians and Genovese fight for dominion. Construction of the first forts.

✓ 1283–1299: Alexander Kallergis' revolution ⇒ land allotment ⇒ improvement in the economic position of the Cretan people.

✓ 1363–1364: Cretans are driven away from the fertile plateaus of Lasithi, Omalos, and Askifou.

✓ 1415: Visit by Buondelmonte the Traveller ⇨ archeological interest.

✓ 1451: Birth of Dominicus Theotocopoulos (El Greco) in Fodele, near Heraklion. Foundation of University.

✓ 1628: Famous buildings appear, like the Loggia in Heraclion and the Morosini's fountain, but the end of Venetian occupation is near, as the Ottomans expand towards the Mediterranean Sea.

✓ 1645: Ottoman occupation of Chania.

✓ 1648: 21 year-long siege of Handakas! Morosini versus the Great Vezir Koprulu.

✓ 1669: Peaceful surrender of the city.

✓ 1770: Daskaloyiannis' rebellion in Sfakia (with British and Russian aid) suppressed. Crete is sold to Mohammed Ali of Egypt as compensation for the Egyptian help to the Ottomans.

✓ 1840: Return to Ottoman rule that leads to many bloody rebellions.

✓ 1866: Arkadi Monastery holocaust.

✓ 1878: Halepa Treaty gives administration to Greeks. Greek becomes the official language.

✓ 1885–1957: N. Kazantzakis.

✓ 1896–1897: End of the Greek-Ottoman War. The island is not united with Greece, but remains autonomous (with English-Ottoman supervision).

✓ 1898: Prince George II. As Crete's administrator, Eleftherios Venizelos, in a political dispute with Prince George, wants union with Greece.

✓ 1913: Crete and Macedonia unites with Greece, as a result of the Balkan Wars.

✓ 1941–1945: Nazi occupation. Continuous resistance, destruction of villages (such as Anogia and Kandanos) and mass executions.

PRACTICAL INFORMATION

Getting to Crete

There are two ways to get to Crete, flying and sailing, and it has been that way for thousands of years. Let's not forget that the first flight to Crete was undertaken by Daedalus and Icarus, although the latter was not very good at landing!

You can fly to Crete from Athens, Thessaloniki and Rhodes, as well as from many European capitals using charter flights. Olympic Airlines and Aegean Airlines have several daily flights to Crete. Charter flights usually start in March, peak during the summer months, and stop near the end of October.

The island's international airports are at Heraclion (Halicarnassus) and Chania (Akrotiri). Although they are well organised airports, you will need some patience at peak times, when a large number of charter flights come and go, and the airports are full of people.

The ferry is your other solution to get to Crete. The island's four major cities, Chania, Rethymnon, Heraclion and Agios Nikolaos offer daily ferry services to Piraeus in the summertime. Ferries leave Piraeus every evening during the summer, usually at 18:00 for Agios Nikolaos, 20:00 for Rethymnon and Chania, and at 21:00 for Heraclion. There is also a morning service to Heraclion and Chania in the high season. The shipping companies that service Crete are ANEK, Minoan Lines and Blue Star Ferries.

The port for Chania is not in the city but at Souda Bay, a 20 to 30 minute bus ride to the centre. In the other cities, the ports are near the centre.

Finally, we should add that there is another ferry service connecting the city of Gythio in the Peloponnese to Castelli Kissamou.

Moving Around

Mass transit in Crete is the same as in the rest of Greece, with the familiar KTEL coaches. In the island's tourist spots, the coaches are luxurious and offer frequent services, although they are more expensive than in other places of Greece.

In small off-of-the-beaten-track villages though, things are not so easy. Usually there is an early morning bus and, in the best of cases, an early afternoon one. If you are really lucky, you might catch one of the KTEL coaches which are used as school buses, that is if schools are open.

Another problem with KTEL coaches is that most of the people working on them do not seem very happy with their jobs. This becomes obvious the minute you ask them something ("C'mon guys, give a smile and show some courtesy...").

If you carry fragile goods, don't hand them over to be put in the luggage compartment. Take them inside with you in a small bag, because luggage is piled high and gets very dirty.

You can also travel by taxi. Normally, taxi fares are determined by kilometers travelled and by minutes waited, but here, as well as everywhere else in the world, there are people who want to get rich quickly and set their own prices!

Usually at the airports you will find lists of taxi prices for the most popular routes. Nevertheless, for a long trip, negotiate the price beforehand.

Another way to get around is to rent a car, motorcycle or moped. In all touristic areas, you can find any car you want. Except for high summer, prices are very competitive. However, in winter, it might be more difficult to find a cheap car because most cars are withdrawn, and only big companies with high prices remain in business.

Here we must issue a warning — if you decide to drive in Crete in your own car or a rented one, you have to be careful of several things. First, the locals with their brand-new 4X4 trucks have always priority! Second, the roads, apart from the main road that runs along the north coast, are really difficult with a lot of tight bends and poor surfaces. Third, in the summertime, near touristic spots, you will come across a lot of tourists with rented motorbikes who do not have the slightest idea how to ride them.

Choosing Accomodation

On an island that is so hospitable and has a tourist infrastructure, the only thing you don't need to worry about is where to sleep. Even in the high season, you will be able to find a bed. If you are lucky, you might be offered one by some local guy in his own home!

Even though traditional Cretan hospitality has not entirely disappeared, it is better not to rely on it completely. Hotels, large and small, rental rooms and campsites are almost everywhere. What would these people do if all visitors were offered free beds?

Luxury hotels are very expensive. Even 4 and 3 star hotels are not exactly cheap, and are mostly booked by the large tour operators. 2 star hotels in big cities are moderately priced, and cheaper in the villages. A typical price for such a room in high season is around €25–€40 per person per night including breakfast.

Rooms-to-let are the next cheapest solution. Their prices vary according to area and season. It could be around €15–€25 pppn. Of course, prices are lower in the springtime and after mid-September.

If you want to find a room and nobody has already approached you the moment you got off the bus, just ask at the cafe where you take your coffee. They will usually make more than one suggestion. Ask for the price before actually going there to check it out. If it is not high season, they will certainly lower it.

Although Cretans have the best of intentions, it is possible that some rooms will not cover the necessary conditions for rented rooms. If they have an EOT (the Greek National Tourist Organisation) badge, as they are obliged to, they must at least offer clean sheets, blankets, soap, towels and hot water, and they must clean the rooms daily. This is what is legally required of the owners, and not a favour to you.

In some of the descriptions of walks in this guide, we mention rooms that we have used and regard as more than adequate. Another reason we have picked them is that they are owned by friendly families. At the end of the day, you will certainly find a room to stay in. Just don't expect jacuzzis, cable TV, and all that jazz.

There is not a large number of campsites in Crete, and most of them are near big cities. In the places that interest walkers there aren't any, and free camping is, theoretically, illegal. But, as you might have to spend a night in your tent, the locals will not cause any trouble, as long as you are not on a really busy beach in a touristic area and you have obtained permission beforehand. It goes without saying that you have to take all your rubbish with you and dispose of it in the next small town, because in villages there is no refuse disposal agency. Pay attention to the site you use as a toilet. Don't use a place near a spring or in a cave, and take away any used toilet paper with your rubbish. Also, avoid lighting fires, especially in the summertime when the dry surroundings combined with sudden strong winds can turn a small fire into an uncontrollable forest inferno in no time at all.

Finally, on Lefka Ori and Psiloritis, there are mountain huts that make climbing these mountains easier. However, only the Omalos hut is always open and can cater for individual walkers. For the other huts you must contact the Mountaineering Club of Chania or of Rethymnon, but only if you are in an organised group. The Kallergis' hut in Omalos (28210 54560) is open from early spring until November, offering food and beds, not only to hikers since one can reach the hut by car on a gravel road. The hut's warden is an Austrian, Josef (Sifis to the locals), who speaks German, English, a bit of Greek with a heavy Cretan accent, and French.

Eating – Cretan Cuisine

The Cretan diet is considered one of the healthiest in the world, but today it is not what it used to be. One could say that part of a people's culture is what they eat and how they eat it. Food for the Cretan was a ritual, always enjoyed with family or friends: A little food, a little wine, a lot of talk and, sometimes, some traditional singing. They never ate on the run; there was always time for meals, regardless of their frugality.

Usually, people who choose walking as a means of getting to know a place are also interested in the lifestyle of its inhabitants. So, chek out the real Cretan cuisine and try to enjoy it the way a Cretan does.

Part of Cretan cuisine is, of course, its ingredients. In the old days, they were only what the land produced. Nowadays we cannot be sure that everything a taverna offers is made from Cretan ingredients, or, from a different point of view, that Cretan products are what they used to be.

The general rule applies here: when possible, eat where the locals do. It is certainly better and cheaper, and you will have the chance to talk to a local and not some foreigner who works as a temporary helping hand.

If, on the other hand, you are not used to this kind of food and don't want to change your habits, look for a more "international" cuisine. This will not be difficult in big cities, where you will be able to eat whatever you feel like.

Holidays and Festivals

The 28th of October and the 25th of March are national holidays, the same as all over Greece, and all shops are closed. Other holidays are Christmas, New Year's Day, Epiphany (6th January), Easter Monday, the Day of the Holy Ghost (a moveable holiday), and the Virgin Mary's Day (15th August).

Depending on the area(s) you visit, if you can attend a local festival, don't miss it. Some of these are:

23rd April – St. George's Day in Asi Gonia.

23rd April – Holy Ghost Day on the summit of Mount Vryssinas.

20th July – Elias the Prophet Day in Trypiti (between Sougia and Agia Roumeli).

26th July – St. Paraskevi Day in Sisarcha.

27th July – St. Pantleleimon Day in Omalos.

15th August – Virgin Mary Day in Axos, Eleftherna, Kalyves, and other places.

24th August – St. Kosmas Day in Kallikratis.

29th August – Agios Yannis Gionas Day (on the Rodopos peninsula).

14th September – Holy Cross Day at the summit of Psiloritis.

15th September – St. Nikitas Day in Frangokastelo.

Walking on Cretan Terrain

Zeus' gift to King Minos was Talos, a bronze giant who could run around the island three times a day. When you look at the Cretan terrain for the first time, you will want to be like Talos. But Cretan mountains are among the most difficult and demanding hiking terrains. In our descriptions of the walks, we al-
ways state the kind of terrain you will have to travel on.

Gravel Roads

Over recent years, gravel roads have spread like a pest. The misuse of subsi-
dies has helped create a lot of totally useless gravel roads that criss-cross the Cretan mountains. Don't be surprised if, walking in an area that we describe as having no roads, you find a new gravel road! Many of these roads are in a really bad condition due to lack of maintenance, but they are alright for walking. The problems are that the new roads are built on old trails, thus destroy-

ing them, and second, they are built in the cheapest possible way, so all the debris is just thrown down the cliff destroying everything that existed downhill of the road. Another thing you will encounter on these long gravel roads are endless fences. These are not there to mark private property. They are there to stop sheep from getting out or getting in, depending on which side of the fence you are. You will find kilometers of these fences, even on the high mountains. To cross them, search for the "gate" which is usually located where the end of the fence is tied to a pole with a small piece of wire. Undo the wire, go through the gate, and close it again.

If you cannot find the gate, search the fence carefully, find its weak spot, and go through there. You can have a small competition with your friends. "Who is going to cross the fence first?", "who can do it without tearing his shorts apart", and so on!

Cobblestone Trails

Before building roads connecting villages, there were trails that were built by the villagers themselves through many hours of work. These trails, covered with cobblestones, helped people and animals not only to get to the villages but also to their fields in comfort and safety, following the smoothest route possible.

Today, most of these trails have become roads and, those that still remain, are almost destroyed by time and neglect. But in some places, like Aradena, these cobbled roads do still exist in a very good condition. They are certainly worth a visit and a walk.

E4 European Trail

The E4 European trail goes along the North/South axis of mainland Greece, and, from the town of Gythio in the Peloponnese, crosses to Castelli Kissamou. From there, it continues due South and then splits into two branches. One branch follows a mountainous route, while the other an almost seaside route. Both branches end at the southeastern corner of the island in Kato Zakros, through the Gorge of the Dead.

The trail is marked by a yellow and black strip, as well as by square yellow and black signs. You have to be careful though because in many places the signs have not been maintained for a long time, and could even be missing. For some strange reason, especially in many areas in the Rethymnon region, the signs have been removed. So you have to improvise and follow the general direction, using a map and a compass.

Trails

There are many other trails that people and animals were using, and they are clearly visible on good maps. Many of these are still used for walking, and some of them are even signposted. Of course, the not so popular ones are partly blocked by stones or bushes, and so, if you want to walk them, you'd better wear trousers and long sleeves.

Goat Tracks

These are the trails made by goats and sheep when they move about on the mountain. They are never reliable, do not lead where you want to go, and cross thousands of other goat tracks forming a chaotic tangle. Although it is best to avoid them, you will often have to use them as the last resort before "no trails".

"No Trails"

Many times, especially when climbing mountain tops, the trails disappear, either because the terrain is rocky or because the vegetation has covered the old trail. Here it is time to follow the advice an old shepherd once gave me "Follow your eyes". In these situations, especially in bad weather, you might get lost. Therefore it is good to use prominent landmarks as signposts, or to use a map and a compass.

Beware!

Lefka Ori is one of the last trully wild areas of Europe. Although it might sound funny to a Greek hiker, Lefka Ori is a place in Greece where a lot of mountaineering accidents happen. A sea of look-alike mountain tops with steep gorges in between make for ideal surroundings in which to get lost, especially when there is snow. But that's not all, the summer heat with the lack of fresh water springs make even experienced mountaineers reach their limits. This is Lefka Ori.

Some Walking Tips

It is not only Lefka Ori where you have to be careful. Almost all of Crete's trails are on sharp rocky terrain, and those which are not, go across screes. The icing on the cake is that every thorn bush in the Mediterranean grows in Crete, especially at the very spot you are most likely to fall onto when walking carelessly!

When hiking, it is good to use a walking stick, or a "katsouna" which is Cretan for a wooden walking stick. Also, wear trousers, not shorts, to protect your legs from thorns.

When you don't know where the trail starts, and you are near an inhabited area, the most natural thing to do is ask the locals. When they understand where you want to go, they will show you the nearest road. When you tell them that you actually want to walk, their first reaction will be to look at you as if you were sick or something. Don't forget that, until recently, all the villagers had to walk to their place of work or wherever else they wanted to go. So walking is still considered something you have to do rather than something you choose to do. Explain to them that you are hikers and want to walk. If possible, cross-check your information with more than one person, since even shepherds today don't walk a lot.

Finally, take enough water with you, start early in the morning, and don't walk alone.

Dangers

Hiking in Crete does not pose any particular dangers. Hippos and elephants disappeared from the island a few hundred thousand years ago. Nevertheless, you should pay attention to some things.

Sun: The sun, as we all know, is a life-giver, but can be tricky, as we also know. Crete lies more south than Tunis and it is very hot in the summertime. Even when you are on the mountains, where the temperatures are lower, the sun's rays are more intense. That has two consequences. First, the ultraviolet rays will bake any part of your skin that is not covered, and second, you could easily experience sunstroke. Always use sun protection with a high protection factor, always wear a hat and prefer to walk in the early morning hours or, even better, plan your trip in spring or autumn.

If you feel significant discomfort and exhaustion, and your body temperature is very high, you are probably experiencing sunstroke.

Sit in the shade, take off any restrictive clothes, cover yourself with a towel, and drink salted water.

Water: Lack of water and electrolytes is the main cause of heat exhaustion, when walking in hot weather. Through perspiration, the method our body uses to adjust its temperature, huge amounts of liquid and salt are lost. There is only one remedy, drink water with glucose or salt. On mountain walks in Crete, the most difficult part is finding water! Always carry with you enough water. On some routes you may find rainwater reservoirs. If the reservoirs are covered, and there is no goat or sheep excrement in it, it might be safe to drink, especially if you boil it beforehand. Avoid water from small surface streams, especially if there are any villages upstream.

Insects and Snakes: Although a bee sting hurts, there is no other danger, unless you are allergic to it. If swelling starts, especially near your throat, you must quickly get to the nearest Medical Centre for a shot of adrenaline. Generally, there are a lot of insects, but if you follow the old principle "I don't mess with them, so they don't mess with me", you will have no problem. Avoid lifting rocks barehanded, and don't stick your hands into cracks in the rocks.

As far as snakes are concerned, there is just one thing you have to remember, there are no venomous snakes in Crete.

Dogs: Crete's sheepdogs are not fierce like their cousins in the mainland. Although they bark a lot, it's probably because they are afraid and not in order to frighten you. One move from your part is enough to make them run away. Just bend down and pretend you are picking up a stone. Without having to throw it, the dogs will disappear. You may also meet some poor dogs chained to a tree with a barrel for home, a barrel so hot you could bake bread in it. If you see one of these poor creatures and you can spare some food, throw it to them and they will be grateful for their lives. Be careful though, for you might meet a dog that is actually fierce.

Lightning: This is a real danger, if you are on the mountains during a storm. Several Cretan shepherds have been hit by lightening. If you are caught in a storm and cannot get down to lower ground, throw away any metal objects (like walking sticks) and avoid solitary trees and very shallow caves or rock cavities. Find a more or less level spot and sit on your rucksack.

Theft: In Crete you have nothing to fear about theft, unless you are a sheep or a goat. Although goat thieves are many, most thefts are limited to that. Although there has been a rise in petty criminality recently, rural areas are generally very safe. However, during the high season, many different people come to the island, so you should not leave your valuables unattended.

In conclusion, we would like to point out that dangers come in two categories, the ones that are independent of our will and abilities, and the ones that actually depend on them. In the first, there are lightening, landslides, etc. In the second, we have dehydration, exhaustion, and other things caused mainly by our own foolishness.

Even general objective dangers can be avoided with a bit of planning and care. This means that, if the weather is changing for the worse, we do not press on regardless, but find shelter or move to lower altitudes to minimize the danger of lightening. If it's raining, it is not wise to hike in a gorge, and so on. Let's enjoy our hobby without subjecting ourselves or others to danger.

Emergencies

One thing everybody visiting the mountains of Crete should know is that out there, on the rough peaks and in the deep gorges, you will be practically alone. This means that if you face an emergency, there is no organised mountain rescue. You can call the emergency number (112) or the fire department (199), but it is not at all certain that the poor firemen will know how to come and rescue you. If you're planning a dangerous route, we suggest you inform somebody of your itinerary and your estimated time of return, especially if it includes a visit to a cave or walking in a gorge.

Equipment and Clothing

I believe that by now you will have realised that in Crete you will find three things in abundance: stones, thorns, and sun. We need to organise our equipment baring this in mind.

Long sleeves and trousers give you an advantage. Another good thing is to wear light-coloured clothes.

Your walking boots must have tough soles and cover your ankles. Do not walk in sandals, even in walking sandals, unless you are really used to them.

Choose your rucksack according to your walk. If you are planning a walk over several days, you will need a big 65 litre sack with a good suspension system and back ventilation. If you plan to use a permanent base and do daily walks, a smaller 30 litre pack is enough. Even then, choose one with a good suspension system. Useful things to stuff in your pack are: one water bottle (make that two), head torch with spare batteries and bulb, Swiss army-style knife, first aid kit, mirror, compass, map(s), whistle, waterproof jacket, thermal blanket, sewing kit, spare clothes and toilet paper.

Wherever you walk in Crete, you will definitely need a walking stick, or, even better, a "katsouna" as the locals call it. Old Cretans say that the best "katsounas" are made from Abelitsia wood, a tree unique in Crete, but there is not a lot of it left these days!

Maps

The best hiking maps are the ones published by "Anavasi" (www.anavasi.gr): 3 maps 1:100,000 covering the whole island and 3 maps 1:25,000 for parts of the described regions. The next best are the Harms Verlag maps. Their scale is 1:100,000. They have 50 m contour lines, and there is one for Western and one for Eastern Crete. They include E4 and a lot of other trails.

Other hiking 1:100,000 maps are the G. Petrakis Maps, printed in 1996. They include E4 and the most important mountain trails. Another 1:125,000 map is by Leadercom's. It includes E4, but has no contour lines.

Finally, we have to mention a 1:50,000 Freytag & Berndt map. Unfortunately it doesn't include the whole of Crete or one particular area. It only includes those parts of the island that have trails on them, but one cannot see the whole picture, therefore it's a map that is useful only to very experienced hikers.

Photography

It is not uncommon for people who like the outdoors to have an interest in photography as well. In general we would like to suggest that in Crete you have to carry your camera in a good bag, because there is a lot of ultra-fine dust on the island.

As for as your photographic equipment, the general rules apply. As elsewhere, to photograph landscapes you must have a wide-angle lens. A polarizing filter is also highly recommended. If you want to photograph people, it is better to have a telephoto lens. This is not because Cretans do not like being photographed. It goes without saying that if an old man or an old woman does not want you to photograph them, you must respect their wishes.

Since light is very intense, especially in the summertime, contrast is very low. For better pictures, take them in the morning between 8 and 9 o'clock, or in the evening after 6. Lighting conditions are better in the autumn, when the air is more transparent and the light not so harsh.

Time

Greek time is GMT +2, which is CET +1 or USA Standard Time +7. Time changes to daylight-saving time on the last Saturday of March (+1 hour) and it changes back on the last Saturday of September.

Use of this Guide

In Crete there are many trails for walking and hiking. It would not be possible or practical to include them all in a guide. Therefore, we chose hikes in Western Crete. The selection criteria were natural beauty and accessibility, as well as some historical or cultural elements. All walks described here were checked a few months before this guide's publication.

Although they have been checked, continuous road construction can change the landscape. If you come across something like that, please let us know. We apologise in advance, should we have missed something that might cause you any problems.

At the beginning of every featured walk you will find a short summary of key facts. These include the following:

Difficulty: This is graded from 1 to 4. The first grade includes simple walks, usually just a few hours long, with very easy navigation. The second grade includes walks that need a reasonable fitness level, have a few ups and downs, are shorter than four hours long, and do not need experience. In the third grade things get more serious. You might have to use your hands in some spots, and navigation isn't really easy. The fourth grade includes long, 6 to 12 hour hikes, requires walking for long hours under difficult conditions, a good sense of direction and, many times, the use of compass and map.

Duration and Elevation Changes: Every walk is divided into stages. The time given for each stage is usually the time needed by an average walker with a small backpack, not including any stops. Elevation changes for each stage are also given.

Terrain: Here we give you information about the hike's profile as well as the trail's condition, i.e. if it's rocky, if it's a gravel road, if it crosses screes, etc.

Signposting: If the trail is signposted, we inform you what kind and how frequent it is.

When to Go: This is the recommended season to do the walk without encountering extreme conditions.

Water and Shade: These are two very important elements of a hike, if and where you can find water, and if, where, and when you can find protection from the fierce Cretan sun.

Popularity: Learn how possible it is to meet other walkers on the trail.

Where to Sleep and Where to Eat: In Crete there are many rooms for rent. Here we point out the ones that are near the walk. Sometimes we may suggest a place that we think is exceptional. We also tell you if you have to pack food or if you can find tavernas near the walk.

Access: The way to get to the trailhead.

Sights: Crete has other interesting things to see besides its natural beauty, like historical, archaeological, and cultural sights. We will provide you with information about anything worth a visit in the area.

In addition, every walk is accompanied by a short text, and often a small appendix with additional background information, which may contain a story, an event, a monument, a local recipe, a description of a plant or something about the local social life. We believe that this way we will give you a motive to pick up as many pieces as possible of the puzzle called Crete, and not confine yourselves to a superficial visit of the island.

Description of Routes

WESTERN CHANIA REGION

The northwestern part of the Chania Prefecture is one of the most distinctive places on Crete's map, with its two rectangular peninsulas stretching deep into the Cretan sea. In this area, from Kolibari to Chania, the tourist industry has created a modern production line of standard vacations and standard pleasures. There is everything you might need; hotels (large and small), rooms-to-let, restaurants, fast food outlets, bars, supermarkets, mini-markets, car rentals, motorbike rentals, bicycle rentals... whatever you can possibly imagine.

In this area, with the exception of the two peninsulas, farming is relatively limited even though there is a lot of water. Farms produce a few oranges, some lemons and some olive oil. West of Chania City, avoiding the tourist rabble, it is worth taking a brief stroll in the Agia area. There is a small artificial lake there, its water supplying Chania. Near here runs the river Keritis (its ancient name is Iardanos) flowing out to the sea in Platanias. At the nearby Alikianos village, nothing special nowadays, there used to be a tower where Kantanoleon's rebellion* ended ingloriously and tragically.

Past the river Tavronitis and the historic village of Maleme, where the first invasion of the German parachutists took place during the famous Battle of Crete, lies the Rodopos Peninsula ending at Cape Spatha (its ancient name is Tytiros). On this stony area, a temple dedicated to the ancient goddess Dyktinna was built. Worshippers had to visit barefoot the rich temple. Relatively close by lies the small church of Ai Yannis Gionas. If you happen to be here on the 29th of August, you will have the opportunity to attend a really good festival.

The other peninsula, which is called Gramvoussa**, lies a bit to the West, and, together with Rodopos, forms Kissamos Bay. The wildness of the area is described very well in an old folk song titled "stis Gramvoussas to akrotiri" (at Cape Gramvoussa) about an old captain lost at sea. At the periphery of Gramvoussa is Cape Vouksa and two islands, the "tranquil" and the "wild" Gramvoussa. On the tranquil Gramvoussa there used to be a very well fortified Venetian castle which in the end didn't prove very useful to the Venetians when they were at war with the Ottomans. The area is unique and it is a pity that the gravel road, which nowadays reaches close to the beach, brings with it a lot of ugliness (and I am not referring only to the shop selling hand-made snacks at the end of the road).

The region of Western Chania has a lot to offer: ancient Falassarna with a white sandy beach and some of the most impressive wild gorges (like the one at Sirikari and the one at Topolia). The road that leads to Elafonissi passes from the Topoliano Gorge through a narrow tunnel excavated at the edge of the cliff. When you reach Chryssoskalitissa and Elafonissi, you will be impressed by the white rocks. However, they are nothing other than plaster. There are quarries in the area which of course are very ugly, but they are essential for the local economy. In the name of the local economy though (or is it better to say "personal interest"?) the area around Elafonissi*** has increasingly more ugly rooms-to-let, tavernas and restaurants. But, this mess apart, strolling in the area is a unique experience, especially in spring before the tourists have arrived.

   * See appendix page 51
  ** See appendix page 46
*** See appendix page 57

1. GRAMVOUSSA PENINSULA

DIFFICULTY 📈	■ ☐ ☐ ☐
DURATION 🕐	2 h
ELEVATION CHANGE 📊	2 h, 150 m ascent, 150 m descent a) Kalyviani – chapel: 60', 100 m ascent b) Chapel – parking area: 40', 50 m ascent c) Parking area – beach: 20', 150 m descent
TERRAIN ⛰	Mostly gravel road and partly well defined path.
SIGNPOSTING 🚸	Signs only on the path (unnecessary).
WHEN TO GO 📅	All year round.
WATER 〰	Take water from the cafes in Kalyviani or from the shop next to the parking area.
SHADE 🌤	There is no shade at all.
POPULARITY 👥	It is crowded from May–October.
ACCESS 🚗	Bus from Kastelli Kissamou to Kalyviani.
SIGHTS 🏛	One of the most beautiful Mediterranean beaches, unique landscape, blue crystal-clear waters.
DRAWBACKS ❎	It can be crowded. The tourist boats tend to bring a lot of people from Kissamos.

As a walk it has almost nothing to offer, no landscape variety and no particular difficulty. But what it does offer is a great view across to Kissamos Bay and to the Rodopos Peninsula. The main attraction, though, is one of the most magnificent beaches in the world.

The walk starts from the scenic little village of Kalyviani, which offers scenic views to Kissamos Bay. Follow the descending paved road which starts from the square. There is a sign there indicating "Balos Beach" or "Hotel Balos". 10–15 minutes later, you will see a boat on your right, a shipwreck on the beach leaning on its side, and immediately after that Hotel Balos, where the tar road ends and the gravel road starts, heading to the eastern side of the Gramvoussa Peninsula. You will get beautiful views to Kissamos Bay, Lefka Ori and the Rodopos Peninsula on the way. When you pass a quarry, the road winds between high rocks and the beach below getting steep and rocky. The landscape is typical Cretan seaside with phrygana, bushes, stones and lots of goats and sheep that graze happily. The slopes above lead to steep rocky summits (Gerosky-nos is the highest, 762 m) with sparse vegetation. After almost an hour of walking, you come to the Agia Irini chapel. Continue on the road to your left. After 40 minutes, the road ends at a clearing with a basic shop (simple food, coffee and refreshments) and a parking area. The route goes left now on a well signed path among stones and phrygana, de-scending smoothly, and in 10–15 minutes you reach a spot with marvelous views to the Balos-Tigani Beach, with its magnifi-cent blue waters, fine light-coloured sand, a round-shaped island and numerous rocky islands dotted around the sea.

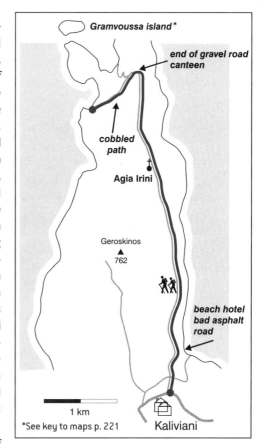

Gramvoussa island*

end of gravel road
canteen

cobbled
path

Agia Irini

Geroskinos
▲
762

beach hotel
bad asphalt
road

1 km

*See key to maps p. 221   Kaliviani

This beach is one of the best in Crete. The water is crystal clear and everything around resem-bles a tropical island. The path now is stone built and easy, leading you to the beach in 10 minutes. After you have enjoyed your swim, you can walk to the island opposite (50 m of swallow water divides the island from the mainland) and explore its shore. Balos Beach has no shops, water nor road (except for the path you walked). Unfortunately, it is very well known and in the summer, tens or even hundreds of visitors come here using every possible means of transport (tourist boats from Kastelli, rented cars, on foot or bicycles). It's worth the pain, though. Return on the same path (unless you prefer to take the boat to Kastelli). Another option is to walk across the west shore to Falas-sarna, but this is not recommended (8–9 kms, 3–4 h). There is no road nor path going there apart from some undefined goat tracks, and at some places the shore becomes steep and rocky, often forcing you to go up and down.

Gramvoussa Peninsula

Chania's northwestern border is called the Gramvoussa Peninsula. There, at the far side of the cape, lie two small islands under the same name, with the only difference that one of them gets the adjective "wild" and the other the adjective "tranquil". That is actually a joke, because one cannot tell which one is wilder, especially when the sea is rough.

Anyway, there, at the steep and impregnable shores of tranquil Gramvoussa (its other name is Agios Nikolaos), the Venetians built a fortified castle. They knew that the Turks were approaching, but what can one do with a single castle? When they finally lost Crete to the Turks, Morosinis, a Venetian official, made a deal to keep this castle as well as the castles at Spinalonga and Sousa. At first the Turks agreed, but of course they actually wanted to get hold of this strongly fortified castle. After second thoughts, and without spending extra money or men, they decided to subjugate it the usual way. The solution was extremely easy; they just had to bribe the right man. So, in 1692, the Italian garrison commander took the bribe money and gave the castle to the Turks.

The Turks did nothing in particular with it and never fired one single cannon ball from its 24 canons. The Cretan rebels, on the other hand, in 1821 decided to conquer it to use it as their military base. So, during a cold winter night in 1823, Mpouzomarkos, a war captain from the Sfakia area, first set his foot on the island. More rebels followed, killing every guard they happened to find in their way. They also killed the garrison commander who was sleeping happily with his mistress. But unfortunately they were too gallant. The Turkish woman shouted loudly enough to wake up the rest of the guard. Before the Cretans could find time to open the castle gates from inside, the canons killed them all and Gramvoussa remained under Turkish rule.

2. FALASSARNA – PLATANOS

DIFFICULTY	■ ☐ ☐ ☐
DURATION	Almost 2 h
ELEVATION CHANGE	250 m ascent a) Falassarna – greenhouses: 1 h b) Greenhouses – Kavoussi: 30', 120 m ascent c) Kavoussi – Platanos: 30', 120 m ascent
TERRAIN	Seaside route without path and a narrow path uphill.
SIGNPOSTING	No.
WHEN TO GO	All year round.
WATER	Water from the beach-front shops and from the spring at Kavoussi.
SHADE	There is no shade at all.
POPULARITY	Only at the beach you'll come across a few people (swimmers, not walkers).
ACCESS	There are 3–4 daily bus services from Kastelli Kissamou or by taxi.
SIGHTS	The ancient city of Falassarna, amazing little beaches dotted with short bushy cedars and fine rocks and the Kavoussi village.
DRAWBACKS	The people on the beaches (and some of the shops there) and the greenhouses before the ascent.

Simple and easy walk offering a variety of landscapes and beautiful views towards the sea.

Start your walk at Falassarna's bus terminal. Continue on the gravel road, parallel to the shore, to the North for almost 2 km, till you reach Ancient Falassarna. It used to be a very significant city and port during the Minoan Era. First you come to the cemetery with the graves scattered around and then to the ancient quarry next to the sea. The city was further north, but nowadays all that is left are some parts of the walls, some ruins of the acropolis and cisterns hewn from the rocks. When you finish your visit, return to the Falassarna coastal road and start walking along the sea. The route is on flat ground in beautiful sunshine, but a bit tiring, because you often have to walk on sand. The sea on your right is magnificent with deep, blue water and fine sand whereas, on your left, the shore is full of high and low wild cedars, dunes, short mossy plants, grey eroded rocks and golden sand. If you come here in early May or October you'll meet just a few swimmers, whereas in the summertime the beach is full of people. When you pass a wide sandy beach with two wooden corridors leading from the sea to the shops, the beach becomes pebbled, and hundreds of greenhouses appear, altering the landscape completely. You soon come to a gravel

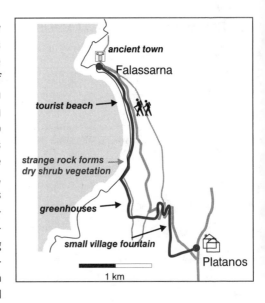

road and after 300–400 m you turn left among the greenhouses. At the second paved road you turn left again, and soon it becomes a gravel road ending at a slope. Follow a goat track uphill, and in 15 minutes you will be on a paved road. A bit to the left and straight ahead you see Kavoussi's small settlement.

Most houses here are old and ruined, but at the entrance of the village stands an enormous villa surrounded by high walls, a shock to the tranquil atmosphere of the old settlement. The road turns right, becoming a gravel road. You will reach a spring with abundant refreshing water. 50–100 m further, on the left, the old route to Platanos begins. It is a pleasant walk among the trees (figs, pears, olives). The path is partly cobbled and ascends passing in front of old houses and turning smoothly to the right. It is a goat track now and it's moving among dense phrygana and grass. You soon come to a beautiful country chapel with an attractive veranda overlooking the sea and Falassarna's Bay (and, unfortunately, the greenhouses as well).

From there on, the goat track becomes a path again, turns to the left and is partly cobbled. Some minutes further on, you are below a taverna (and its rubbish of course) and minutes afterwards up the road, where you turn right heading to the village centre.

3. TSIHLIANI GORGE – POLYRINIA – SYRIKARI

DIFFICULTY	■ ■ □ □
DURATION	2 h, (3:30' return)
ELEVATION CHANGE	250 m ascent/ descent a) Polyrinia – water tower: 30', 100 m descent b) Water tower – little bridge: 15' c) Little bridge – sheep pen: 45', 100 m ascent d) Sheep pen – farmhouse (road): 30', 150 m ascent e) Return to water tower: 1 h 30', 250 m descent
TERRAIN	An easy well-defined path. On the way back you walk in the river-bed which is stony, full of plants and with some easy downhill passages.
SIGNPOSTING	Sparse red marks on the path.
WHEN TO GO	All year round.
WATER	From the fountains at the villages or from the water tower at the start.
SHADE	Enough shade, mainly inside the gorge.
POPULARITY	You will meet no one outside the villages.
ACCESS	One bus daily from Kastelli Kissamou or by taxi.
SIGHTS	The scenic Polyrinia village with its traditional houses and the ruins of the ancient city among them. The ancient acropolis on top of the hill, the Ai Yannis country chapel and the steep and distinctive gorge with its stony bridges.
DRAWBACKS	The walk on the paved road, the fences in some parts of the gorge and the difficulty of the return journey from Syrikari (if you don't want to return the same way).

A really pleasant walk off the beaten track. The gorge is beautiful and shady, with typical local vegetation, and you'll have a small adventure in its riverbed. It combines history and architecture with solitude and serenity.

The walk starts from the traditional village of Polyrinia. Simple, stone-built houses, remnants from another era, some cement walls here and there, and the ruins of the ancient Minoan city in between. It is a pleasant walk climbing up the hill to visit the ancient acropolis, passing through the village. It will take almost half an hour going up and down, but the strategically built acropolis as well as the great views will certainly reward you.

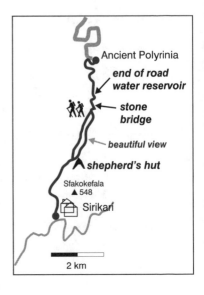

You can see Ai Yannis country chapel and the gorge below lying among olive groves from the edge of the village and the parking area (cars can't drive through the village's narrow streets, thank goodness!). Turn left when you exit the village (you can visit the ancient cemetery, if you like) walking on the paved road which descends by the school on your right. The road keeps on descending and later it becomes a gravel road till you reach Ai Yannis chapel, 30 minutes on. You can do this part by car or motorcycle (assuming you have one and you want to come back the same way). At the last bend to the right before the chapel, open the fence gate and go towards the water tower (don't get too close because, especially during summer, the area is full of wasps, bees and other heavily gunned insects).

The road continues left from the water tower in the gully, and, when you pass two fences (on the road) and some peaceful sheep, it becomes a path (signposted with red marks) leading soon to an old stone bridge. Walk across it and climb up. The vegetation is sparse now (phrygana only), and the gorge opens up before your eyes. It is a large, wide gorge with relatively smooth slopes (and some vertical bits here and there). The route heads high above the left of the riverbed. 45 minutes after the bridge, the path leads you down to the riverbed. Cross it (passing a fence with plastic pipes and water troughs), move to the other side and cross another gully coming from the right. The path ascends and the vegetation is denser now (trees, high bushes). The route is more demanding at this point, leading you below a farmhouse and a sheep pen (the dogs bark but are tethered) to a gravel road. Follow this road to the left. After a while, it becomes a cement road, climbing a bit more, and in 15 minutes you will arrive at Syrikari.

The Tragedy of a Cretan Wedding

At the beginning of the 16th Century, Cretans rebelled one more time against their Venetian masters. Leader of this rebellion was Georgios Kantanoleon, a descendant of a great Byzantine family.

The rebels soon had a lot of land under their control. Venice, losing the taxes from these areas, was displeased with the new situation, but it wasn't easy to quell this rebellion. Then somebody made a fatal mistake. Kantanoleon believed that he had absolute control of the situation and, in order to secure it even further, took a great risk. He sent a message to the Venetian feudal lord, Da Molin, asking him to give his daughter as a bride for his son. Da Molin thought twice about it, but decided to accept the proposal. He set a date for the wedding, which was to take place at the family castle in Alikianos.

When the date came, Kantanoleon with his men and his whole family, 450 people in all, arrived at the castle. The Da Molin family welcomed them with all the nobility the situation required and the wedding began. Soon after, the bridal feast took place with singing, dancing and gallons of wine.

But the guests drank so much they passed out. The drums gave the signal from the tower, and the Chania garrison, notified beforehand by Da Molin, arrived with 200 men. It was then easy to arrest and tie up the drunken men and lead them all to Chania. Kantanoleon and his son were hanged together, whereas many of the others were hanged at four other sites outside the city. The rest were sent to the galleys.

Nobody really knows if this story is true. How can one say? The truth was buried in the castle's ruins and scattered around the stones that can still be seen across the fields...

You can follow another route to get back. Take your time to enjoy the view, the gorge's vertical walls and the typical vegetation. When you feel ready, it is time to practise your climbing skills a bit. Go back on the same, now descending, path to the water troughs, pass the fence and continue along the dry riverbed (unless of course it has rained heavily). The hike is easy and shaded at the beginning, with some small stones and attractive plants around (mainly oleanders), a small gradient and great views. 25 minutes later, the middle section becomes more exciting, with large fallen rocks jammed in the river bed and some low, vertical walls, easy to descend. At two points along the way, it becomes really interesting. The jammed rocks create small tunnels and shallow wells, and for some meters you have to walk under these naturally built archways and between openings. Then the gorge opens up, the riverbed becomes flatter turning to the right and the plants are dense, making your walk more difficult. Soon afterwards you see the stone bridge ahead. Climb up, following the path to the left and reaching the water tower and the road after 15 minutes.

4. RODOPOS PENINSULA

DIFFICULTY 📈	■ ■ □ □
DURATION 🕐	4 h 30'
ELEVATION CHANGE 📊	500 m ascent, 500 m descent a) Rodopos – end of the road: 1 h 30', 500 m ascent b) Trail start – Ai Yannis Gionis: 30', 250 m descent c) Ai Yannis Gionis – end of the road: 40' d) End of the road – prefab house: 1 h, 200 m ascent e) Prefab house – Rodopos: 45', 100 m descent
TERRAIN ⛰	At the beginning you walk on a gravel road and then on a narrow, rough path/goat track.
SIGNPOSTING 🔼	Partly signposted with red marks.
WHEN TO GO 🗓	All year round, but avoid hot summer days.
WATER 〰	Take water from Rodopos village.
SHADE 🌟	There is no shade at all.
POPULARITY 👥	You'll meet almost no one, except perhaps some locals in Ai Yannis chapel.
ACCESS ➤	There are 8–10 daily bus services from Chania to Kastelli Kissamou (10–12 daily bus services from Chania). Get off at Rodopos junction and walk 3 km, or take a taxi from Kolybari (6 km).
SIGHTS 🏛	The old, simple, almost deserted Ai Yannis Gionis Monastery and the beautiful view to Kissamos Bay and the Gramvoussa peninsula.
DRAWBACKS ✖	The first 1 h 30' hike on the road, the lack of shade and the dust (when it's windy).

The starting point is the village square. Leave it to your right heading North. Pass by the church and, after a while, leaving the last village houses behind, you will come to some smooth cultivated slopes. The paved road ends (after 1 km) on a bend and becomes a gravel uphill road. Follow the road for almost an hour walking among sparse cultivation and slopes full of

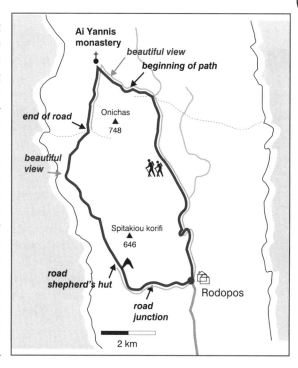

phrygana and bushes with views to Chania Bay and the Akrotiri Peninsula on the right. Ignore any junction you meet continuing straight on, and in 20 minutes you will reach a water tank with a sign on it indicating "to Ai Yannis". Take the road to the left and in 10 minutes you will find a house built on a wide ridge. If you walk further, you will see red marks and the trail which descends the steep slope to a small plateau, the Ai Yannis plateau. The view unfolds before you. You see the buildings and the church of the small monastery, the sea, Kissamos Bay, the Gramvoussa Peninsula and the houses of Kastelli behind. Descend the winding path and 30 minutes later take the road which, in a few minutes, will lead you to the monastery.

Leaving the monastery behind, head south following the gravel road you left before. The road descends gradually, winding among pastures and phrygana with the steep rocky seashore always on your right. 40 minutes later you will see the Agios Pavlos chapel on the beach below and the road becomes a trail (goat track), well signposted with red marks on rocks and trunks, traversing the slope above the seashore to the North. The trail, though narrow

Battle of Crete (Operation Merkur)

It is the dawn of the 20th of May 1941, and the famous German Stuka bombers are incessantly shelling the three big Cretan cities. The main target is Maleme, the area where the Chania airport is. There are only a few English and New Zealand soldiers with the order to defend it. 150 bombers mercilessly bomb its defensive positions, preparing the place for invasion.

The sky is full of aeroplanes and smoke. The sound of the propeller-engined planes and the screams of the bombs is scary. Through the smoke, 600 transport planes, Junkers Type 52, endlessly drop white parachutes with guns and ammunition and black parachutes with soldiers. The parachutists fall 200 at a time to the Cretan ground where they are repulsed by the exhausted English battalions. The Cretans use every weapon they have to help the soldiers. This fierce defence by the residents themselves is unprecedented and the invaders are not prepared for it.

But, although brave and fierce, it is not enough. The line of defence falls on the 25th of May. The Germans invade Maleme, Chania and finally the rest of the island. The German operation under the code name Merkur ends here, but the losses are extremely large, 5,000 dead and 12,000 prisoners from the defenders, and 6,000 dead, 4,500 of them parachutists, from the German side.

The self-sacrifice of the Cretan people was not in vain, since it delayed the famous Operation Barbarossa for 18 months, giving enough time for the allied forces to be prepared. Moreover, handpicked parachutists were not used again as the main force in any other invasion attempt.

Von Strudent himself (the parachutists' commander) said characteristically: "Every one who fought in Crete's battle in 1941 ought to be proud, the attacking Germans as well as the defenders, English and Greeks alike."

and stony, is clear and offers great views. The last part gets steeper heading SE, and in about an hour it will lead you to a road next to a sheep pen (no dogs here!). Follow the road which turns left and continues on the wide ridge, leaving the sea behind and the mountain top on your left. The road runs among pastures and vineyards with lovely views across the surrounding area. Remain on the main road until you meet a junction with a vineyard and then turn left. 40 minutes later, you will reach the edge of the slope which descends smoothly to Rodopos. You'll see the houses below and, 10 minutes later, turn right after the soccer-ground entering the village.

5. ELAFONISSI – PALAIOHORA

DIFFICULTY	■ ■ □ □
DURATION	3 h 45'
ELEVATION CHANGE	a) Elafonissi – Ai Yannis: 2 h 30', 60 m ascent b) Ai Yannis – Krios beach: 1 h 15', 60 m descent
TERRAIN	A bit of the walk is on a gravel road, some on a relatively good trail, some on stony ground and finally on a beach.
SIGNPOSTING	E4 signs.
WHEN TO GO	March–May, September–November.
WATER	There is a fountain in the middle of the route, at Ai Yannis.
SHADE	There is practically no shade. It is better to start early from Palaiohora (Krios) or early in the afternoon from Elafonissi.
POPULARITY	Considering how many people visit Elafonissi, the trail is very quiet, if not desolate.
WHERE TO SLEEP WHERE TO EAT	There are three or four basic guesthouses in Elafonissi. In Palaiohora you will find plenty of rooms for every budget. There are three tavernas in Elafonissi and countless more in Palaiohora. You will find good food and very gentle people at Manolis and Maria's taverna, at the end of the beach.
ACCESS	There is a bus daily from Chania to Elafonissi and four from Chania to Palaiohora.
SIGHTS	Elafonissi is a beautiful wildlife habitat. Visit also Selino, the Venetian castle, built in 1282 in Palaiohora.
DRAWBACKS	The inadequate signposting at critical points.

A relatively short walk with interesting views over the sea, starting with Ino and Apollo Island. You must cross the sea to the island and walk towards the lighthouse among dunes and strange rocks, where seagulls build their nests. In order to cross the nar-

row passage that divides the island from the shore you must walk in the shallow water for almost 100 m. Avoid going there in July and August for obvious reasons.

Leave the island and the beach behind and head east. At the end of the beach, you will see an E4 sign (if it is still there). The trail, even though not particularly clear, runs along the beach. Half an hour later you come to a rare cedar tree forest and in less than an hour to a well with brackish water and a building. The path is a bit confusing here, but it climbs up to the foot of Vitziloharako. Ahead of you lies a beach. Descend there and then walk up along a dry stream for 200 m. From there, turn right, reaching a small beach after almost 2 hours. Climb gradually and, 30 minutes later, you will be at the Ai Yannis chapel, which you could see in front of you throughout your walk to this point.

100 m above you in the gully, there is a spring with some running water. Before you reach the spring, turn right and continue on the clear path which circles the steep slopes of the peninsula. At some point (the worst, of course) a rockslide has destroyed the path so you should be careful. After a while, you climb down to a nice little beach surfaced with huge rocks. If you look carefully, you will see some half

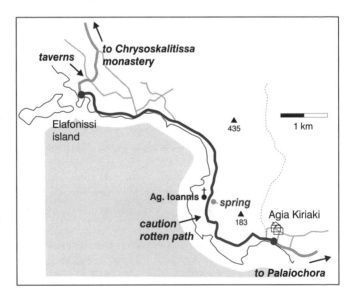

Tragic Elafonissi

What a beautiful beach with pink and golden sand, emerald waters and a small channel dividing the island from the mainland! Who can imagine nowadays that two very tragic events took place here, in this small piece of heaven?

The first took place in 1824, when the blood-thirsty Egyptian, Ibrahim Pasha, slaughtered 800 women and children on these same gold sands. 40 warriors tried to keep him away from the island, which they had foolishly believed to be a safe hiding place. It was Easter Day when the Turks found their way across, and only one man managed to escape the butchering that followed, swimming to Palaiohora.

The second event was in February 1907. The south wind (Livas) causes tremendous storms in the area, some of the worst in the Mediterranean, it is said. During a tempest like this, a ship named Imperatrice sank in these wild waters taking 300 people to their deaths. Some years later, in one of those twists of fate, Captain Philosophof of the Russian ship Hividits, who had saved more than 300 people from this tragic shipwreck, came to Greece after the October Revolution. Using the influence of Queen Olga, he succeeded in getting a position in the navy. They made him lighthouse keeper in Elafonissi, without even knowing who he really was.

made columns, probably Roman. (If you do the hike the other way round, climb the stream to the right before the end of the beach and head west).

Before the end of the beach, among the bushes, you'll find the path which climbs up again, ending at a col you could see above you to the East. You come to a road which ends at the long beach of Krios. Another option is to descend soon after you pass the col, and then turn right to a small gully which will lead you to a smaller beach and then to Krios Beach.

From there on, the only interest is in the red tomatoes which decorate the plastic greenhouses. So it is preferable to continue to Palaiohora by taxi (you must book it in advance). Otherwise you have only 10 kms to go...

Western Chania Region

6. PALAIOHORA – SOUGIA

DIFFICULTY	📈	▪ ▪ ☐ ☐
DURATION	🕐	5 h 15'
ELEVATION CHANGE	📊	a) Palaiohora – trailhead: 1 h 15' b) Trailhead – col/gravel road: 1 h 45', 240 m ascent c) Gravel road – Lissos: 1 h, 230 m descent d) Lissos – Sougia: 1 h 10', 160 m up – 160 m down
TERRAIN	🏔	Gravel road at the beginning, a relatively good path with a few ascents and descents and partly on the gully bed.
SIGNPOSTING	🔼	E4 signs.
WHEN TO GO	📅	March–May, September–November.
WATER	〰	There is a spring in Ancient Lissos, but it may have no water in the summer.
SHADE	🌿	Shade only inside the gorge near Lissos.
POPULARITY	👥	You meet people walking on this trail, especially in the section between Sougia and Lissos.
WHERE TO SLEEP WHERE TO EAT	🍴	In Palaiohora and Sougia, there are plenty of rooms for every budget. There are countless tavernas in Palaiohora. You will find good food and very gentle people at Manolis and Maria's taverna at the end of the beach. In Sougia go to "Polyfimos" taverna and ask for Yannis. Apart from the food, he can arrange rooms, transportation and much more. Drink a cool raki on our behalf.
ACCESS	⟋	There is a bus daily from Chania to Elafonissi and four from Chania to Palaiohora. Palaiohora is connected with Sougia, Agia Roumeli and Sfakia by boat.
SIGHTS	🏛	Visit the ancient city of Lissos, the ancient Asklipiion, the Roman graves, the small chapel of Agios Kyrkos and Agios Nikolaos and the short Lissos Gorge.
DRAWBACKS	⊗	Even though Ancient Lissos is a place of great beauty, it is abandoned. Somebody really should take care of the rubbish.

This is an easy walk, most of it next to the sea. The ruins of Ancient Lissos and the cobbled path add to its charm.

Walk to the East, following the eastern seaside road or on the pebbles of the beach after the last tavernas. If you choose to walk on the pebbles, go as far as you can, then move to the road which runs parallel to the shore. Again, you have two options. The first is to follow the road and the other to climb the path which goes left from the road and then, in about 1 km, return to the road. The road ends at the last beach, and from there you must try to find the end of the path east of the beach, among low rocks and lentisk shrubs. At some points, due to the dense vegetation, the path disappears. Head eastwards to the col which can be seen ahead of you between the Vardia peak and the Flomos Peninsula.

You'll reach the col after 1 h and 30′ on the path. Descend until you find a road. Follow it for 15 minutes passing in front of a small sheep pen up to the point where the path divides. Go straight on along the path. After a while, you'll start descending to the bay where Ancient Lissos lies. You will see it 10′–15′ after you started on the path. A relatively steep descent starts there and continues for almost 20 minutes, till you reach the ruins of the ancient city. The first stone built houses you see on the west slope of the bay are remnants of a Roman cemetery. You should take a break here, leaning under the shade of the huge locust trees a few metres away from the Asklepiion. The spring usually has running water till July. Apart from the Asclepiion, visit the Agios Kyrkos Byzantine church which is built with the remnants from the ancient city. If you descend to the sea, look up and see the huge overhanging cliff above you. Imagine how the area would have looked before the 5th Century B.C.

The path that leads to Sougia is well hidden, and you need to struggle to find it. Go to the fence that circles the Asclepiion to the east side, just before the vertical rocks. The path climbs among olive trees and old cultivation terraces. If you look closer, you'll find some signs as well. It will take you less

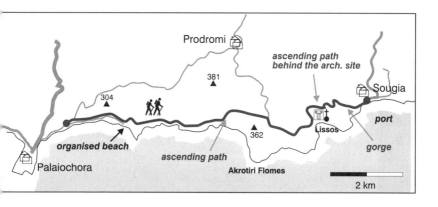

than 15 minutes to get to the edge of some really steep slopes with great views to the small bay below. Continue to the East for a while towards the big pine trees. The path winds and descends to the gorge's riverbed. This is a small but beautiful gorge, full of pine trees, acorns and oleanders offering dense shade. On its vertical walls you will see the famous dittany and maybe also a hawk circling above your head.

Watch out, because at some points the rocks are slippery. In less than 30 minutes, you will be at Sougia port which looks like a nuclear bunker with all those cement buildings around. 10 minutes more and you are in Sougia village. Nowadays, this seaside village has become highly touristic without harming the surrounding area, thank goodness. In Sougia you can put your tent up on the beach for free with the local permission.

The hike to Ancient Lissos can be a pleasant excursion from Sougia, and if you don't want to return the same way, you can arrange for a boat to come and take you back.

Ancient Lissos

In 1957, Lougiakis, a local peasant, was trying to find a spring of curative water west of Sougia. Luck made him dig the ground exactly above the point where some hundreds years earlier Asclepius' doctors had used the same water for medical purposes.

Archaeological excavations directed by N. Platonas brought to light the Asclepiion, that is to say the infirmary of Ancient Lissos. Lissos, even though a small city, managed to survive for many years and also had its own gold coins, a sign of prosperity and power. It isn't yet known exactly when the first settlers came here, but its naturally fortified location and the curative water got them under its spell. Imagine that, before the growth of Western Crete, this small settlement was certainly much bigger. From this bay, ships sailed to many Mediterranean harbours. It is known that they had made an alliance with the Kingdom of Cyrenia.

The era in which the city flourished is long ago, before the Doric period, from the 11th century B.C. to the Roman era and the early Byzantine years. A big earthquake destroyed the city and the Asclepiion, so we are not sure exactly for how long.

What a visitor can see today is surely completely different from what Pashley saw when he first came here in 1834, a lot of ancient ruins scattered around, but not the Asclepiion, with its excellent mosaic floor. He saw the theatre, the tombs (the most impressive ancient cemetery in Crete) and of course the two small churches of Agios Kyrkos and Virgin Mary, which are built on the ruins of previous 4th and 5th Century churches .

LEFKA ORI REGION

Lefka Ori in Greek means White Mountains, but the Cretans, especially the ones from the Chania region, call them the Madares (in Cretan it means the bald or the naked ones). They may be lower than the Alps, but they are equally beautiful and massive, as the English traveller Pashley observed, when he first saw them from a distance.

With more than fifty peaks towering over 2,000 m high and dozens of rugged gorges, Lefka Ori is a mountaineering paradise and more. The difficult terrain makes them inaccessible to people who do not know them. They have been the perfect hiding place for hunted people ever since the Venetian occupation. This was where rebels took refuge, as late as World war II. The Ottomans never marched to the heart of Lefka Ori, and the city of Sfakia had a kind of independence. It was through these difficult mountain passes that English soldiers were helped to escape to the Middle East.

Most of the high peaks are clustered together around Pachnes (highest peak is 2,452 m high), forming a peak-valley-peak-gorge pattern. The renowned Samaria Gorge divides Volakias and Gingilos peaks to the West from the central cluster of high peaks, where the Omalos plateau is. A bit more to the West, the Agia Irini Gorge forms the western boundary of Lefka Ori. To the South, the high peaks drop steeply down to the cold waters of the Libyan Sea. The Libyan Sea itself is not cold, but it is here that the cold underground mountain rivers flow directly into it. To the East, Castro peak is the last bastion of the mountains, before they drop a little to the Askifou plateau. There, the Imbros Gorge forms their eastern impenetrable boundary.

One main feature of Lefka Ori is its many gorges. As well as the famous and now crowded Samaria Gorge, there are many others worth a visit. Most have not been "developed", and therefore Cretan nature has a chance to expand to all its majesty. They include the Tripiti Gorge where, if you know the way, no abseils are needed, the Klados Gorge where you have to abseil even if you know the way, the Eligias Gorge where a rope is also necessary, the Illigas Gorge which you can walk without a rope, and many others, all awaiting your respectful visit.

Besides gorges and peaks, Lefka Ori features another unique gem, the little villages that surround the peaks, sometimes at a low altitude near the sea and sometimes on the high plateaus. Some of them, like Hora Sfakion and Sougia, still prosper, mainly due to tourism. Others, like Anopoli and Koustogerako, still hold on despite the difficulties they face. Some will be history in a few decades, though, like Mouri and Kali Lakki, or they will become "traditional" and be transformed into resorts.

It is well worth meeting the remaining old timers who still live in these villages. Few people experience this side of Crete.

Lefka Ori Region

7. AGIA IRINI GORGE

DIFFICULTY	📈	■ ■ ☐ ☐
DURATION	🕐	3 hours 30′
ELEVATION CHANGE	📊	460 m descent a) Starting point – "Ai Yannis" rock chapel: 20′ b) Ai Yannis – Fournaki: 40′ c) Fournaki – Gorge exit: 2 h 30′
TERRAIN	🏔	Defined path, partly destroyed due to falling rocks.
SIGNPOSTING	🔼	E4 signposting.
WHEN TO GO	📅	April–October.
WATER	〰	Only near the gorge entrance.
SHADE	🌲	A lot of shade inside the gorge, even at high noon.
POPULARITY	👥	Enough walkers and tourist groups as well.
WHERE TO SLEEP WHERE TO EAT	🍴	Sougia offers a lot of accommodation for every budget. There are two tavernas at the entrance and two others at the exit of the gorge, but a lot more in Sougia.
ACCESS	🚍	Take the bus to Agia Irini from Chania or Sougia.
SIGHTS	🏛	The gorge itself. See also Fygou ravine.
DRAWBACKS	✖	Lots of people and unfinished improvement works.

There is a small village on the way from Chania to Selino, after the junction to Omalos, that lies among green slopes. The gorge that lies below took its name from the village. Apart from its natural beauty, the gorge gave its name to some of the fiercest battles during the Ottoman occupation. Though some of its natural fierceness is lost due to the "improvement" works, Ageriniotiko Gorge (the first gorge) is still a sample of Crete's natural grandeur. The gorge used to be part of the productive life of the people here. They used to have bee hives producing very nice honey. You can still find some in the surrounding area. Ovens worked continuously to produce lime, while pine tree trunks gave tons of resin that was used in tanning. Apart from felling timber, they used to collect lots of balsam, especially the so-called miraculous dittany (diktamo).

The most usual walk is the descent from Agia Irini, but it can be done the other way round. On the main road from Chania to Sougia, soon after the village, there is a sign indicating the start of the trail. You can't miss it. A road descends from there to the tourist pavilion. 100 m beyond that, there is a pretty bridge with water flowing underneath. Unfortunately, the water disappears after a while. The lovely wide trail is covered with huge plane trees (nobody knows how old they really are) which offer their generous shade.

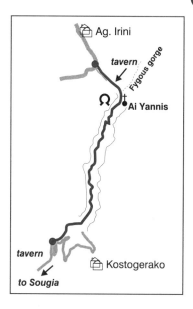

Walk for 15 minutes and you'll see a sign pointing to the Fygou (fugitive) ravine. The name comes from a historical incident. Women and children were hiding inside the gorge as a cruel and merciless Janissary, named Kaouris, decided to enter the gorge and pursue them. Women and children finally managed to flee to Omalos passing through this impassable gorge. It is a very attractive walk to or from Omalos.

20 minutes after the entry, you'll reach the Ai Yannis rock chapel. This is a huge rock that resembles a chapel. Further down, the stone-paved trail climbs up the slope of the gorge to Fournaki, a well made recreation area. You have already spent one hour inside the gorge. From this point on, the narrow section of the gorge begins.

The trail descends to the creek bed moving up and down several times, trying to avoid the huge rocks lying inside the bed. Be careful on the rocks, as they are very slippery. The trail is partly destroyed due to recent harsh winters, but you'll find no difficulty continuing.

Vegetation is really more than enough. Some brave pine trees are perched on the gorge's slopes. The riverbed is full of oleanders, chaste trees and a lot of wild flowers, which decorate the area from March until the end of April. Look carefully at the sides of the gorge to find wild lettuces, verbasko and Cretan ebony, all of them endemic species.

In three and a half hours, you'll exit the gorge from its left side onto a gravel road. You'll find another tourist pavilion there, nicely built inside an olive grove. You can continue until Sougia following the riverbed to the Koustogerako Bridge. From there, take the paved road leading to the village.

Dittany or Erontas

There are a lot of indigenous plants on Crete. One of them has been really famous from ancient times up to today: DITTANY. They say it is miraculous and its name derives from the Dikti Mountain or from the goddess Diktina (the Greek name is "Diktamo"). They also call it Erontas or Stomatohorto.

Its distinct, fluffy leaf can be picked out easily on the steep chalky slopes, a very pleasant drink for us these days, a miraculous panacea for our forefathers.

Twenty four authors have written about it, among them Theofrastos, a pupil of Aristotle. Aristotle said that when the wild goats were wounded by poisoned arrows, they looked for Dittany. Not only did Dittany made the body exude the poison, but it also cured the wound. You will hear the same story from shepherds up in the mountains all around Crete.

Hippocrates used it to cure bile and kidney cysts and he also made poultices out of it. Dioskouridis thought it was good for many things, while Aphrodite cured Aeneas' wounds with it ('The Aeneid' by Virgil, 12.412).

Dittany is gathered usually in August when in full blossom, because the leaves then have a very pleasant scent. Many local people used to gather and sell this herb at high prices to merchants from Chania, who in turn exported it. In the Middle Ages, Benedictine, the acclaimed liqueur, contained dittany, and even today vermouth is scented with dittany.

8. KOUSTOGERAKO – OMALOS (THROUGH GINGILOS)

DIFFICULTY	📈	■ ■ ■ ■
DURATION	🕐	6 h 30', 14.5 km (to ascend to Gingilos add another 1 h 30')
ELEVATION CHANGE	🛗	a) Koustogerako – cistern/kiosk: 1 h 10' 340 m up b) Cistern/kiosk – Ahlada's Mitata: 2 h 15' 670 m up c) Ahlada's Mitata – Gingilos col: 2 h 190 m up d) Gingilos col – Xyloskalo: 60' 470 m down
TERRAIN	🏔	Ascending trail through a tree covered gully. Then you walk on limestone (partly slippery and exposed).
SIGNPOSTING	🔼	E4 signposting.
WHEN TO GO	📅	May–June, September–October.
WATER	〰	Take enough water with you, because the Linoseli spring below the Gingilos col is at the end of the walk.
SHADE	🌿	Shade only in the wooded part when ascending the gully after Koustogerako. From this point on, you'll be exposed to the sun.
POPULARITY	👥	You'll meet practically no one, because this part of the E4 trail is not on the map.
WHERE TO SLEEP WHERE TO EAT	🍴	Sougia has accommodation for every budget. There are some good places in Omalos as well. "Polyfimos" taverna is a good food option in Sougia, but there are a lot more. While in Omalos, try "Drakoulakis" (New Omalos has rooms to let as well), where they serve good traditional cuisine.
ACCESS	✏	Take a taxi to Koustogerako from Sougia or walk there. Four buses travel daily from Chania to Omalos. The first one leaves Chania at 6 am.
SIGHTS	🏛	Stunning views over the Trypiti and Samaria gorges. Formidable geological formations on the way from Gingilos to Xyloskalo. Lots of orchids, tulips and crocuses after the forest.
DRAWBACKS	⊗	The gravel road above Koustogerako has spoilt the trail.

This is a demanding hike, offering landscape variety. It ascends from 500 m to 1,800 m and descends again to 1,200 m, passing through forests, gullies, gorges, screes, exposed passages and old trails. The first exposed passage, at the entry to the Trypiti Gorge, is secured with a wire rope, but, if you find snow remaining there, you'd better avoid it. There are stunning views from Gingilos col to the South and to the North. If you have time to spare, climb to Gingilos' peak before going down to Xyloskalo.

Before starting the hike, have a coffee in Kyria Sofia's coffee shop to breathe in the calm village atmosphere. From the small square, follow the cement road uphill to the mountain. An E4 sign informing you of the hike's duration should be there. After leaving the village, the road turns into a gravel road, and you'll come to a stone-built spring with refreshing water, the last one before Linoseli. 2,200 km away from the village, after passing two bends past a cement cistern, the trail turns left, away from the road. Soon enough you return to the road. Turn left again 100 m after that, following the trail (almost northeast). After an hour's walk you will arrive at a country church, a kiosk and a water tank, where the gravel road ends for good. A good stone-built trail traverses downwards on the pine-forested slope, heading northeast. Soon the trail leads you to the gully. Walking under the trees is more than pleasant. Pine trees cover the sky offering their desirable shade.

The gully turns east now. It widens and the trail continues on the right for a while. You may see some red signs on your left which head northeast. This is the trail leading to the Seliniotiko loop. Continue east following the gully. 1 h 30´ after the kiosk or 2 h 45´ from the beginning of the trail, the gully seems to end up on the Ahlada slopes. You are already 1,350 m above sea level. Take the left side of the gully now, where you'll come to a cement cistern full of water for animals, and an old mitato (shepherd outpost). Go east towards the col. In less than half an hour, you'll arrive at the old shepherds' mitato built in a small hollow at an altitude of 1,500 m, between Ahlada (South) and Psilafi (North). It takes almost 3 h 30´ from Koustogerako to here.

At the eastern exit of the basin gap lies Trypiti Gorge, offering a taste of what follows. At this point, follow the trail that heads north, parallel to the gorge, which is not the Trypiti Gorge itself, but one of its branches. Walk north, always on the left side of the gully towards the col ahead of you. The steep gorge becomes a small gully until it completely disappears. Meanwhile, you climb up to a col and Volakia and Gingilos peaks stand in front of you.

From this point on, you must move carefully. The trail turns left and traverses the steep slope. In less than 10´ you'll come to an unstable and exposed part that is secured with a wire rope. Try it before you use it. In addition, test every step before you take it in order to avoid

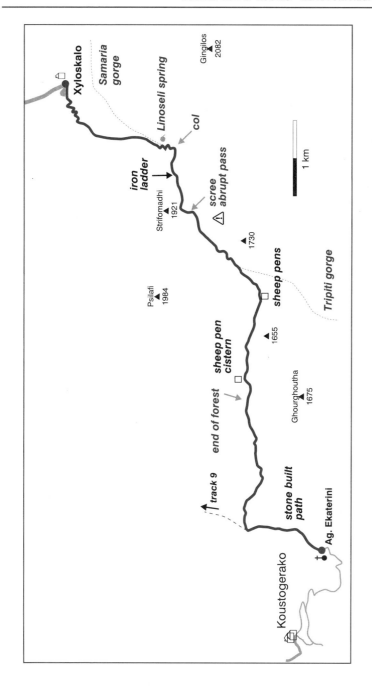

unstable rocks. You will probably find snow here until the beginning or the middle of May, depending on the snowfall during the winter. If you don't have the appropriate equipment, don't try this trail.

After the scree, climb until you reach a height of 1,850 m. Then you descend continuously on a relatively unstable and ill-defined path to Gingilos Ridge. At some point, you will scramble for 4–5 m (there are iron steps to help you). The last part is stony and heads mostly downhill. It can be confusing. Try to move just below the ridge on the southern slope. It will have taken you 5½ hours to reach Seli from Koustogerako.

The view from the col is magnificent, even if you don't climb to the summit of Gingilos. It is less than an hour walking from here to Xyloskalo. The spot is ideal if you want to marvel at the view, adore the eagles flying above you and enjoy the beautiful wild flowers that grow only on these rough Cretan slopes. Find the small "glory-of-the-snow" (white petals with purple ends) and the even smaller Anhoussa (blue-purple petals with white stamens).

Below the ridge, the path is well defined, and it descends gradually. So, in 15 minutes you will lose 250 m of elevation and be at the Linoseli Spring. One can usually find water here all summer long. The path descends more, passing through beautiful rock formations like man-made sculptures, and climbs again for 10′ until the final descent to Xyloskalo, covering the trail's last 1,200 m. Looking northeast you see Kalergis' hut and to your east Pachnes, the highest peak of Lefka Ori.

There is a restaurant and a tourist pavilion in Xyloskalo, because from here one can enter the famous Samaria Gorge. Prices are a bit high, but not outrageous. If you want to sleep here, there are two options. You can keep walking for almost 1½ hours until Kallergis' hut, or follow the road to Omalos (5 km).

The Coffee Shop (Kafeneio)

Let's imagine that we have walked for hours on the Cretan mountains (or beaches for that matter) and we end up in a village. What is the first thing we try to find there? The coffee shop (kafeneio) of course!

Coffee shops are at the centre of life in Crete (and everywhere around Greece). They are the gathering places, the feast places, information centres, social centres, places where one makes trade agreements and, of course, places where one can find a drink and grab a bite. Some of them (in small mountain villages) also sell basic supplies justifying the term "coffee shop-taverna-grocery".

The coffee shop's history is long (maybe from the Byzantine Empire or even older), even though there was no coffee back then. They offered wine, raki and herbal teas. They took on their current form during Ottoman times, when coffee was introduced as a drink. The evolution of the coffee shop has been continuous, and nowadays we have cafeterias and bars enriched with electronic games, video projectors and much more, even in mountain villages. Today it is difficult to find a traditional coffee shop. Coffee shops are still male dominated (apart from Sundays after mass and at festivals, when one can also see women). What men do there, apart from drinking various tipples, is discuss (and dispute of course). They discuss politics, football, and European Union subsidies. They play cards (even though it is officially prohibited), chequers, backgammon and watch football games on TV, all together. In older days, there used to be a political division among the coffee shops (and there is still in some places): coffee shops for the leftists and coffee shops for the conservatives, more like a club.

What coffee shops are actually offering doesn't stop here. Even today many different events, like political speeches and meetings, informative lectures about the European Union and other subjects of interest (like pesticides or agricultural devices), local festivals, commemorative gatherings and many other events are held here, making cinemas, meeting rooms, concert halls and such multifunctional places unnecessary for most villages.

Lefka Ori Region

9. KOUSTOGERAKO – OMALOS

DIFFICULTY	■ ■ ■ □
DURATION	6 h total time
ELEVATION CHANGE	a) Koustogerako – cistern/kiosk: 1 h 10′ 340 m up b) Cistern/kiosk – trails junction: 30′ 170 m up c) Trails junction – cistern: 3 h 30′ 230 m up d) Cistern – Omalos paved road: 50′ 150 m down
TERRAIN	Ascending trail through tree-covered gully at the beginning. Then you walk on stony terrain through a forest.
SIGNPOSTING	E4 signposting and some red marks.
WHEN TO GO	April–October.
WATER	Take enough water with you, because water can be found only on the last part of the walk.
SHADE	Shade only in the wooded part at the first third of the route.
POPULARITY	You'll meet practically no one, because the route is long and not well marked.
WHERE TO SLEEP WHERE TO EAT	Sougia has accommodation for every budget. There are some good options in Omalos as well. The "Polyfimos" taverna is a good choice in Sougia, but there are a lot more. While in Omalos try Drakoulakis (in New Omalos with rooms-to-let as well) serving good traditional cuisine.
ACCESS	Take a taxi to Koustogerako from Sougia or walk there. Four buses travel daily from Chania to Omalos. The first one leaves Chania at 6 am.
SIGHTS	Stunning views over the Agia Irini Gorge. Lots of orchids in the spring time.
DRAWBACKS	The gravel road above Koustogerako has spoilt the trail.

This trail is really old and pleasant, and it was used to connect Koustogerako with Omalos. Moreover, it is an alternative route when there is snow on the roads after Ahlada and Gingilos. This trail, with its fantastic views, ends as another gravel road losing all its wildness and beauty, because it crosses the slope very smoothly.

At the start the route is much like the one that goes to Ahlada (Route 8). While walking inside the forested gully, the gully's direction

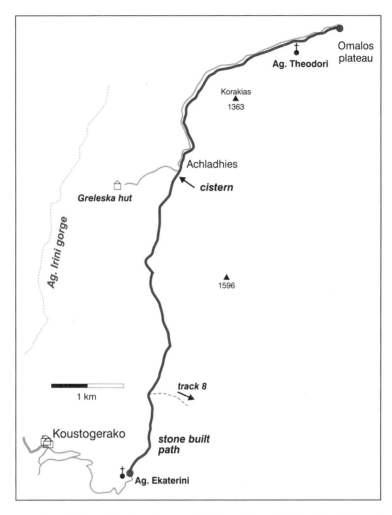

turns abruptly from North to East and widens. Take the left side of the gully (North) and you will find some red marks heading north-northeast.

Follow these marks and you exit the densely forested gully climbing slowly. Traverse at the top, keeping a steady route above the rocks that hang over the Agia Irini Gorge. It is a long traverse on the west slopes of Mount Psiloritis, and it'll take some time, but you will be rewarded by the beauty and the stunning views. At some point, you will come to a small valley with a stony riverbed. Follow any of the uphill goat tracks for a while, until you reach the next hill.

From there, continue to the North descending to the shallow gully at the bottom. You will find a cistern and a cement water tank. There is water here, although you are almost at the end of the hike. Follow the gravel road that descends northeast. In less than an hour, you come to the small church of Agios Thodoros. The walk really ends here because the rest of the path leading to Omalos became a paved road a long time ago. To reach Omalos follow the road northeast, but you can also hitchhike avoiding the boring walk on the road.

The Cretan Lyre

The lyre was a musical instrument in ancient Greece, but does not seem to have any close relationship with the Cretan lyre of today. They just happen to have the same name. It belongs to a class of arch-shaped instruments, which can be found in many places around Greece, Middle Eastern countries and the Balkans. The word lyre is often found in literature, but the first specific references to stringed instruments with the use of a fiddlestick are in Digenis Akritas' epic drama, which is dated back to the end of 10th or early 11th Century. Historians tend to agree that playing the strings of an instrument with a fiddlestick or bow, and not with the hand, dates to the 9th Century A.D. This technique with a continuous melodic line passed to the Byzantines and the Arabs during the same era.

The bow is made, as in the olden times, from resinated horse's tail hair. Gerakokoudouna, the small round bells which decorate the bow, are part of the old musical techniques. There are no frets, and the musician has to press the strings with his or her nails and not with the fingertips, unlike the violin. Up to the beginning of the 20th Century, lyres were constructed by the players themselves who used trees from the area, and made bows from horse or donkey tail hair. But western influences helped to replace the lyre in Greece with the more popular violin. The Cretan lyre though, is not only alive, but is also a part of everyday life and the Cretan mentality.

10. SOUGIA – AGIA ROUMELI

DIFFICULTY	📈	■ ■ ■ ■
DURATION	🕐	Almost 9 h, 22 km
ELEVATION CHANGE	📊	a) Sougia – first col: 1 h 20′ 135 m up b) First col – Pikilassos: 1 h 30′ 100 m down, 280 m up c) Pikilassos – Tripiti beach: 40′ 300 m down d) Tripiti beach – Klados gorge ridge: 1 h 50′ 150 m up e) Klados gorge ridge – Domata beach: 40′ 150 m down f) Domata beach – gully: 1 h 40′ 500 m up g) Gully – Agia Roumeli: 1 h 30′ 500 m down
TERRAIN	🏔	Relatively difficult to find the route on limestone and various rolling stones. The going gets better in the wooded areas.
SIGNPOSTING	🔼	E4 signposting, though scarce.
WHEN TO GO	📅	April–May, September–October.
WATER	〰	Before Pikilassos there is a spring that may have some water. At the exit from Tripiti Gorge, behind the small church, there is also water. Take 3 litres with you.
SHADE	🌳	There is enough shade on most parts of the walk, but not particularly dense. When climbing the big ascent, you will be exposed to the sun for a long time.
POPULARITY	👥	Even though it is a difficult hike, you will meet some other walkers.
WHERE TO SLEEP WHERE TO EAT	🍴	Sougia and Agia Roumeli have a lot of pleasant rooms to let. Try "Galini" or "Artemis". Take a good snack with you. When in Sougia, try "Polyfimos" taverna, which has good food and most of the people working there are locals. In Agia Roumeli they are more touristy, but you can always find decent food. Try to find Roussos Tzatzimakis; he is a great cook.
ACCESS	➤	Take the bus, one service per day, to Sougia and then the boat from Palaiohora or Agia Roumeli. To go to Agia Roumeli, take the boat from Palaiohora, Sougia or Sfakia.
DRAWBACKS	✖	Lack of time. There is never enough of it to enjoy a hike like this!

This is one of the toughest hikes in Crete. It isn't due to the technical difficulty of the hike, but to the fact that it is a very long one and the sun is merciless for most of the route. What you will see is so beautiful that it really is worth all the pain. The landscape alternates constantly, changing from pine forests on the slopes to rocks, and then to marvellous beaches. One moment you linger on the trail up on the slope looking down at the sea like a bird, and the next you are by the sea wetting your feet in the waves, looking at the steep slopes above. You go up and down like this five times.

Maybe it would be better to make this hike a two day excursion, in order to make the most of it. Either way, wear a pair of good boots and take plenty of water with you. If you are afraid of heights, you can check out the route from the boat that sails from Sougia to Agia Roumeli. Above all, don't attempt it if the weather is bad or if strong north winds are blowing.

Even if this description is from Sougia to Agia Roumeli, as a natural successor to the walk from Palaiochora, it is probably better if you do it the other way round. By doing so, the burning sun will catch you when walking the easy parts between Pikilasso and Sougia. Your greatest concern is to avoid the heat of the day, so you need to get up before dawn. There is a creek bed at the east side of the village which you follow for 200 m uphill. Pass by the fenced archaeological site of Syia, and you'll find an opening on your right with a pine tree signposted with E4 signs. Climb on a well-defined path. Pass trough olive trees, locust trees and small rocks until, 15´ later, you turn right onto a gravel road. Climb for 20´ to the end of the road, and then turn east on the clear path. The view to Sougia behind you is magnificent. From this point on, the signs are as scarce as the pine trees.

Your first aim is the col that can be seen to the East, below a stony hill. 15´ later you'll find a junction. Turn right and after a while you'll find yourself between two gullies. Take the one on your right heading east, and in less than 15´ you will be at the col. Follow the clear path and descend to the bottom of the gully. Keep on for a while and you will pass in front of a small cave on your left. 300–350 m inside the gully you turn east again. After a while, you will see the scenic bay of Agios Antonis below you.

Continue east for 25´–30´ among short pine and locust trees. Be careful not to lose the path because of the numerous goat tracks. Prophet Elias' hill can be seen in front of you. Descend gradually one more time to a point where there is a distinctive split in the slope on your left. A huge fallen pine tree forces you to divert a bit from your route. Follow the gully bed for 200 m. The landscape becomes wild now. East, that is on the right side of the gully, you'll see the ascending path. Find your way among dense pine trees and, after a while, you reach abandoned fields. There is a spring with a little running water next to a stone-built shrine. The path climbs again and in a while you'll reach a distinctive col, almost two hours away from the point when you left the gravel road.

The ancient Cretan city of Pikilassos used to be here. On your right is the old Turkish castle. The path that climbs to the South leads to Prophet Elias' country chapel after 15´. Every summer, on the eve of the saint's feast, believers disembark at Trypiti Bay and climb here to honour the saint. Holy mass and good food all night long! The path heading north leads to Trypiti's abandoned settlement.

It will take you 20´– 30´ to descend or, even better, roll down the scree and you are in the gorge's riverbed. Trypiti is a wild gorge, therefore very difficult to cross. You must rappel with your rope to descend it, and it isn't easy to find your way out. When you reach the river bed, continue to the sea. Just before the gorge's exit, at its east foot, there is a small church and the last water spring.

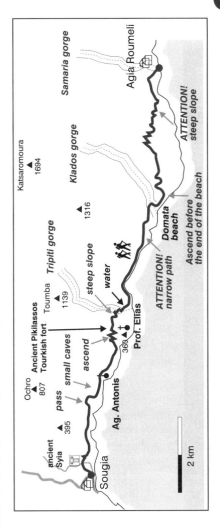

Following the path is becoming adventurous now. Walk on the rocks next to the sea, and pray for the sea to be calm. If the sea is rough, don't attempt to walk here. Walk towards a large hollow in the rocks, cross it and after a while you reach some small shepherds' houses. Though they are hospitable, they don't really bother about keeping this beautiful place clean.

Leave the sea behind you as you cross round the bay. Turn your back to the bay and walk along the rocky edge. Look on your left to find the stone steps that will help you climb up the cliffside. Be careful while walking on the next part until you reach Klados Gorge.

Continue east for almost an hour. The path climbs to an exposed passage. Go past a small wooden gate and you are at a balcony which hangs above an impressive cliff overlooking the sea. Continue a little more on a path eroded by rain and goats, and descend steeply before reaching Klados Gorge, 45´ later. This is one of the most beautiful beaches in Crete. It is called Domata. The name (rooms in Greek) derives from the multiple levels formed by soil erosion. One can come here by sea or by this route. Traverse the beach for 15´ until you reach the eastern end, where you can see a huge rockslide. You have covered 2/3 of the route so far and you are almost 6 hours away from Sougia.

The most demanding ascent of this hike starts here. At the only point where the high vertical walls come down to the sand, you can see something that resembles a path. This path climbs steeply up the slope above. Climb for almost 1 h 30´, until you reach a height of 500 m. You walk through pine trees, which offer precious shade at this time of the day, when the sun is at its zenith. Volakias peak appears to the North.

At some point, you will reach a gully. Descend to its bed and immediately start the last ascent of the hike. The old path, clear at first, heads east through a dense pine tree forest. As soon as it starts descending at the first gully, navigation will get confusing again. Climb down for 20 m to the gully and then turn east.

At some point you will see the best view of Agia Roumeli lying ahead of you, though it seems closer than it is. You will need 50´ more, climbing down a steep slope. When this descent is over, you must traverse left passing some fences until you reach a distinctive gutter of fallen rocks. Climb a bit more to find the path. WARNING – If you keep on descending you'll find yourselves falling over into the void! Traverse continuously under the rocks, which have many small caves. From there, climb down to a pine forest and the fence that can be seen below. After a while, you reach Agia Roumeli's first houses or, to be more precise, the first rooms-to-let. It took you 9 hours to get here from Sougia. For statistical purposes the hike is 21.9 km and the total elevation gain is 1,500 m.

11. SAMARIA GORGE

DIFFICULTY	downhill: ■ ■ ☐ ☐ uphill: ■ ■ ■ ☐
DURATION	5 h 30′ – 6 h
ELEVATION CHANGE	1,220 m elevation gain a) Agia Roumeli – gorge's entrance: 30′, +50 m b) Entrance – Portes: 30′, +100 m c) Portes – Samaria village: 1 h, +220 m d) Samaria village – small church: 2 h, +300 m e) Small church – exit: 1 h 30′, +550 m
TERRAIN	Well laid, wide, easy path on a smooth terrain. Part of it is on pebbles on the riverbed.
SIGNPOSTING	It is signposted, but this isn't necessary because you can't miss it.
WHEN TO GO	Early May–October.
WATER	At 6–7 points there are artificial stone built water sources.
SHADE	Most of the hike is under shade in the forest.
POPULARITY	During summertime 40–50 people climb up the gorge, whereas 1,500–2,000 people descend it.
ACCESS	Take the boat from Hora Sfakion (2h) or from Palaiochora (2h) or walk following Routes 10 and 12. There are 3–4 daily bus services during summertime and a bus service to Chania.
SIGHTS	The hike is one of great beauty, with gorgeous walls, rich flora and beautiful views during the last part.
DRAWBACKS	Crowds of people.

The biggest and the most famous Cretan gorge. There is nothing more to be said.

The usual way of going through the Samaria Gorge (the locals call it "faragas") is by descending it. Large groups of people, all together, walk down using the easy path. Our suggestion is to walk it the other way round, to enjoy solitude while others move in crowds, to turn what is easy going into an adventure, to change what is common to something of beauty and diversity. What you must pay for all this is burning a few more thousand calories (which is actually good) and sweating a bit more than usual, but we are sure you will feel rewarded. It will be something to remember. If you still have doubts, think of solitude and tranquility.

You must of course start very early in the morning from Agia Roumeli. For the first 2 hours until you reach Samaria village, you will be alone with the trees, the birds, maybe a kri-kri and naturally the gorge. Then you will meet hordes of people coming down (you won't believe your eyes). Be patient, it will be over soon and after 2 hours, when you have the climb ahead, you will be alone again. Another advantage is that during the morning at low altitudes, where the gorge is wide and open, it is cool and shady. When you reach higher altitudes at noon, you enjoy the freshness of the forest, whereas all the others are freezing when they start the hike from Omalos in the morning and after 5–6 hours, when they reach Agia Roumeli, they are being burnt by the sun (at least 20^0C temperature difference). If you are a photographer, you will have plenty of opportunities to photograph animals and landscapes without unwanted people in your frames. And, last but not least, sleeping in Agia Roumeli the night before the walk and in Omalos (that is if you wish to) the night after the walk is an experience by itself. Sensational beauty, tranquillity, almost no other people and lovely, new hotels. If you are still not convinced, think of your mountain ego: what is an 1,200 m ascent? Just one more challenge.

Either way, this walk is one of the most impressive in Crete. The path is clear, wide and well laid, there are a lot of fountains and places to rest and clear waters for a refreshing cold swim (but you must not be seen, since it is strictly forbidden!).

The starting point is the Agia Roumeli main road, the road that heads upwards from the wharf, passing among tavernas, rooms-to-let and mini-markets. It is easy to find, as there are signs to the Samaria Gorge or to the provincial Medical Centre. Turn right and then left on a small gravel road. Straight ahead you see the entrance (or the exit) to the gorge. Beside you, flows Samaria's river (there is water even in the summer). You cross it twice using small bridges. The first 2 km are not very pleasant. The interesting thing is the riverbed, 2–3 m deep and narrow. The multi-layered rock is eroded by the water.

Half an hour later, you come to some small shops and the ticket office, where you must pay the entrance fee. Keep the ticket because you will need it at the exit. As you move forward, the gorge becomes wilder, the rock face becomes more vertical and the vegetation becomes denser. Sometimes you walk on the left and sometimes on the right side of the gully, and in less than 30′ you will be at the most photographed spot of the gorge, the "Portes" (doors). The gorge here is only 3 m wide, and the cliff face is 200 m high, rising vertically above you. Avoid passing through the water (if you wish) by using the

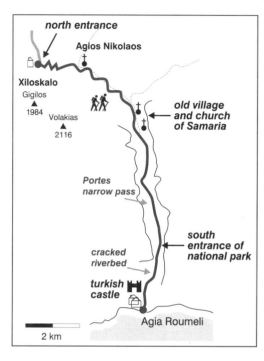

wooden platform. In the winter or during a flash flood, the water can reach a level of 3 m. The water flow is particularly rough and it is impossible to cross it (it is forbidden). Some years ago 3 tourists drowned here, while trying to swim across this passage after heavy rain.

Continue on the path inside the now wide riverbed, and then on the right side of the gully. Take a look at the vertical walls of rock with their wild vegetation and the local flora, pine trees, cedars, maples and numerous other plants and wild flowers. After reaching an organised recreation area (stone-built fountain, benches and tables, toilets and rubbish bins) go to the left hand shore and you will find the abandoned Samaria village (it lies on the right side of the river). You are now 2 hours away from Agia Roumeli and at a height of 320 m.

The village with its ruined houses, the recreation areas, some national park wardens, mules and tame kri-kris are the only signs of civilization you'll see (thank goodness there are no stores or other such intrusions). Here you might meet people who descend the gorge and are really fast trekkers.

The path is getting steeper now. It often crosses screes moving always

Chamois ("Kri-Kri")

Chamois, or simply wild goat, belongs to the goat spe-cies as is obvious from its name, or, if you are a scientist, to the even-toed Ruminantia family. It lives on the mountainous terrain of southern and central Europe, central Asia and Africa. In many places it is endangered because of the unrestricted hunting, the habitat limitations and interbreeding with the common goat. There are a lot of subspecies which differ in shape and dimension.

Some of its characteristics are the ability to jump a long way, its high speed, the ability to climb or stand on steep slopes and sides of rocks, and the ability to endure the cold. They live in small herds up on the mountains when the snow melts and they feed on alpine pasture, whereas during the winter they come down to low-er altitudes in the forests. Pregnancy lasts almost five months and they give birth to one or two offsprings at the end of the spring. Calves are able to follow the rest of the herd after a few days. The most common species in Europe are the wild alpine goat (ibex) and the wild Pyrenees goat. They are related to the Greek wild goat that lives in Pindos and on Mount Olympus. The Cretan subspecies is unique and lives only in Crete. Its local name is Kri-kri. It lives freely on Lefka Ori and on Psyloritis. Their number is decreasing for the reasons given above. Samaria's national park is their main habitat and one can see them on its slopes. Many come down to the main guardhouse of the uninhabited village of Samaria to get food from the forest guards. One can photograph them easily as they don't run away from people that cross the gorge.

In the Greek folklore Kri-kri is considered a very special animal, a symbol of freedom, and for that reason is frequently mentioned in traditional songs (rizitika and mantinades) where it is spoken of highly, often as a companion to rebels and partisans.

in the forest, crisscrossing the river from the left to the right shore. Unfortunately, for the next 1–2 hours you will constantly meet people moving in the opposite direction. You may as well forget the usual "good morning" and "hi", unless you like repeating the same phrases again and again or you are practising your elementary English. Pay no attention to the usual rude people who stop in the middle of path or decide to stay there. Wear your best smile, enjoy the beautiful surroundings and perhaps a lovely swim in the refreshing waters of the river among the rocks. Move away from the path, following the riverbed to enjoy it the most.

Finally, the path turns towards the right-hand shore leaving the gully (1 h 30'–2 h from Samaria village) and climbs up the slopes. Trees are bigger now, huge pines and cypresses, and they offer their shade generously, water is plentiful (through artificial but beautifully built fountains), and you come to the old country chapel of Agios Nikolaos. You have left the hordes of people behind now, and you can enjoy nature's tranquility once again.

The path is very good, wide but steep in parts. There are some steps supported by small wooden trunks. As you move upwards, the grandeur of the White Mountains (Lefka Ori) is revealed before you. Gingilos and Volakias are on your left, Pachnes and Zaranokefala are on the right and behind you, whereas in front and above is the gorge entrance at Linoseli. Before you know it, you are at the end of the walk at the Omalos outpost, the gorge exit, and the parking area after an ascent of 1,250 m and a unique experience.

Lefka Ori Region

12. AGIOS YANNIS – AGIA ROUMELI

DIFFICULTY	📈	■ ■ □ □
DURATION	🕐	3 h 30'
ELEVATION CHANGE	📊	750 m descent a) Agios Yannis – cobbled path's start: 45', 180 m descent b) Cobbled path's start – Agios Pavlos: 1 h 15', 570 m descent c) Agios Pavlos – Agia Roumeli: 1 h 30'
TERRAIN	🔺	Ruined cobbled path at the beginning. The last part is tiring, as there is no path and you must walk on sand and pebbles.
SIGNPOSTING	🔼	Red marks on the first section (sparse). In the third section there is no path, and you must walk on sand and pebbles signposted with piles of rocks.
WHEN TO GO	📅	All year round.
WATER	〰️	Take water from the cafe in Agios Yannis, in Agios Pavlos from the little store, or from the spring on the beach.
SHADE	☀️	Shade is sparse, some trees below Agios Yannis and some when approaching Agios Pavlos.
POPULARITY	👥	Practically no one from Agios Yannis to Agios Pavlos. You will meet some people on the section near the beach from Sfakia to Agia Roumeli.
ACCESS	↗️	A paved road connects Hora Sfakion with Anopoli (12 km) ending in Agios Yannis (18 km). There is no bus going there, so you must take a taxi from Sfakia.
SIGHTS	🏛️	Agios Pavlos' Byzantine country chapel built in the 10th century A.D. on the beach. The hike is of exceptional beauty, offering stunning views and landscape diversity.
DRAWBACKS	✖️	Lack of shade, Agia Roumeli tourist development (things are quiet only in the early evening) and the heat (from June to September).

An easy-going beautiful walk offering landscape and terrain variety. It combines walking through a pine and cedar tree forest with a coastal walk. One can swim, visit historical monuments and observe samples of the rich Cretan flora.

The walk starts from Agios Yannis, a secluded village lying on the south foot of Lefka Ori. The village is almost abandoned with just a few people remaining there, mainly shepherds. The road leading to Agios Yannis from Aradena was paved some years ago. If one wants to walk there, one must try to find parts of the old trail that still exist (most of it is lost, as

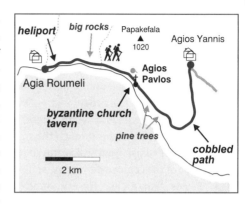

the road was opened just above it). The old school with its attractive yard lies at the entrance of the village and is sometimes open offering coffee (take water from here). On the opposite side, you will see the red marks that lead to the Agia Roumeli path. The path is well-defined at first, descending, stony, moving among dry stone walls next to the shallow bed of a dried stream. After a while you come to the Agios Yannis country chapel, which you can visit. It is a typical example of island architecture. Short cedar and cypress trees are all over the place, offering shade mixed with other kinds of the Cretan vegetation (oregano, thyme, rock roses, etc). In half an hour you reach a large plateau full of cedars, fenced to protect it from the animals. Other paths meet here as well, goat tracks mostly, but they are not very clear anymore. Stay on your path and go straight ahead, heading south, and in a while the path clears again, descending and crossing a gully. Climb to the other side (there is a fenced animal pen on your left).

The walk continues among brushwood (thyme, sage, thorny burnet), small bushes, and scattered rocks. The air is full of scents from the aromatic plants that grow all over the place. The path, a goat track, ends at the edge of the cliff, with a great view to the southern shore of Crete. The steep green slope descends 600 m into the blue waters of the Libyan Sea. On your right, far away, you see the Samaria Gorge exit and the village of Agia Roumeli, crowned by the Lefka Ori peaks. On your left, you have a steep mountain side, whereas far to the South you can see Gavdos Island.

At this point starts an old stone-built path which has recently been rebuilt and used to connect Agios Yannis with Agios Pavlos. They carried food and other products to and from the village using mules to the seashore, and from there they used boats to Sfakia or Agia Roumeli and Sougia. The path was abandoned and partially destroyed, as practically no one lived in the village. The path descends steeply, from time to time turning into steps, until it flattens and you walk on soil again. There are many pine and cedar trees. Follow the slope to the sea below you. When you have lost enough height, turn right (west) and move parallel to the seashore through the forest. The path connects with the one that comes from Sfakia and Loutro (E4 signposting, 45´ from the start of the cobbled path), descending gradually and heading to Agios Pavlos. After a while, the Byzantine church and the beach are right in front of you. Further away are the restaurant and its outbuildings.

For the last 10´ you walk on the sand, descending steeply to the beach. Take a break here (short or long – we suggest the latter). Swim in the crystal clear blue waters (a bit cold due to underground springs), lie on the attractive pebbled shore, visit the small chapel and eat or drink something in the small cafe. Leaving the beach, the path climbs steeply on the sand for a while, until is levels again. You walk on soil, parallel to the sea among sparse pine trees offering some shade. You will see some E4 signs from time to time. The view is beautiful. On your left, the beach with its large rocks and stones, on your right the steep, green, stony slopes of Lefka Ori and straight ahead the Samaria Gorge exit. The path goes up and down gradually, on sand and pebbles or next to large rocks until, 1 h 15´ later, it reaches the Samaria Gorge river mouth, almost always full of water (except at the end of summer). After crossing the gully, you will reach the heliport and Agia Roumeli's first houses (during the winter, go further to the North to cross the river from the bridge).

13. LOUTRO – FINIKAS – AGIA ROUMELI

DIFFICULTY	■ ■ □ □	
DURATION	5 h	
ELEVATION CHANGE	250 m up, 250 m down a) Loutro – Marmara: 60', 50 m ascent, 50 m descent b) Marmara – Crossroads: 2 h, 200 m ascent, 100 m descent c) Crossroads – Agios Pavlos: 30', 100 m descent d) Agios Pavlos – Agia Roumeli : 90'	
TERRAIN	Mostly clear path, part of the walk on pebbles, sand and stones.	
SIGNPOSTING	E4 signs, not very easy to see.	
WHEN TO GO	All year round.	
WATER	From the cafes at the beginning or at the end, in Finikas and Agios Pavlos, or from the fountain in Agios Pavlos (if it is flowing).	
SHADE	The middle part of the hike is through a pine forest, so there is shade.	
POPULARITY	More than a few people in the summertime.	
ACCESS	No road access. You can walk there, or take the boat from Sfakia or Sougia.	
SIGHTS	The Byzantine Agios Pavlos country chapel (11th Century), the Turkish castle in Agia Roumeli. Impressive views at the Aradena Gorge exit, and exquisite beaches.	

One of the most attractive seaside walks in Crete, in an impressive landscape, combining steep rocky seaside cliffs with beautiful beaches, gorges, forests, and the unique Agios Pavlos country chapel.

We leave the small picturesque village of Loutro, heading to the western side of the small bay. We walk uphill on the clear path among cedars and small pine trees on the right side of a fence, still heading west, by-passing the path that leads us to the ruins of the ancient city of Finikas (10'–15') and leaving the old castle and other fortifications on our left. The trail that we see going to the right leads to Anopoli (Route 16). We continue on the gradual slope leaving the small peninsula behind, going downhill towards the small seaside settlement of modern Finikas. It has a few houses, rooms-to-let and tavernas (but more and more appear every year). The trail, for the next 15', continues parallel to the seaside until we reach the picturesque small bay of Marmaras, where the Aradena Gorge exit is. The distinctive marble rocks from which the bay takes its name "Marmara" (marble in Greek) create a fantastic landscape.

The trail goes on heading west, passing by a taverna and is sign-posted with E4 signs. Then it turns steeply uphill for the next half an hour or so. When you are 50–80 m above sea-level, take a course parallel to the seashore, traversing a steep slope. The trail is clear all the time and has no exposed nor very steep sections. There is little vegetation here, so there is little shade, but the views are terrific. As they say, you win some, you lose some!

An hour later, the vegetation is getting denser and the hike continues in a proper, if not really dense, pine and cedar forest.

After crossing over the steep spur that leads to the plateau below the small village of Ai Yannis, two hours walk from Marmara, we find ourselves at the crossroads. On our right is the trail to Ai Yannis and Aradena (Route 12). We continue straight on for almost half an hour until the seaside Byzantine chapel of Agios Pavlos and the small taverna near it. They say that St. Paul (Agios Pavlos in Greek) found shelter here, when a blizzard hit his boat on one of his trips to Palestine.

The walk now continues parallel to the sea, most of the way on the beach, for 1h 15´, crosses the small river flowing out of the Samaria Gorge, and ends in Agia Roumeli.

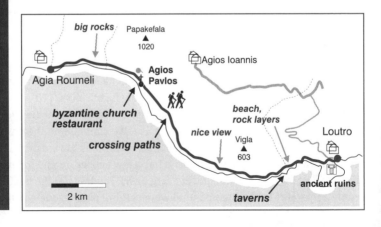

14. ARADENA GORGE

DIFFICULTY 📈	■ ■ ■ □
DURATION 🕐	2 h 30' approximately
ELEVATION CHANGE 📊	550 m down a) Iron bridge – gorge bed: 20', 100 m descent b) Gorge bed – vertical drop: 30', 50 m descent c) Drop – Livaniana junction: 45', 200 m descent d) Junction – Marmara: 45', 200 m descent
TERRAIN ⛰	Riverbed walk on stones and rocks.
SIGNPOSTING 🔼	Sparse.
WHEN TO GO 📅	All year round (not after heavy rainfall).
WATER 〰	Take water from the cafes in Aradena.
SHADE ☀	Enough shade, depending on the hour of the day.
POPULARITY 👥	You may meet some people during the summer.
ACCESS ⟋	With your own vehicle, or walk 3 km on the paved road from Anopoli. 1–2 daily bus services from Chania.
SIGHTS 🏛	The abandoned and half-ruined Aradena village. Its houses are in the traditional style, and are built at the edge of a cliff. The view from the iron bridge. The impressive and wild gorge with its dense vegetation and the lovely beach at the exit.
DRAWBACKS ⊗	Lack of easy access (entering and exiting the gorge) and the descent from the iron staircase (especially for those afraid of heights).

This is a walk through a wild and impressive gorge, with cliff sides up to 100–150 m and some difficult passages that require some rock climbing knowledge. Not recommended for inexperienced hikers or for those who are afraid of heights.

The hike starts from the Aradena Iron Bridge that offers spectacular views. First you should visit the abandoned village of Aradena (some houses and some streets have been renovated in the traditional style and make the visit worthwhile). Then, follow the old cobbled path, starting from the edge of the village at the base of the slope (the path is partly restored) which descends to the gorge's bed (20'). Follow the bed downhill, walking on pebbles, stones and soil. The walls of the gorge rise vertically above you up to 150 m. This part is striking and wild. The slopes and peaks of Lefka Ori and the iron bridge are behind you, and the next part of the gorge lies ahead. It twists between vertical

Lefka Ori Region

walls while trees and large rocks are scattered at its base, which is sometimes flat and sometimes narrow, steep, with slight descents on rocks.

Half an hour later you reach a vertical part of the bed, 10 m high, which you descend with the help of a long iron staircase fixed in the rock. The staircase ends on a large rock some meters high and the de-

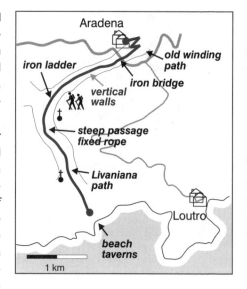

scent continues. Use the carved steps with the help of a rope, until you reach the bed again. This descent is actually easy enough (using the staircase and the rope) and breathtaking, making all the struggle worthwhile. There used to be a wire here instead of the staircase that made the descent difficult, requiring climbing equipment (harness, karabiners and slings). Ages ago there was just a rope (of dubious strength).

If you are afraid of heights, or the ladder is broken, take the alternative route. Some minutes before you reach the difficult part, a narrow marked path goes right on the steep slope (it is partially stone-built, so you may see it from below). It bypasses the difficult passage and comes to the flat bed 10′ later. The hike continues inside the bed with the walls 100–200 m vertically above you twisting from right to left. You will scramble a bit to pass over large rocks and stones. You can consider it a game, and in 30′ you are on the second steep part of the bed, which is just a few meters high (it is not vertical this time, and you descend it with the help of a rope fixed on the rock).

Now you walk in the forested and shaded bed among rocks, bushes, small trees and aromatic plants. If you are lucky enough you may see goats, kri-kris, turtles and vultures flying above you. The bed nar-

Vendettas

A vendetta, or blood revenge, is the most barbaric, cruel and insane custom in Crete. According to the laws of a vendetta, if someone intentionally kills another person, the victim's family must take revenge by killing the killer but, if that is impossible, by killing one of the killer's first degree relatives (brother, father, son). On the victim's side, those who are obliged to take revenge are the men who have a first degree relation (brother, father, son) to the victim. It is well known that vendetta is a male matter. Women do not take part in the killings, but they often encourage men to take revenge in order to honour the family name.

Fortunately, nowadays there aren't many vendettas. It is limited, mainly to the Sfakia region and some mountainous villages of Psiloritis. Once upon a time though, in a large part of Crete but in other areas in Greece as well (mainly mountainous such as Mani where it still exists), it was a rigid common law, leading many families into a vicious cycle of blood and revenge. The consequence was that there were vendettas which lasted for centuries and families that were in a continuous war with each other. There are villages and areas, such as Aradena and other mountainous villages in the Sfakia region, which were deserted by residents out of fear for their lives. They felt forced to emigrate to Athens or abroad and they never came back, not even to sell their properties and collect the money.

Vendetta started as a way of the people taking the law into their own hands during the Ottoman occupation, when justice was unfair and partial, and many killers were acquitted, walking free and ready to kill again. On other occasions the Turks did not punish killers, either intentionally ('let them kill themselves, why bother?'), or due to weakness (it was really hard to chase down people in the mountains), or even because they did not feel like it. So the victim's family had an obligation to punish the culprit. There were certain ways and rules for doing so, with the silent approval and support of the whole village. Vendetta existed and still exists in remote areas and among closed communities in other parts of the world, like Sicily, Corsica, Albania, Calabria and many Romany communities around the world (Romania, Ukraine). Thank goodness it is almost extinct, following the opening up of these areas to the outside world, to education and to fairer judicial systems.

rows and then widens, and in a while you reach the Livaniana junction. If you take the narrow path that climbs up to your left, you reach the village in about 40´. On the main path, 10´ later, you will see a small spring under a large rock. You can take water from here (no luck during the summer though). The bed is flat and wide now, and the gorge's walls get smaller and open up until half an hour later you reach the beautiful Marmara beach. The water is crystal clear and blue, the shore is sandy with slate plaques around as if cut by man's hand. There is also a small shop on the rocks to your right.

Cicadas, the Summer Troubadours

Everybody knows the tale of the hard working ant and the lazy cicada. But perhaps you don't know that cicadas sing without a care in the world because, as the ancient poet Xenarhos said, "happy live the cicadas because they have mute wives". It is indeed true that female cicadas do not actually sing. Male cicadas sing in order to find (or be found by) the female during the short time they live in this futile world.

Have you ever wondered what it would be like to live the life of this fussy insect, the cries of which fill the hot summer air?

Let's start from the beginning. Female cicadas lay their eggs in the bark of trees. From there a chrysalis is incubated. This chrysalis falls to the ground and remains there for one or two months. Nourished by the moisture from the tree's root, the well-fed cicadas break out from their cocoons to see the daylight.

The male cicadas, in order to perpetuate the species, brandish a membrane producing a very sexual sound... this oscillation has a frequency of 300–900 repetitions per second and is amplified by the trachea which works as a resonance chamber. In that way, the female finds her mate and the cycle continues. Some weeks later, the singing gradually stops until the following summer.

15. LOUTRO – LIVANIANA – ARADENA

DIFFICULTY	■ ■ ☐ ☐
DURATION	3 h, 6 km
ELEVATION CHANGE	700 m up, 160 m down a) Loutro – Livaniana: 1 h 30′ 280 m up b) Livaniana – gorge bed: 45′, 160 m down c) Gorge bed – Aradena: 50′, 400 m up
TERRAIN	Cobbled road and path at the beginning and end of the walk, then walking on a stony gorge bed and climb using iron staircases at the steep sections.
SIGNPOSTING	Sparse blue marks at the beginning.
WHEN TO GO	All year round, not if it rains.
WATER	Take water from Loutro or Livaniana. There is a spring inside the gorge, but it might be dry.
SHADE	Inside the gorge there is plenty of shade, especially if the sun is shining from the side. Until you reach Livaniana though, you'll get sunburnt.
POPULARITY	Loutro is a touristic place, so be prepared to see a lot of walkers, especially inside the gorge.
WHERE TO SLEEP WHERE TO EAT	There are several guesthouses in Loutro, budget and expensive. You will find several tavernas as well. Tavernas at Finikas are usually open during the high season.
ACCESS	Take the boat to Loutro from Sfakia, or walk there (Route 17). There is no bus service to Aradena.
SIGHTS	Finikas beach, the Turkish castle, the plain but beautiful Archagelon country chapel in Aradena, the traditionally-built houses in Livaniana and Aradena.
DRAWBACKS	The gravel road that destroyed the last part of the path before reaching Livaniana.

If there is still anything left from old Crete, then you will find it in this area around Aradena, Agios Yannis and Livaniana. For two thousand years now, people have been going up and down using the same paths from the Ancient Araden to Finikas Bay. With the only exception of Loutro village that has recently became a tourist attraction, the other villages are almost empty and lying in peace. The path, though it moves through wild places, conveys this peace and tranquillity. If the gravel road before Livaniana were not there, this feeling of the past would be complete.

Follow the path above the church which leads to the ruined Turkish castle. Continue west until you reach a hill towering above Finikas Beach. There are some palm trees there and a small church. On this hill the ancient city of Finikas was built, an important city during the Roman era, due to the purple rock shells from which they produced pigment. If you go straight on, the path

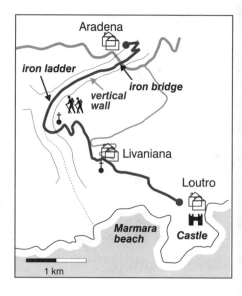

goes to Marmara and Agia Roumeli. You must climb to the gully which lies east of Livaniana. Follow the blue marks and take the old cobbled path, which goes up the steep slope. The well-defined path, two mules wide, used to be the main access to the hinterland.

Nowadays, these paths are of no use to anyone except for walkers. New roads were built in their place. Change sometimes replaces the old in a cruel manner, which is what happened when the new road destroyed the old path that used to go to Livaniana. Climb above the rubble and follow the road's last few meters until you reach the village, almost an hour away from the junction at Finikas.

The village is a row of plain, box-like houses, built that way to protect the residents from the heat that comes from the Libyan Sea. Climb until you come to the white church on top of the hill. The view is stunning. Move a bit further uphill to the ridge where the trail splits, offering several options. Right ahead lies the Aradena Gorge and some abandoned fields.

Heading to the gorge, descend to the fields that are now full of thorny burnets and scarlet pimpernels. Pass through the fence gate and continue to the left, descending the steep slope. The path moves beneath the red rocks and, after a while, you reach the gorge bed.

The "Saint General"

At the edge of Aradena stands a plain white chapel with a strange cupola, like a cap. This is Archangel Michael's chapel, the Ai Stratigos as the locals call it (literally meaning the Saint General), built in the 14th Century. At first it was not designed to be so large. The narthex (vestibule) was added later on. Ai Stratigos is deeply connected with the region's history as well as with its locals. As you can see, this saint holds a sword and the fierce Sfakians respect and fear him at the same time. Their respect is so great that when a man was accused of a dreadful cattle rustling offence, it was sufficient to take an oath of innocence in the name of the saint to be acquitted. He had to put his hand on the saint's icon and say "As this very hand differs from the saint's icon, likewise my soul differs from my body and from God. If I have done something or know something about your cattle, then let God not interfere but let a whole battalion of demons come and take my soul". If, on the other hand, the man didn't want to take this oath, it is anybody's guess what happened to him. He probably went to meet the saint in person!

In this very chapel, Daskalogiannis, the visionary rebel, had his headquarters during the 1770 rebellion. They defended the chapel for three days, until large numbers of Ottoman soldiers succeeded in cornering them, ingloriously ending the rebellion. They burned all the surrounding villages, until Daskalogiannis was forced to surrender to the Pasha.

There is a lone olive tree there. You have two options. The first is to descend to the sea at Marmara, and from there back to Finikas and Loutro. It is an hour's walk to Marmara. In the same direction (10´ on), there is a spring in the rocks, usually dry in the summertime.

The other option is to climb to Aradena. The wide gorge bed narrows, the stones turn to rocks and the path becomes a constant rock climbing game. Sometimes large piles of rocks point the ideal route, and even more often your hands are more necessary than your feet, because you need to scramble to get through. 20´–30´ later, you will find a large iron staircase fixed on the rock to help you go up (or down) the huge rocks. There are basically two staircases, but imagine that people used to travel on this path using only a rope and a chain. Climb for another 20´ and on the high walls of the gorge, you will see the new Bailey-type bridge, which connected Agios Yannis and Aradena with the rest of Crete.

As soon as you pass beneath the bridge, the gorge walls become lower and flatter. There, you will see the path that descends with a lot of switchbacks to the gorge bed and then climbs on the other side, connecting the villages with Anopoli. Climb the west slope. 15´ on, you reach the abandoned (due to a vendetta) Aradena village. At the edge of the rock stands the plain but beautiful Byzantine church of Agios Stratigos, which is actually dedicated to Archangel Michael. This church is very important to the local people. The now abandoned village is the living proof of the harsh life that these people used to endure.

"The Cockfight"

In the Sfakia region, the descendants of a nobleman named Skordilis often caused problems to the Venetians. Bear in mind that the whole Sfakia region is the only one in Crete that has never been conquered by anyone, except for tourists nowadays!

The most comic rebellion that ever took place, as its name suggests, is the rebellion known as "the cockfight". The feudal lords claimed a hen from every family every month, and this hen had to be well fed. Sfakians refused to obey this law. They actually suggested offering an egg instead and said that the Venetians ought to provide the hen to sit on it. This response ignited a war which lasted for three whole years. Venetians issued over 3,000 arrest warrants for Sfakians. The Venetian Commander-in-Chief was replaced without a solution being found. The new Commander came up with the only possible solution; he cancelled all the arrest warrants!

16. ANOPOLI – LOUTRO

DIFFICULTY	📈	■ ☐ ☐ ☐
DURATION	🕐	1 h 30'
ELEVATION CHANGE	📊	650 m descent a) Anopoli – Agia Ekaterini: 20', 50 m ascent b) Agia Ekaterini – junction: 1 h, 550 m descent c) Junction – Loutro: 15', 100 m descent
TERRAIN	⛰	The path is well defined, easy going if a bit stony. A small section is on gravel road.
SIGNPOSTING	🔼	Yes, with red marks.
WHEN TO GO	📅	All year round.
WATER	〰	You can take water only at cafes or from the public fountain (on Anopoli's square).
SHADE	🌴	No shade at all.
POPULARITY	👥	Some walkers in the summer.
WHERE TO SLEEP WHERE TO EAT	🍴	A few rooms-to-let in Anopoli, mainly during high season. Ask Yannis, at Orfanoudaki's bakery, for their rooms. You'll enjoy the stay as much as Yannis appreciates company. Mrs Popi at "Platanos" in the square will always prepare something for you to eat. Many places to stay and eat at Loutro.
ACCESS	⬈	There are 3–4 daily bus services from Chania to Sfakia. From Hora Sfakion (12 km) take a taxi (or hitchhike). Another option is the boat from Agia Roumeli or Sougia (3–4 times per day to Hora Sfakion or Loutro).
SIGHTS	🏛	Country chapel of Agia Ekaterini, the beautiful, unusual Loutro village. The gorgeous landscape and the view to the Libyan Sea.
DRAWBACKS	✖	The lack of shade and the steepness in some parts.

An easy, short walk offering impressive views and beautiful landscapes.

The walk starts from Anopoli's central square behind Daskaloyannis' statue and to the right of the taverna and the guesthouse. Follow the narrow street which passes between the village houses going south. After a while, it climbs and becomes a gravel road leaving the last houses and animal pens behind. 20´ and some bends later, you are on a ridge where a couple of steps on the right lead you to the white country chapel of Agia Ekaterini, with a large veranda and a spectacular view. Even though the chapel itself is of no interest (rebuilt with a lot of cement extensions), the view from its veranda is panoramic. In front of you (to the South) lies a steep slope, the seashore, Loutro and the small Finikas Peninsula. If the weather permits, you can also see Gavdos Island. On your left lies the impressive shore, Fragokastelo, and Psiloritis Mountain, while behind you, you can see the Anopoli plateau with its olive trees and fields, a few houses and the Lefka Ori peaks.

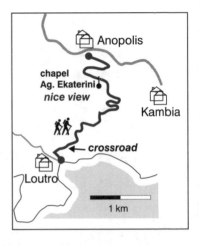

Take the path which is now descending with a lot of bends, offering great views of the steep slope around you. You will see a sheep pen on your left (and a track going there) and on your right, down below, houses of the village of Loutro and the small bay. You can continue descending the last 650 m on this easy and clear path, without any special effort. Just before the first village houses, the path divides. The right-hand branch goes to Finikas, whereas if you go straight you reach Loutro in 10´. From here you can continue your walk to Sfakia or Agia Roumeli or take the boat there.

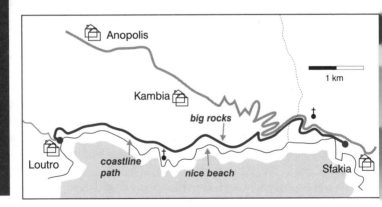

17. HORA SFAKION – LOUTRO

DIFFICULTY	■ □ □ □
DURATION	2 h
ELEVATION CHANGE	200 m ascent and descent a) Hora Sfakion – trailhead: 30', 100 m ascent b) Trailhead – Agios Stavros: 45', 50 m ascent, 100 descent c) Agios Stavros – Loutro: 40', 50 m ascent, 100 m descent
TERRAIN	You walk on road or on easy paths for the most part. There are some rocks and stones on a small section of the path.
SIGNPOSTING	Good E4 marking.
WHEN TO GO	All year round.
WATER	Take water from the cafes in Hora Sfakion and Loutro.
SHADE	No shade except occasionally under the rocks.
POPULARITY	A lot of walkers, especially in the summertime.
ACCESS	There are 3–4 daily bus services from Chania.
SIGHTS	Country chapels and Loutro's main church. Beautiful view to the Libyan Sea and to the scenic village of Loutro en route. The walk is mostly on exciting slopes.
DRAWBACKS	Walking on the paved road at the beginning and the lack of shade.

This is an easy, short and typical seaside walk, ending at one of the most remote and picturesque villages in Crete. You have a lot of opportunities to swim at attractive, small beaches en route to Loutro.

From the bus stop, turn left and follow the paved road to Anopoli. Continue for 30' on the road. After the first 20', you come to a bridge and Iligas gorge which descends impressively on your right and goes down to the beach. 10' on, the road turns right and you see the path which starts just above a fence in front of you. There are E4 signs on the steep slope descending to the sea. Take this clear, signposted path climbing down with several turns under the rocks, offering good views. The path runs several meters above the seashore among rocks. Occasional rockslides can make your walk stony and strenuous.

Half an hour later you reach the wide, pebbled and sandy seashore. You walk parallel to it, climbing a bit until, after 5', you reach the small country chapel of Agios Stavros built on the shore. After a while, you see in front of you the village of Loutro and its wide bay. The walk continues on the steep slope by the rocky seashore, climbing gradually until, 40´ later, you reach the isolated village of Loutro (people can only get here on foot or by boat; there is no road connection). During summer though, the village is full of tourists and walkers, and its shops are all open. When in the village, before moving on, you should visit the Venetian castle, a 15´ walk above the village towards the small peninsula.

18. ASKIFOU – ANOPOLI

DIFFICULTY	📈	■ ■ ■ ■
DURATION	🕐	8 h approximately
ELEVATION CHANGE	📊	800 m ascent, 950 m descent a) Askifou – Kali Lakki: 4 h 30´, 530 m up, 100 m down b) Kali Lakki – Mouri: 1 h 30´, 120 m up, 250 m down c) Mouri – Anopoli: 2 h 15´, 150 m up, 600 m down
TERRAIN	🏔	Gravel road and then old path, dry riverbed and a lot of goat tracks.
SIGNPOSTING	🔼	Signposts are sparse. Don't try to find signs.
WHEN TO GO	📅	March–November.
WATER	〰	You can take water from the Skafidia spring.
SHADE	🌟	There is shade in most parts of the hike.
POPULARITY	👥	No one, except some shepherds.
WHERE TO SLEEP WHERE TO EAT	🛏🍴	There is some budget accommodation at Askifou, and a very attractive stone-built hotel (Lefkoritis). There are a few rooms-to-let and tavernas in Anopoli, mainly during high season.
ACCESS	↗	There is a bus to Askifou (3–4 daily services) and to Anopoli (a bus service daily).
SIGHTS	🏛	The castle on the top of Plana hill is Turkish, built in 1868, by Omar Pasha. There is also an interesting World War II private collection owned by Mr Hatzidakis at Kares.
DRAWBACKS	✖	You must have very good navigational skills.

The hike starts on the Askifou plateau from the small square with the statue. Take the main road for 5´, and then turn right to the small chapel. The road ends at a sheep pen soon after the chapel. Pass the fence (there is a gate there) and walk on the clear path climbing the steep slope for the next 20´ until it reaches a small gully coming from the left. Continue walking inside the narrow, shallow gully bed for about an hour. The surrounding area is relatively clear (no bushes or fallen tree trunks) so it is easy to find your way without a path. Just before the bed ends, it turns right and you leave it, heading to the col on your left (1,080 m elevation). Follow this ridge to the left, descending gradually for 20´, and then turn right walking down the slope passing through phrygana and short bushes until you reach a small dry gully. Take the right side for a few minutes until you see another dry gully coming

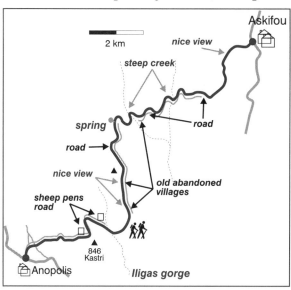

from your right. You will see a goat track marked with sparse red signs. Follow this until you come to a small plateau dotted with bushes and sparse trees. For the next half hour you walk (slightly descending) on this goat track, passing successive small plateaus with a few goats and sheep. At its end, the path becomes a road with a gully on its right. Pass the gully at its start (it deepens after a while) and traverse on the slope, heading south on a goat track for the next 15´.

The landscape is typically Cretan, having sparse vegetation (some cedars and holm oaks), phrygana, stones, smooth slopes, while the air is full of scents from the aromatic plants (thyme, oregano, sage), released when you walk on them. Left and below you, you can see Nimbros village and the gravel road, which climbs up the slope for some hundreds of meters ahead of you. When you reach a shallow, dry riverbed, follow it climbing for 25′−30′, until you meet the road from Nimbros to Kali Lakki. The road follows the west side of the ridge with many u-turns.

After 1.5−2 km, take the right side of the road, pass a large construction which is made to collect rain water for the fire service, and at the next junction turn left. The road ends 15′ later. A goat track leaves to the right, descending the slope for 15′−20′ until it comes to a gully bed and a path that comes from the right (some sparse red marks), which continues for some minutes climbing up the opposite slope to the road above. Continue on the road for half an hour, with Lefka Ori peaks (Kastro and Skoutsokorfi) on your right and the steep forested slopes of Sfakiano Gorge on your left.

The road brings you to Kali Lakki, an abandoned old village with a few dozen half-ruined houses (2 or 3 of them are still inhabited by dogs to protect them. Luckily, they are on a leash or behind a fence). It is worth a stroll among the empty houses. You will observe some really impressive architectural elements (stone-built arches above the doors, large carved stones at the corners, fireplaces, two storey houses). The road ends soon after the last houses. Continue on the well-defined path, climbing down gradually. The path turns into a steeper goat track above Sfakiano Gorge. You reach its bed 30′ later. Take care when descending the last 4−5 m, choosing the easiest way, and pass across the dry bed. Climb the forested steep slope for 10′ on faint goat tracks.

The next half hour is the most tiring of the hike. Traverse, ascending gradually on the slope, with no path, or, on some goat tracks that fade out, moving up and down on the unsteady terrain. The last section is flatter and leads you to a small fenced sheep pen squeezed among the trees. A road begins here. Take it for almost 20′ to the Skafidia spring with its fresh water (there is water here even during the summer). The road climbs up gradually for 10′ to a flat ridge. At the junction, we turn left and go downhill for 15′−20′ till the next junction. Continue left, climbing for 100 m to a large sign indicating some construction work for a water tank, and turn right and then right again on the road that leads to the abandoned and ruined Mouri village. The first 2−3 houses you see are still inhabited in the summer by shep-

Settlements (Metohia)

Metohia are small settlements or small villages, usually consisting of just a few houses. Administratively speaking, they were never autonomous but parts of a nearby village and they were never mentioned on maps, even on large-scale maps. Even though their existence was officially recognized, as birth places for example (in older documents it is recorded that Mister A was born in Metohi X which belongs to the Community Z, part of Province Y), they had no community chairman or administrative offices of any kind. Their residents voted in the nearby villages. Nowadays, under the new administrative law (the Kapodistrias Act), they belong to a greater entity consisting of many villages and forming a Municipality.

Their history and the way they were created are lost in ancient times, when people first gathered to form small settlements. Many metohia though, were created during the Saracen era (8th to 10th Century A.D.), the Byzantine era (10th to 13th Century) and the Venetian era (13th to 16th Century) because of battles between the different invaders and following pirate attacks from the sea. Inhabitants were therefore forced to abandon their cities in areas near the sea and retreated inland.

Another reason for the creation of metohia, especially during the last few centuries, is that many farmers wanted to live near their fields in order to protect them from aspiring trespassers and crop thieves, or to avoid having to walk there and back. A lot of them were founded by a single family which then persuaded its relatives to live nearby. Very often the name of the metohi derives from the name of the family that first lived in the area. Back then, they were independent communities and their relations with nearby villages were limited, sometimes even unfriendly, especially if there were property disputes or long-lasting rivalries.

herds' families and are well preserved, whereas all the other houses which are built on the slope are in ruins. A panoramic view of the village's plateau, the ridge, the nearby gorges, the Libyan Sea and the impressive Sfakia seashore lies in front of you.

Walk on the road for the next 30´, shortcutting some of its curves through a wide ridge which descends gradually. It passes by some houses and sheep pens heading to the ruined village of Kavro at the end of the road. Turn right passing the village's open ground among ruins and high grass, marveling at some of the ruined houses, which must have been amazing when still standing. Continue west on a goat track, and you will come to the edge of a steep slope, the face of the gorge. For the first few minutes, you descend steeply among rocks and on eroded terrain. Then it becomes smoother and for the next 30′ you descend on a spur ridge with steep slopes to the bed of Iligas Gorge. The terrain is partly firm, partly stony and unsteady, but always steep with impressive views. The goat track meets the bed and crosses it to the other side to become a gravel road (the slope here is more gradual).

Some minutes later, above the very steep gully of a tributary of the main gorge, you pass by a sheep pen with dogs guarding it. The road continues climbing up the slope heading west. When the road flattens, in 30′, it passes by a large dairy farm. Continue on the road which descends very gradually, leading you after 20′ to Anopoli's main square.

19. ANOPOLI – PACHNES

DIFFICULTY 📈	■ ■ ■ ■
DURATION 🕐	6 h, 18 km
ELEVATION CHANGE 📊	18 km, 1,900 m ascent a) Anopoli – trailhead: 45′, 180 m up b) Trailhead – Agathopi: 2 h 30′, 860 m up c) Agathopi – Amoutsera: 45′, 160 m up d) Amoutsera – Roussies: 2 h, 350 m up e) Roussies – Pachnes: 50′, 300 m up
TERRAIN 🔺	Gravel road at the beginning, old half-ruined path afterwards, gravel road again and finally a path of unstable rocks.
SIGNPOSTING 🔺	Inadequate and sparse.
WHEN TO GO 📅	May–November.
WATER 〰	There are only two wells. It is better to stock up (min. 2 litres) at Anopoli.
SHADE ☀	Shade only during the first third of the hike until you reach Agathopi.
POPULARITY 👥	It is the shortest hike to the peak, so you might find some other walkers, but you may be by yourselves.

WHERE TO SLEEP 🍴🛏 WHERE TO EAT	A few rooms-to-let in Anopoli, mainly during high season. Ask Yannis, at Orfanoudaki's bakery, for their rooms. You'll enjoy the stay as much as Yannis appreciates company. Mrs Popi at "Platanos" in the square will always prepare something for you to eat.
ACCESS ◪	One bus per day to Anopoli from Chania or take a taxi from Hora Sfakion.
SIGHTS 🏛	Next to Agia Ekaterini chapel, with the panoramic view, you will find ancient Anopoli's ruins, a city with the same name it has today.
DRAWBACKS ⊗	The gravel road that has destroyed the mountainous landscape for ever.

A well planned, rough gravel road climbs from Anopoli to Roussies, 1 h 30´ before Pachnes. This road has destroyed much of the area's wildness. Whether you climb on the road or on the old path, this is certainly the shortest way to get to the peak. The hike's difficulties are its increase in elevation, the rough stony terrain, insufficient signposting in an almost unchanging landscape and the lack of water and shade for most of the walk. On the other hand, it is a scenic, relatively isolated trip, with weird lunar rocks and peaks all around the area.

Even though the road, which was opened only for the sake of the shepherds, goes almost up to Roussies, you can take the old path avoiding this charmless part of modern civilization. Additionally, the road makes a large circle to gain elevation, whereas the path follows a gully going to Agathopi where it meets the road. From this point on, they meet and divide many times until the point where the road works fortunately stopped.

From Anopoli's main square, where the Daskaloyannis' statue is, the road runs west. A little further down, in front of Nikos' taverna/coffee shop, the road forks. The left goes to Aradena and the right to the mountain. Naturally you must take the right. After a kilometer, you see a blue shrine and a gravel road on your left. Olive groves give way to a pine forest, and if you happen to be here early in spring, the place is full of anemones and red neragoulas, an endemic plant. Another kilometer and you'll come to a junction. Follow the right branch; the left leads to a dead end. Keep on for 400 m and turn left on what seems like a path. You bypass the next bend in the road and you come to the road again at a stone-built shrine and an old house. You are now 45´ away from Anopoli.

There is a gully in front of you that climbs more or less northeast. Leave the road for good and enter the gully. You are in a dense pine forest and soon

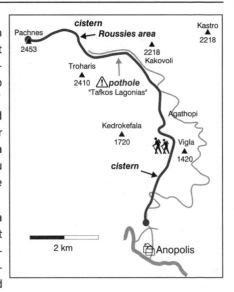

you will find the old path which is very well built. It takes a lot of twists gaining height gradually up the steep slopes. 1 h 30′ later you reach an old sheep pen and a water storage tank above Vigla peak. On some maps you may see a road inside the gully — this is a mistake.

You are already at a height of 1,300 m, but you must carry on climbing. 5′ later, turn a little left, passing an old house on the right, and continue in the gully's tranquillity, until the pine and the cypress trees are behind you and the terrain is almost flat. You meet the road again, 200 m before a spot called Agathopi. Follow the road until its right turn, and at the point where the terrain is completely flat, a shallow gully can be seen on your left.

Leave the road and proceed on the left side of the gully. Climb the path to the North for 15′, avoiding the road once again. You can't of course avoid the inevitable, so you must walk on the road for 10′ to an old sheep pen with a subterranean cistern at Amoutsera.

(Tip for your descent: when you pass Amoutsera and come to the road, follow it for 10′ until you can see Gavdos Island. If you look carefully to your right below the rubble of the road, you will see the path, and in a while you will reach Agathopi. From here, take the road until you see the first sparse trees. Turn right there, entering the gully on your right, following the sparse blue marks).

Pass on the left of the cistern, and head west to a magnificent lunar landscape, full of pools. If the weather is foggy, you may easily end up in one of them; fortunately they are not very deep. When you come to the road again, turn left and continue for almost 20′ until you reach a really weird landscape with pools and peaks. On your right lies the dark peak called Kakovoli (2,218 m).

The Shiniest Gem

"Once upon a time, many years ago, in an eastern country, a king wanted to obtain the most precious and shiniest gem in the world. He called for the five wisest men and asked them to tell him which gem that was. The five wise men gathered together and said that the most precious and shiniest gem of all was in the raindrops of April."

A shepherd heard this story one day in his village, Anopoli, and decided to look for this precious gem. It was April and the golden raindrops fell on the Cretan mountains. The little shepherd climbed up the great mountain, and he saw something shining, half buried in the wet ground. So there it was! What he wanted so much was actually there in front of him! He ran towards it, but his immense joy turned to horror. The bomb, forgotten since the war, exploded in his hands with an astounding shine.

Years went by, and the little shepherd grew up with only one hand and his sight almost destroyed (5% of normal).

I met this man once, on the southern slopes of Lefka Ori when he was gathering his goats and he invited me to his pen. "Let's share our stories" he said to me and began to narrate his life story.

He was illiterate, but he had great reserves of energy and, with faith in the world around him, he had not given up. He had tried to repair his eyesight, but the doctors could do nothing. Despite all this, he got married, raised his children, and helped them to start their own businesses. He achieved all that with only a few goats and his unquenchable zest for life.

It was difficult for me to find a story to tell him...

A small valley opens up in front of you, with peak Troharis (2,410 m) above it. Leave the road which continues north and goes to the right side of the valley, and climb on the left side. Find the ill-defined path and move along it as long as possible, because shortly you must walk alongside Tafko Lagona, a precipice which looks very steep indeed. After the precipice, continue straight on for 100 m, and then climb to the right, until you meet the road again in front of you. The rocks are dark in colour and eroded by the water. There are almost no plants; it's as if you are in the desert.

Follow the road for 400 m and 80 m before it ends, climb to the right side and climb the vague path, which is sparsely marked in many different places.

Basically there is not just one path, but a lot of goat tracks. Continue the climb heading northwest, and in less than 30′ you will reach Roussies. The cistern there usually contains water, but you will need a bucket and a Primus to boil it. Walk along the path from there to the peak, following the directions for the Katsiveli – Pachnes trail (Route 23°C).

(Tip for your descent: in Roussies, climb down the left slope. As soon as you get to the road, walk 400 m and after a left turn, try to find the path which is at the lower side of the road, covered with rubble. When you come to the road after the precipice, and walk for 10′ – 15′ on it, you will see an open space like a quarry. Turn right there, taking a short cut to Amoutsera).

20. ANOPOLI – HORA SFAKION

DIFFICULTY	■ ■ □ □
DURATION	2 h
ELEVATION CHANGE	650 m descent, 50 m ascent a) Anopoli – road bend: 30′, 50 m down b) Road bend – Iligas Gorge: 1 h 30′, 450 m down c) Iligas Gorge – Hora Sfakion: 30′, 50 m up, 150 m down
TERRAIN	Paved path, goat track, road, gorge bed.
SIGNPOSTING	Sparse, mainly with piles of rocks.
WHEN TO GO	All year round (avoid it after heavy rain).
WATER	No water, apart from the shops in the villages.
SHADE	Shade only under the rocks.
POPULARITY	Almost no one.
ACCESS	There are two bus services daily in summer from Chania and Hora Sfakion. Otherwise, take a taxi from Hora Sfakion.
SIGHTS	Spectacular views at the start of the walk, the paved path just before Hora Sfakion and the wild and beautiful gorge.
DRAWBACKS	Lack of high vegetation and scrambling in some sections of the trail.

The hike starts from Anopoli. For the first 500 m, you walk on the main road to Hora Sfakion. On your left, just before the last houses, there is a gravel road. Follow this road, which climbs gradually up a hill next to a big antenna. A stony path full of phrygana runs down the slope heading east. Enjoy the view of Sfakia seashore and the wild mountainous landscape. In a few minutes you reach the paved road which goes to Sfakia. Cross it and follow the stony path, signposted with sparse red marks, until you come to a pump house and a gravel road (10´–15´) which leads to a sheep pen on your left. Keep going east, leaving the gravel road behind, and enter a small dry gully. For the next 30´ you follow the gully's bed, which turns into a small gorge with narrow walls and easy "staircase" descents. Now you can see only the nearby slopes. There is a goat here and there, and the bed is occasionally full of bushes and other plants. A narrow goat track follows the gorge from the left side, but it's much more pleasant to walk inside the gully.

Half an hour later, the gorge becomes steeper with continuous easy descents (you must use your hands), while the walls are now higher and closer together. Rock passages have weird shapes looking like doors, arches, or small tunnels. If you want to avoid a passage, there is always the goat track on your left. This small gully/gorge is the tributary for Iligas Gorge, ending in the main gorge an hour later.

However the last section has steep and difficult passages. So, leave the riverbed 10´ before the last big drop and take the paved and partly built path on the left, which ends gently in the wide stony bed of Iligas Gorge. It crosses the bed and continues on the other side. The path has disintegrated for the first few meters of the climb, which makes your walking more difficult, but

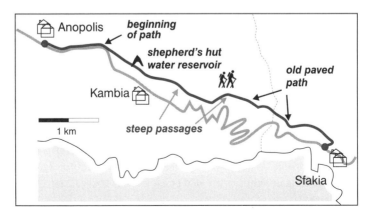

after a while it widens again. It is cobblestoned and climbs for 50 m to a passage among rocks. This is a pleasant and impressive part of the walk. The path continues on the slope for a few minutes, and then descends to the road some hundred meters, before the large parking area of the village of Hora Sfakion.

21. ILIGAS GORGE

DIFFICULTY	◪	■ ■ ■ ☐
DURATION	◷	3 h 30'
ELEVATION CHANGE	▥	700 m ascent, 100 m descent a) Hora Sfakion – gorge entrance: 20', 50 m ascent b) Gorge entrance – sheep pen: 2 h, 500 m ascent c) Sheep pen – Anopoli: 1 h 10', 150 m ascent, 100 m descent
TERRAIN	◮	Walking on stones and pebbles in the gorge (some easy climbing passages inside the gorge) and on gravel road.
SIGNPOSTING	⬆	No.
WHEN TO GO	▦	All year round (avoid it after heavy rain).
WATER	〰	Take water from the cafes in Anopoli and Hora Sfakion.
SHADE	✲	Depending on the hour of the day, you'll have enough or perhaps a lot of shade inside the gorge.
POPULARITY	👥	Very sparse. Unlikely to meet others.
ACCESS	◹	There are 3–4 daily bus services from Chania to Hora Sfakion.
SIGHTS	🏛	A really impressive gorge with dense vegetation and a variety of rock formations. A beautiful beach at the beginning and lovely views from the last section towards Anopoli's plateau and Lefka Ori.
DRAWBACKS	✕	Walking on stones and pebbles.

A very scenic walk following the gorge's bed.

The walk starts at the point where the gorge meets the main road from Hora Sfakion to Anopoli, at a distance of 1.5 km (20' walk) from Hora Sfakion. On your left lies the isolated and beautiful Iligas beach, while on your right sits the wild and impressive gorge. You walk in the

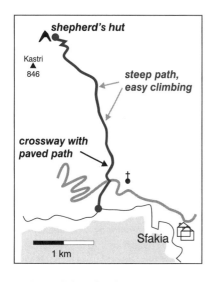

gorge's bed which is full of stones and pebbles (sometimes there are also fallen trees as well as some rocks), more or less level, with a few ascending passages. In 20´ you will find the old paved path, coming from Anopoli and going to Hora Sfakion, which crosses the gorge and continues climbing on the right. You keep on walking inside the gorge's bed. At this point it is a wide, flat area with vertical walls, around 100–150 m high, and quite a few trees (mainly cedars), some of them fallen. There is seldom water in this riverbed (it has to rain heavily for some days), so the walk is safe with no unexpected dangers.

After 40´–50´ of walking, the gorge narrows. It is only some meters wide now with high, vertical walls, fallen trees and some easy climbs. Follow the gorge's bends (it follows a meandering path), and in an hour you will reach a small rocky wall, which you must climb. Soon afterwards, you will come to the difficult part. It's a steep 10 m high climb, up on the left side underneath the trees. You will see marks (piles of stones) indicating the way. The gorge's walls open up again after 2–3 easy climbs, and you walk on the flat but tiring bed (it feels like walking on scree). 15´–20´ later you come to the last low (4–5 m high) rock wall which you get past with an easy climb in the middle.

Continue this easy walk for half an hour. The gorge is wilder and more impressive now. Carry on to a point where a road comes from the left, almost reaching the bed. On the right, there is a steeply ascending goat track. This marks the end of your hike inside the gorge.

You have two options now. Either turn back until you come to Iligas beach and have a nice swim there, or climb the narrow road on your left to the sheep pen and then on to Anopoli (1 h climb on the goat track on your right takes you to the first houses and to the road leading to the small isolated Mouri settlement).

Gun Possession

Gun possession is a very popular hobby (more popular than football and backgammon) in Crete. It appeals to every income and age group. Bullets are a bit expensive of course, if one uses the gun often. It is said that every Cretan has one gun (don't count on it though). The truth is that there are thousands of guns of every type and category. There are guns from the World War II. Most of them are out of use and can be found as decorations in houses, sheep pens and warehouses, and their value is historical. There are also modern guns (pistols, rifles, automatic guns) used mainly by younger people who continue the tradition. Gun possession is not spread evenly across the island. There are areas where people possess a lot of guns and others in which guns are practically nonexistent. Most of them can be found in the western part of the island and in the highlands, whereas you'll seldom find them in big cities and in the eastern part. In the villages of Sfakia, Anogia, Psiloritis and Lefka Ori almost every house has at least one gun. They are usually used at weddings, baptisms and feasts, and sometimes just for fun and practice with road signs as targets. Mathematically, the holes in the road signs are proportionate to the number of guns in the area. So, if you see a road sign that looks like a strainer, you should understand that you are entering a war zone (with no victims). Sometimes though, they are used as a means to resolve unsolved disputes (vendettas, property disputes, threats) or just for hunting.

Even though gun possession is widespread in Crete, the crime rate is one of the lowest in Greece, in terms of the number of murders, robberies and thefts. This contradictory fact has mainly to do with the Cretan mentality as well as with the fact that all these guns intimidate those who want to be thieves! They know very well that most Cretans will not hesitate to shoot, if they feel threatened. Most of the guns come from eastern European countries, new and used, but there are also guns from Western Europe and America, usually more expensive. Of course, all of them are illegal and not registered. From time to time, police makes spot checks in houses or in the streets and cars, and are often very successful in finding a lot of guns, but nothing seems to change. Unfortunately, these past few years, some people have been killed at weddings and funerals by stray bullets. This motivated a section of the population (politicians, artists and professors) to campaign in an attempt to convince people not to use guns at weddings and festivals.

22. GINGILOS ASCENT

DIFFICULTY	📈	■ ■ ■ □
DURATION	🕐	3 h ascent
ELEVATION CHANGE	📊	860 m ascent a) Xyloskalo – end of winding path: 40', 260 m ascent b) End of winding path – Linoseli spring: 45', 50 m ascent, 50 m descent c) Linoseli spring – col: 40', 200 m ascent d) Col – lower peak: 40', 260 m ascent e) Lower peak – main peak: 20', 80 m ascent
TERRAIN	⛰	Clear path, signposted, narrow, easy-going. A large part is on scree and rocks. The earthen parts are also stony.
SIGNPOSTING	🔺	Dense at first, then red marks here and there.
WHEN TO GO	📅	April – end of October.
WATER	〰	Take water either from the restaurant at Xyloskalo or from the Linoseli spring (1,450 m height) in the middle of the hike.
SHADE	☀	Almost no shade at all.
POPULARITY	👥	20–30 hikers climb every day, due to its easy access.
WHERE TO SLEEP WHERE TO EAT	🍴	There are 3 small hotels offering everything, including food at Omalos and some rooms-to-let. You can also eat at the tourist pavilion next to the parking area or at the restaurant 20 m above it. The balcony offers great views.
ACCESS	➤	A paved road leads from Chania to Omalos plateau (35 km) ending at Xyloskalo. Regular daily bus service (2–3 times), in the morning and early in the afternoon.
SIGHTS	🏛	Very scenic hike with a great variety, unrestricted views, and impressive rock formations.

This is a classical ascent to Lefka Ori. It is one of the most beautiful and spectacular in Crete. The view from the peak is amazing and the walk is enchanting. The view changes all the time and so does the path. It is unusual to find anyone else at the peak, even though some tourists do come here in the summertime. An advantage of this walk is the easy access to the starting point, Omalos, with daily bus services from Chania. It can easily be combined with other walks, so one can make different trips which end in villages of the region.

The hike starts from the tourist pavilion, which lies above the parking area at the end of the paved road, as you will see from its highly visible signposts.

Lefka Ori Region

The first part is a good path that winds up the slope, right by the fence which encloses the Samaria Gorge. As you climb, the view is getting better with Omalos plateau to the North, the Lefka Ori massif to the East, and Kallergis' refuge hut on the ridge to the South at a height of 1,680 m, the Samaria Gorge further to the right, while on the left (West) lies Gingilos' vertical wall. Half an hour and some 30 criss-crosses later, the path flattens and heads west, leaving the ridge and passing on the left of the upper end of the Samaria Gorge,

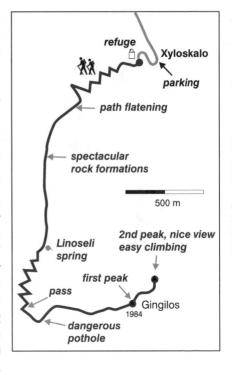

over unstable rocks, steep and eroded slopes and vertical rock formations. The vegetation is sparse, bushes and cedars, the gorge's steep and wild slopes lie below you, and Gingilos' bleak wall is ahead of you.

The path descends now, passing over and among fabulous rock formations, arches, needles and unsteady rocks, in one of the wildest areas of Crete. At this point the path is rudimentary, narrow, mainly on scree, and some parts of it have disintegrated. Here and there some old cedars and cypresses add their trunks as art objects to the surreal landscape.

Half an hour later, you come to a small shallow cave, an ideal spot in which to protect yourself in case of a sudden rain or thunderstorm. The path climbs again, and 10′–15′ later it reaches the Linoseli spring at a height of 1,450 m. This spring, considered the point at which the Samaria Gorge begins, always offers water flowing slowly among the stones. Fill up your flasks from the spring or from the hose beneath.

Dances

The origins of Cretan dances are lost in time. Minoans considered dance as a divine gift, and dance was an important way to worship. As **Sophocles** writes in one of his tragedies, the main characteristic of these dances was their orgiastic nature, and Plato divides dances into three categories: religious, peaceful and war dances.

Until the 18th Century A.D. and before the arrival of modern guns, Cretans used to dance armed. In the Middle Ages, they danced wearing a quiver and holding a bow and a sword.

Modern Cretan dances are divided into quick and slow, with a lot of step variations.

Quick dance is the oldest. The steps follow a very complicated and variable system, which lends elements to all the other dances. Experts say it resembles the ancient dance "pyrrihios". It is quick and lively, its tempo allegro agitato.

The names of the dances are chaniotikos, rethemniotikos round, kastrinos, maleviziotis, prinianos quick dance, slow sousta in hold, pentozalis etc.

Good dancers make simple imposing symmetrical movements, with grace and beauty. They improvise with turns and springs. Being a good dancer is considered a great asset. Dancing gives many opportunities for individual expression to dancers because, through the dance, they can improvise and express their inner selves. At the same time, a relationship develops between the dancers and the musicians. When the dancers are good, then the fingers and minds of the musicians are on fire as well as the feet and minds of the dancers.

Written by Kostis Moudatsos

Have a rest while trying to ignore the cement wall, the tin cans and the plastic bins (yes, they bring sheep and goats up here). Continue on the path climbing on the scree and zigzagging for the next 30´. At the end of this steep ascent, you reach the col. It is always windy up here and the view is spectacular. You can see Klados Gorge, Gavdos Island, Lefka Ori's highest peaks (Pachnes, Zaranokefala etc) and the Omalos plateau to the East.

Take the path to the left, avoiding the opening of a hollow cave (a walker was killed here recently!). The rock at this point is an excellent example of transparent calcite with different mixes and different colourings, resembling quartz. The hike is getting steeper. Follow the red marks on the rocks using your hands in some of the passages. For the next 30′ you walk on different terrains; rocks, stony and narrow paths, and stone slabs. In 15′ you reach a smooth slope leading to a wide area in front of the peak. Most walkers stop here.

You can continue (after resting for a while) to the main peak on the left. Now you can see the real lunar landscape. For 20′ you scramble on rocks, stone slabs, broken stones, and in small lakes – depressions(there is no path here), going up and down gradually until you reach the main peak. It is not easy; you need to climb a bit and have a good sense of balance. Take the right-hand side, which is a bit easier, and you will be rewarded by the spectacular view below. Everything is at your feet: two seas, the Aegean and the Libyan, two mountains, Lefka Ori and Psiloritis, gorges (Samaria Gorge the most impressive of all, just below), plateaus, villages, cities and the wild and variable Cretan landscape.

23. ASCENT FROM OMALOS TO PACHNES

THE ASCENT IS DIVIDED INTO THREE PARTS

> **A. OMALOS – KALLERGIS' HUT**
> **B. KALLERGIS' HUT – KATSIVELI**
> **C. KATSIVELI – PACHNES**

23A. OMALOS – KALLERGIS' HUT

DIFFICULTY	■ ☐ ☐ ☐
DURATION	1 h 15′, 3.4 km
ELEVATION CHANGE	370 m ascent a) Xyloskalo – path's end: 35′, 130 m up b) Path's end – hut: 40′, 240 m up
TERRAIN	The path is stony to start with and the vegetation is low. Then you walk on a gravel road.
SIGNPOSTING	Red marks and E4 signs.

WHEN TO GO	May–October.
WATER	Xyloskalo spring at the Samaria Gorge entry.
SHADE	No shade at all.
POPULARITY	Many walkers because of its location.
WHERE TO SLEEP WHERE TO EAT	There are small hotels in Omalos, like "Neos Omalos" offering tasty local dishes such as tsigariasto, different kind of pies, or stamnagathi. At the hut (reservations on 28210 74560), apart from sleeping (€10) you can enjoy breakfast, lunch and refreshments.
ACCESS	Four bus services daily from Chania to Omalos.
SIGHTS	Amazing view!
DRAWBACKS	The gravel road is ugly, but you will need it.

The ascent to Kallergis' hut, the most famous in Crete, is not challenging, but it is the first step to discover White Mountains.

The Omalos plateau has hundreds of visitors every day. Luckily, most of them visit the Samaria Gorge, so the area is relatively tranquil after all these people vanish inside the vast gorge. The plateau has an elevation of 1,100 m and can be the start for many walks, like the one that climbs to Lefka Ori's highest peak, a two day hike. For that reason, you will meet some walkers at the hut who plan to climb to Melidaou, Gingilos and Pachnes.

Buses arrive early in the morning at the end of the road below Gingilos' stunning mass, where the hordes of tourists get off to cross the gorge. Xyloskalo is the entry to the Samaria Gorge as well as the starting point for climbing Gingilos (route 22) and for going to Kallergis' hut.

Right at the entry, there is a cypress tree with horizontal branches and beneath it a spring. It is the only place you will find water, before you reach the hut. Near the fountain, on your left, you'll see an opening in the fence and a sign to Kallergis' hut (1 h 20').

The path is easy and well defined despite climbing. It heads mainly to the North. 35´ later, you will find a gravel road that passes by the hut on its way to shepherds' pens on the north slopes of Melidaou. The road is easy, but long and tiring. The most interesting part is the open view to the Omalos plateau. In about 40´ you reach the most popular hut in Crete.

The hut is built in a very beautiful spot and the view is wonderful. Joseph Schemberger, an Austrian hiker and yachtsman, who has spent so many years in Crete that Cretans call him Sifis, a local nickname, is the man responsible for the hut's operation. He rents it from the Chania Mountaineering Club and has managed it with love and care for many years. If you are planning to stay for the night, it is better to call beforehand to book your stay.

Kokalas (Lammergeier)

The "dominant" species in nature, man, obviously decided to exterminate some other animals which he considered harmful and vicious. The Lammergeier was on this list, thus signing its death sentence. Only a few pairs remain in the whole of Europe. They live in the Pyrenees, in Corsica and in Crete. This impressive bird, its wing span reaching 2.8 m, scared the peasants who thought that it was eating their young animals. So it became their worst enemy without in fact having any responsibility for the crime it was accused of.

In reality, 90% of its food comes from bones and from this fact it derives its name "kokalas" ("kokalo" in Greek means bone). Its stomach contains highly acid fluid, and it can obtain sufficient nutrition from bones. The way it breaks large bones is impressive. As it flies above rocky areas ("spastres" in Greek), it plummets down vertically at full speed and drops the bone onto the rocks, watching it by flying in a spiral above. It repeats the process as many times as necessary and ends up eating it all, starting with the marrow.

Its scientific name is Gypaetus Barbatus, which refers to the long black hairs below its beak that look like a beard. It can be distinguished very easily by its long, spiked wings and the rhombus shaped tail. Its breast and belly are usually orange from the iron oxides picked up, as they rub on the chalky rocks. Even though it is nowadays considered an endangered species and is protected, it faces new dangers from all the poisoned baits which are widely used to destroy other "harmful species" such as wolves, foxes, and ravens, from illegal hunts and from the deterioration of the whole habitat.

23B. KALLERGIS' HUT – KATSIVELI

DIFFICULTY	■ ■ ■ ■
DURATION	6 h 45'
ELEVATION CHANGE	1180 m ascent, 450 m descent a) Kallergis' hut – Poria: 1 h 10', 4 km, 100 m down b) Poria – Melidaou: 2 h 15', 985 m up c) Melidaou – (before reaching the peak) – Potami: 1 h 30', 340 m down d) Potami (North) – Katsiveli: 1 h 45', 200 m up
TERRAIN	At the beginning you walk on gravel road and then on stony terrain.
SIGNPOSTING	Sparse E4 signs.
WHEN TO GO	May–October.
WATER	Take water from the hut and from Katsiveli. There is water at the cistern, but you must boil it.
SHADE	No shade at all.
POPULARITY	Only few hikers.
WHERE TO SLEEP WHERE TO EAT	At the hut (reservations on 28210 74560), apart from sleeping (€10) you can enjoy breakfast, lunch and refreshments. At Katsiveli there is a small hut and, if you are a party of hikers, there is also the Svourichti hut in which 25 people can sleep (reservations: E.O.S Chania 28210 44647). Take food for two days.
ACCESS	Four bus services daily from Chania to Omalos.
SIGHTS	Amazing view!
DRAWBACKS	The gravel road is ugly, but you will need it.

An ascent to Madares, the most difficult to reach but maybe the most enchanting area of Crete, involves a difficult walk to a remote area of fifty and more peaks above 2,000 m high. Until recently, there were no roads leading into the heart of the mountains. Only a few shepherds and some brave hikers climb close enough to see the white lime rocks which, together with the black volcano rocks, form a perfect lunar landscape. Apart from some small but strong plants, nothing else grows up here. Water is so sparse that you think you are in a desert. A lot of gorges, most of them impassable and inhospitable for amateur walkers, start from these peaks and cut through the rough decayed slopes of Lefka Ori. How can one describe this imposing mountain that Cretans call Chania's bald peaks (Chaniotikes Madares)?

This climb presents no particular difficulties, but it is long and exhausting, with no shade nor water. The terrain is stony and crumbly, making progress difficult for amateur walkers. This sea of peaks can confuse even experienced hikers. Before starting, make sure that you carry plenty of water, enough food, sun protection, warm clothes as temperatures tend to fall during the night, as well as a compass and a map in case of fog or low clouds.

Take the road on your right when you leave the hut, following the E4 signs. After 300 m, there is a path to your right which helps you avoid the gravel road. The road, which was made for the shepherds, will in 70´ lead you to a basin, where there are some sheep pens and a lot of ferns. The road continues north and later turns northeast, but you leave it when you see a wooden kiosk with marks pointing to the East inside a gully. This gully lies above the basin.

From here on, there is no path, but it is easy to find your way among the goat tracks. Follow the left gully with the red and black/yellow marks and you'll come to some small basins, which, if you come at the beginning of May when the snow melts, are full of crocuses. Keep on climbing and 1 h 30´ later you'll reach the Mavri (or El. Venizelos) peak and the col to the Melidaou peak. The view to Chania and especially to the gorge is amazing.

Continue climbing up the ridge, following the E4 signs. Half an hour from the col, you will be near the double peak at a height of 2,133 m. You can climb up to the peak from here to see Pachnes to the Southeast, which you cannot otherwise see. Return to the hut the same way.

The other option is to keep walking east on the faint path until Potamos, and from there to Katsiveli. The path traverses across Melidaou's steep southern slope and continues east, climbing constantly down until Plakoseli, a small valley, at a height of 1,850 m. There is an open cistern here. If you want to use this water you should boil it first. It takes 3 h 15´ from the path to Plakoseli or 1 h 10´ from Melidaou.

The Lines peak is on your left, and a shallow gully to the Southeast. Signs will lead you through the gully to the next valley in 20´. Papasifi's sheep pen is on your left, where the shepherds are always eager to help. Don't be surprised, if you find out that the little ones are not Greek but Albanians! Continue, crossing the gully ahead. The gully to the right leads to Potami, a basin dotted with sheep pens. Potami is the entrance to the Eligias Gorge. This gorge descends west of Zaranokefala to Agios Yannis, but you need a rope to make it.

So, continue straight on to the opposite side, climbing up to the right, to circle Kefala peak which lies ahead. At the ruins of a sheep pen, the path turns east climbing constantly through an amazing landscape. You can see Pachnes to the East, with a lot of peaks around, while an impressive black and white peak, Modaki, lies ahead to the right. You can see the path from time to time, going up and down winding among small caves. An hour later it turns northeast, and 15´ later you reach a wide open space, Katsiveli.

This is the Lefka Ori junction. The E4 path continues north, either to the Volikas hut or to Askifou (you can get there by walking straight east for 10 hours). Another path to the Southeast, between Modaki and Svourichti, climbs to Anopoli and Pachnes.

In 1992, the Chania Mountaineering Club built a stone hut here (Christos Houliopoulos), which is closed unless you book it in advance. There is also a hut in case of emergency, but usually it has to be cleaned. Unfortunately people don't always respect the place in which they find shelter and hospitality. At Katsiveli sheep pen there is fresh water, usually until autumn, pumped up here from the Karavonero spring.

Lefka Ori Region

23C. KATSIVELI – PACHNES

DIFFICULTY	📈	■ ■ ■ □
DURATION	🕐	3 h 15', 7.7 km
ELEVATION CHANGE	🏔	a) Katsiveli – col: 50', 210 m up b) Col – Roussies: 50', 40 m down, 160 m up c) Roussies – Pachnes: 50', 320 m up d) Return: 40'
TERRAIN	⛰	Stony terrain mostly without paths.
SIGNPOSTING	🚩	Sparse.
WHEN TO GO	📅	May–October.
WATER	💧	Water from Katsiveli until autumn. There is also water at the Roussies cistern but requires boiling.
SHADE	🌤	Shade only when it's cloudy.
POPULARITY	👥	Only a few hikers climb to the peak.
WHERE TO SLEEP WHERE TO EAT	🍴	At Katsiveli there is a small hut and there is also Svourichti hut, which accommodates 25 people but only for parties (reservations: E.O.S Chania 28210 44647). Take food for two days.
ACCESS	🥾	Different paths ending to Katsiveli.
DRAWBACKS	❌	Vandalism at the refuge huts from unscrupulous people.

Katsiveli is the main Lefka Ori junction. Almost all the walks which cross Lefka Ori meet here, and climbs to some of the most famous mountain peaks also start here. If you walked up to this point you will have already sensed the area's special nature. Until the time when more useless roads destroy the mountain further, you have the chance to experience the vastness and solitude of the place. At this final section of the hike, the mountain reveals its grandeur. Pits, peaks, cols, weird geological formations and dolines adorn the surroundings, perhaps in an attempt to leave you satisfied.

Southeast from Katsiveli is the twin-coloured Montaki peak (2,224 m). Its black volcanic rocks hug the white limestone. On the left side of the peak, the path climbs to Pachnes. From Katsiveli, turn your eyes southeast and start climbing left from the gully. Don't expect to find many signs here. If the weather is foggy, beware of the hollows and the pits; they are countless. It's like walking on a big colander.

Keep climbing, until you come to a col at a height of 2,090 m. From there continue south until the next col, 45´ from Katsiveli. The path is difficult to find in this lunar landscape. The massif of the highest peaks can be seen to the Southwest. Straight ahead, you see a whitish peak. You must go towards the north col of this peak, initially climbing on a ridge and then left to the gully. 1 h 10´ from Katsiveli, you reach the col at a height of 2,150 m and from there, following the same route, traverse across the weird landscape trying not to lose height.

20´–25´ minutes on, and you are on a col passing the basin from the left. Welcome to Roussies. On the shoulder there is a sign pointing west to Pachnes. Right behind it, there is a small empty cottage where three people can sleep in the event of bad weather. There is also a cistern, but you need a bucket and a rope to access its precious content. The low stone walls lying around are very useful if you intend to sleep outside without a tent when a north wind is blowing.

If you are heading for the peak and Anopoli, then you must return to Roussies. You can leave your backpack somewhere here and climb to the peak, without carrying extra weight. Return to the col where the sign is. Climb west (no signposting – just some piles of stones). In less than 10´ you will see a small basin. Cross it to a flat area, climb a bit more and follow the slope to the Southwest. The final ridge is ahead, and you have two options. The first is to climb directly to the first peak and from there to traverse the ridge to Pachnes. The second is to climb diagonally, heading straight to Pachnes. The first choice is better, if the northern slope has snow.

Either way, in 50´ from Roussies, you will conquer Pachnes, the Lefka Ori summit (2,453 m). There is a visitor's book there. Unfortunately, the southern view isn't as spectacular as you might imagine, because the peaks to the South hide the seashore. The view to the Samaria Gorge though, as well as to the north side of the island, is very beautiful. You come down to Roussies the same way in 40'.

Lefka Ori Region

24. LAKKI – POTAMI (VRYSSI GORGE)

DIFFICULTY	■ ■ ■ ■
DURATION	9 h, 17 km
ELEVATION CHANGE	a) Lakki – Vryssi spring: 3 h, 260 m up b) Vryssi spring –1st col: 2 h 30', 900 m up, 40 m down c) 1st col – 2nd col – sheep pen: 1 h 10', 200 up, 90 m down d) Sheep pen – Melidaou ridge: 1h, 280 m up e) Melidaou ridge – Potami (Koumi): 65', 330 m down
TERRAIN	Relatively good path (cobbled) at the beginning, no path afterwards. Walking on stony terrain.
SIGNPOSTING	Certainly not.
WHEN TO GO	May, June, September and October.
WATER	You'll find water at Vryssi spring and in cisterns at Potami. Take some water from Lakki and then fill up at the fountain.
SHADE	The first third of the hike is in shade. After the fountain, wear your hat and sun protection cream.
POPULARITY	You may meet a shepherd at the beginning or at the end of the hike.
WHERE TO SLEEP WHERE TO EAT	In your tent at Potami or under the stars. Take enough food for two days.
ACCESS	Catch the bus to Lakki until it gets to Omalos. Usually 4 bus services per day. The taxi from Chania costs about €15.
DRAWBACKS	This hike has no drawbacks! Good navigation skills are necessary.

If you like solitude, if you want to be off the beaten track and if you have good navigational skills, then this is the hike for you. You'll be excited even if you just walk through the Vryssi Gorge to the fountain with the same name. From there, you will have complete freedom to choose your own path to your final destination. There you will realize the actual size of the Lefka Ori Mountains and you'll understand why rebels used to hide up here away from their enemies.

The historical village of Lakki lies 24 km from Chania, on the road leading to Omalos. This is Hatzimihali Giannari's home village. He was the ringleader of the Cretan rebellions of 1866, 1878, and 1896 against the Ottomans and later became Crete's Convention Chairman, a convention which heralded Crete's unification with Greece in 1912. At Lakki, between the "Nikos" taverna and the traditional coffee shop, descends a narrow cement path. Ignore the rubbish and follow the path and then the gravel road to the last house. It takes you 15'. If you look southeast, towards the mountain you'll see two ravines running down from there. You should follow the one on the left.

Some meters beyond the last house there is a fence. Climb down the steep slope before that fence and head east to reach the gully. As soon as you reach the gully bed, continue left. 5´ later, you will see marks on your right and a path that runs south to Omalos.

Walk inside the gully on its right-hand side. Shortly you'll see a stone-built path which climbs gradually leaving the gully behind. After a while, you'll see metallic covers on the path. Underneath them, lies a water pipe carrying water from the spring to the village. Continue southeast on the path which is on the right side of the riverbed, a bit higher than the bed itself. You may lose the path, but you can always find it again after a while. The more you climb, the better the route. The path winds round like a belt on the gorge's steep slope.

After a 3 hour walk from Lakki, the gorge narrows down, while the path disappears leaving the pipeline exposed. Further up and to the left, fresh water flows from a small cave following its ancient route to the sea. There is no path from here, only some goat tracks.

This description will be based on some natural features in the distance. Sometimes, you might decide to follow something that looks like a path, only to return to search for a better one.

Continue inside the bed on the left side, this time scrambling over some fallen rocks. Try to gain height and keep a southeastern direction, always remaining on the left side of the gully. The route climbs up, moving on screes among trees and branches, and you might need to use your hands at some points. It will take you 1 h 45´ to climb this section, and you will exit to an open space, gaining 600 m in height in just 2 km! As soon as you are up on the open slope, you'll see Melidaou peak in the background. Continue traversing the slope climbing gradually in a southwestern direction. Your aim is to pass behind the slope that is ahead of you, traverse around a gully and find yourself below Melidaou.

Climb continuously for 45´, until you find yourself above a basin where

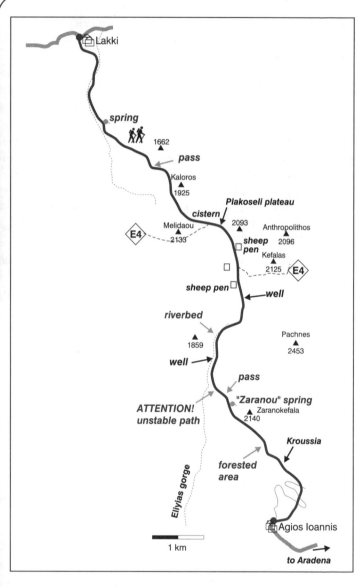

there is a sheep pen. To the East, left from Melidaou, is Kaloros, your next target. Follow the shape of the slope and head east, traversing above and around the basin, to the col which lies to the Southeast. It will take you 40´ to cover the 1.5 km of this amphitheatrical traverse. Try to cross below Kaloros, without losing height, to the col which lies between you and Melidaou. You'll get there 30´ later. Unfortunately, there is now a gully between you and the peak, and you must descend into it, losing 150 m in height. In order not to lose too much, turn a bit to the Southwest to meet the gully high up. There is an old sheep pen there. Climb again heading east, following the terrain. East and higher up, you will see rock formations covering the slope almost vertically. Above them there is a col, Melidaou's crest. The real difficulty in climbing this slope, and all the other Lefka Ori slopes for that matter, is the slope's formation which is actually a scree consisting of small and large irregular stones. Even though you might be tired now, it will not take you more than 40´ to reach the crest. From there, descend to the other side heading southeast. You'll walk among large, very impressive, tectonic submersions, heading to the gully and the alpine meadows. You will meet the E4 path there. Keep descending following the gully. Pass by Pyros' sheep pen and you will come to another gully which opens to the South on a large alpine meadow. From there, the E4 ascends to Katsiveli. This area is called Potami. It is a 50´ walk from the crest to this spot. If you keep descending to Koumi, you'll find water in one of the cisterns and you might meet some shepherds to keep you company.

25. POTAMI – AI YANNIS

DIFFICULTY	■ ■ ■ ■
DURATION	6 h 30' – 7 h, 16 km
ELEVATION CHANGE	a) Potami – mule track: 1 h 45', 100 m down b) Mule track – Mavra Harlara: 1 h, 170 m down, 250 m up c) Mavra Harlara – Seli: 1 h 15', 110 m up d) Seli – Kroussia: 1 h 10', 650 m down e) Kroussia – Ai Yannis: 65', 430 m down
TERRAIN	You walk on scree or on rough, stony and crumbling terrain. A large part of the walk is on a mostly damaged mule track.
SIGNPOSTING	Some piles of rocks or nothing at all.
WHEN TO GO	May–October (avoid August as it is very hot).
WATER	You will find water at Koumi (wells and cisterns) and at the Zarani fountain, beneath Zaranokefala.

Lefka Ori Region

SHADE	🎇	Shade only inside the forest at the part between Seli and Kroussia (first third). After the fountain, wear your hat and sun protection cream.
POPULARITY	👥	A shepherd now and then.
ACCESS	📐	Walk to Potami (Routes 23b, 24, 27). Take a taxi from Anopoli to Ai Yannis or use your own vehicle.
SIGHTS	🏛	Amazing view!
DRAWBACKS	✖	Difficult access (it might not be such a drawback actually!).

This route connects Potami area with the isolated village of Ai Yannis. It is one of the best hikes on Lefka Ori and follows the natural lines of Zaranokefala's steep slopes in one of the wildest areas in Crete. A very old cobbled path connects the mountainous pasturelands with the winter quarters. The magic of the hike is completed by the small fountain with its water running out of solid rock. The view to the southern seashore over vertical slopes is expansive.

This hike will be described from Potami to Ai Yannis as an alternative route to the South (instead of Route 19 from Roussies). Easily enough though (or maybe not so easily since it is an uphill hike), it can be reversed. Using the same route, you can ascend to Zaranokefala and the Pachnes peak.

The E4 path descends from Melidaou to Katsiveli (Route 23b), crossing a wide gully with some sheep pens around. This area is called Potami. The gully goes south, getting wilder and steeper as it approaches the sea. This is Elygia's Gorge. If you want to do it and enjoy its wildness, you must have a rope and know how to use it, because there are waterfalls inside the gorge (they might not have water though) but to reach Ai Yannis, you don't need to go into it. Follow the gully passing Kriarades' sheep pen and the covered cisterns. These cisterns are masterpieces, because they have water until the end of the summer. You will need a bucket and a rope to take water from there. 30´ after the start, you'll find a tank with a bucket but, if you use some water, take care not to pollute the rest.

After a while you have two options. The first is to continue in the gully and the second to follow the left branch of the path. If you keep straight on, you'll come to another sheep pen and a cistern. From there, climb to the East on a scree and, when you reach the rocks, you'll see the mule track on your right.

Rizitika Songs

In Crete there are three song categories: rizitika, folk couplets (mantinades) and historical songs. Rizitika can be heard mainly in Western Crete. They started in the areas at the foot (rizes) of Lefka Ori. Researchers can date their lack of rhyme, and their affinity with other songs, back to the Venetian occupation. However, some of the best songs (hunting songs, rebel songs and songs about nature) were composed under Ottoman rule.

The content of Rizitika varies: historical, heroic, religious, social and erotic. Their melodies are unique. Cretans divide rizitika in two categories, those that are usually sung around a table (tavlas) and those that are sung when on the road (stratas). The former are sung at festivals when everybody sits around a table, with no musical instruments to accompany them. They are sung by two groups of men, those on one side being the first choral group and those on the opposite side being the second. A singer from the first group starts singing the first verse of a song he likes, covering the fifteen-line verse, while the rest of the group accompany him with softer voices. The same verse is repeated by the second group in exactly the same way. This procedure continues until the song is finished, when the lead singer of the first group raises his glass and says "geia mas".

Stratas songs are sung when on the road and are accompanied by musical instruments. They are usually sung when relations go to collect the bride from her mother's house and accompany her to the church. Each verse of these songs (and there are a lot) is usually repeated two or three times, so a single song can last for an hour or more.

If you continue left you'll climb up to Gremnara, passing the remains of a Belgian Mirage fighter plane which crashed here back in 1973 and now decorates the area with the shell of its fuselage and makes sheep pens with parts of its engine. The path almost disappears brushing the vertical rocks. After passing the two spurs, look below you to the sheep pen and the cistern. The so-called path moves through very steep areas now. Look south below you to the opposite side of the scree, and you'll see the cobbled path climbing the steep side of a spur.

It is almost 2 hours from the start to the mule track, regardless of the option you have taken. You have a continuous climb now from here to the foot of Zaranokefala, which will take almost 2 hours. Nevertheless, it is the best part of the hike. The harsh lined slopes of Lefka Ori end in the sea. You will walk on terraces, feeling like you're flying above this magnificent scenery.

When up on the spur, the path keeps traversing up to a smoother slope, like a plateau. The direction is southeastern now, and the path can be easily seen among all the stones. Walk an hour or a bit more until the terrain becomes black, looking like it has been burned. This is Mavra Harlara, and you see a round low peak to the South in front of you, with its col and Zaranokefala behind it. Pass this col and with the help of some piles of stones, you'll find your way and the path that climbs winding round up to Zaranokefala.

Before reaching the wall, something like a path goes up the steep crumbled slope. This path leads you to the Zaranokefala and Pachnes peaks. 20′ after you pass the col, you will be at the path's highest point on ledges that traverse the wall. Some small caves and peaks add to the gorgeous scenery. In one of these small caves there is a small but steady spring, "Zarani water", which provides you with water for the rest of your hike. Shepherds have built a small covered cistern to gather the precious water. Try not to spoil the little cistern and cover it again. Think how precious this gift is.

The walk on the ledge and the view are fantastic. Look west to see Agia Roumeli. This small walkway can be impassable in the early spring because of the snow. In a while you start descending, and, after 15′, the path turns east. You climb down for another hour. You see Anopoli to the Southeast. You soon reach a wide col and the end of the rocks on a slope, where pine trees and cedars are forming a forest. Descend carefully through the rolling stones that wind down inside the wide gully. You will see two black pipes carrying water from above, moving parallel to your route. The roof tiles of Ai Yannis can already be seen below. After 15′ or 1 km downhill, the path goes east to Anopoli. Keep walking south next to the black pipes. You will find a wide forested area called Kroussia. A road runs here from Ai Yannis. Ai Yannis is still far away, but it is a piece of cake for anyone who has walked this far now. Continue in the gully always heading south. You'll pass some abandoned fields, while a cobbled path is visible on the eastern side of the gully. You come to a large cement cistern. Keep on the road, and after an hour from Kroussia, you are entering the village.

No transport gets to this quiet Cretan village, one of the last really tranquil ones. Walk to the village's entrance, closed with a big iron gate, and notice the school that was closed down, but now opens occasionally as a coffee shop. The road from Anopoli comes to this point. If you are lucky, a car may come to take you to Anopoli. The other option is to go to Agios Pavlos following Route 12. Try to stay overnight at Ai Yannis if you can.

Lamb Haircut (Koura)

Whenever there's a festival there's at least one Cretan. There is always a good cause to celebrate, to gather your friends and relatives around a table to eat and drink. Since ancient times, Cretans have managed to combine work with pleasure.

A good opportunity is when sheep need to be sheared at the end of May or early June. The shepherd will say 'This Sunday morning we are going to shear our sheep; anyone available is welcome to help us...'

On the given morning, scissors will come out of drawers, they will be sharpened, their handles will be modified so they don't hurt the hands, and an order will be given to the lady of the house to cook stew with rice or pasta for the guests.

One by one the "barbers" arrive, drink the necessary amount of raki and the scissors are on fire. Some of the guests catch the sheep, tie their legs tightly and leave them in front of the barbers, while others put the wool into sacks.

Some on one knee, some on both their knees and others seated, they cut the sheeps' wool really fast. Thick wool comes from quick and skilful hands working on the tufts. From time to time, a clumsy barber wounds a poor animal, which springs up and screams. Once sheared, the sheep jump around as soon as they are freed and run away as if they are ashamed of their nudity.

When noon comes, the table is laid and the stew is served with the rice or pasta boiled in goat's broth. Salads, pies and kaltsounia (small Cretan pies) are also served, accompanied by stories of the old days, jokes and teasing. If the wine is good and the company enthusiastic, you'll soon hear some singing and if a lyre is available...

26. KASTRO ASCENT FROM ASKIFOU

DIFFICULTY	📈	■ ■ ■ ■
DURATION	🕐	8 h
ELEVATION CHANGE	📊	1,450 m ascent a) Ammoudari – Tavri hut: 1 h 30', 450 m ascent b) Hut – ridge start: 30', 70 m ascent c) Ridge start – peak: 2 h 30', 930 m ascent d) Return: 3 h 30', 1,450 m descent
TERRAIN	🏔	The first part to the hut is easy and signposted. The second part is a gravel road, but there is no path on the third part.
SIGNPOSTING	🔼	Good enough (E4), but sparse until the ridge's start.
WHEN TO GO	📅	April–October.
WATER	〰	Take water from the coffee shops in Ammoudari or from the hut if it is open.
SHADE	🌟	You will have shade up to the hut, because your walk will be in the forest.
POPULARITY	👥	Only some shepherds.
WHERE TO SLEEP WHERE TO EAT	🍴	Some budget rooms in Askifou and a very good new stone-built guesthouse.
ACCESS	🚗	3–4 daily bus services from Chania to Sfakia.
SIGHTS	🏛	The amazing view to Chania from the top and the mountainous landscape with its continuous plateaus.
DRAWBACKS	✖	The great change in elevation, the rough terrain and the lack of shade.

A very impressive ascent to one of the Lefka Ori peaks offering great views. You will see a panorama of the mountain range, all of the Chania region with distinctive landscapes (plateaus, dolines, peaks), vegetation variety and scenes of agricultural life. The ascent during winter is a real alpine hike.

The hike starts from Ammoudari on the Askifou plateau. Go to where the statue, the bus station and the coffee shops are, and then take the road climbing to the right of the statue and turn right again into a smaller road. 300 m away, at a left-hand bend, you will see an E4 sign on your right, with a map indicating the hiking routes and a small wooden fence. The path starts there, at the right of the fence and continues uphill following a shallow gully. The signposting is good, and in 15′ you reach a gravel road. The path continues on the opposite side in the forest (pine, cedar and oak trees). It is a wide easy path, which winds continuously and leads you (1 hour later) to a low col and to the Tavri plateau at a height of 1,200 m.

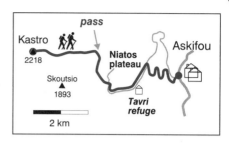

A small plateau lies ahead, while in the background you can see the peaks of Kastro (2,215 m) and Skoutsokorfi (1,893 m). On your left, you see a hill with a hut on it. Follow the E4 signs descending gradually to the road, turn left, and in 20′ you will be at the hut. It is an attractive, new, large building with great views to the mountain and the plateaus. The road bypasses the hut and continues to the right, reaching the Niato plateau in 10′.

This is a large plateau with sparse vegetation, full of sheep and goats at a height of 1,200 m. Cross the plateau, following the road to the right at the next junction (the left road goes to Kali Lakki) and then turn left on the ascending road. 20′–25′ afterwards you will be at a small col. The road and the E4 path go straight on. Leave them and climb the steep ridge to the left (West) on a goat track. This ridge stands out and goes straight to the peak without any more ups and downs. The Lefka Ori grandeur lies all around as you climb. Kastro is ahead, with other small peaks next to it, while at your back you can see the Niato and Tavri plateaus, the hut, and Agathes, with Lefka Ori slopes on your left, the sea and the Vamos region on your right.

The hike continues on small goat tracks which disappear after a while, and you walk among small rocks, phrygana, stones and bushes on a ridge that is sometimes steep, sometimes flat. Choose the side you walk on according to the direction of the wind. If a north wind is blowing, take the left side of the ridge (10–20 m lower) to protect yourself from its fierceness. If there is a south wind (it is usually very strong), take the right side. The shape of the mountain's relief (relatively smooth slopes, view to the mountain top) will help you with these choices.

As you are getting closer to the peak, the ridge will get steeper and far more tiring, as sometimes you have to walk on screes. In 2 hours you will be at the foot of the peak, and you'll climb the steep slope. This is the route's most tiring section, with a steep incline and small screes, but impressive views. It takes almost half an hour to climb this final slope, on the last bit of which you move along a smooth ridge leading you to a wide peak with the typical small column and the unobstructed view of the Lefka Ori massif clustered with tens of peaks, of the small valleys, of the two seas and of the villages and cities of the region.

Leave the peak behind and, if you don't want to go back the same way you came, you can descend the north slope. Climb down walking on screes and goat tracks until the distinctive hollow (doline) underneath the peaks (20′–30′). Then, turn east and follow the wide valley which is formed by the two saddles. To the right lies the right saddle you followed earlier on, and to the left another one almost parallel and a little to the North. The descent is on stones, soil and phrygana, not particularly difficult. Stay on the right slope under the south saddle (always descending) and pass above some steep low rocks. 1 h 30′ later you reach the road and the E4 path, just a few meters away from the col where you left it and you continue to the right following the same route (Niatos plateau – hut – Tavri plateau – E4 path) to return to Askifou. An alternative route is to continue left on the road and the E4 path, heading to the Svourihti hut at a height of 2,000 m (6–7 h hike).

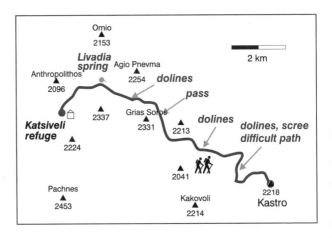

27. KASTRO – KATSIVELI

DIFFICULTY 📈	■ ■ ■ ■
DURATION 🕐	7 h
ELEVATION CHANGE 📊	850 m ascent, 1,100 m descent a) Summit – plateau: 1 h 30´, 80 m up, 650 m down b) Plateau – 1st col : 30´, 150 m up c) 1st col – 3rd col : 2 h , 420 m up, 150 m down d) 3rd col – mountain hut: 3 h, 200 m, 300 m down
TERRAIN 🏔	A rough, stony terrain mostly with no path.
SIGNPOSTING 🔼	Some sparse E4 signs, then only some piles of stones.
WHEN TO GO 📅	April–October.
WATER 〰	Only a spring with no water in the summertime.
SHADE 🌴	Shade only if you are a reptile.
POPULARITY 👥	No one.
WHERE TO SLEEP WHERE TO EAT 🍴	In the huts, if they are open.
ACCESS 🛣	3–4 daily bus services from Chania to Sfakia.
SIGHTS 🏛	The amazing view to Chania from the top and the mountainous landscape with its continuous plateaus, peaks, dolines and rocks.
DRAWBACKS ❌	The rough terrain and the lack of shade.

This is one of the toughest and most tiring hikes on Lefka Ori, but also one of the most wild and beautiful ones. It is recommended only for mountaineers. A mountaineering paradise with a lot of wild peaks, steep slopes, screes, basins, lunar landscapes and green valleys, streams and amazing views. A hike to remember, really unique.

Start descending southwest from Kastro's peak, following the relatively steep saddle on earth and stones for almost half an hour. You reach a basin between two saddles. Continue north, climbing for 15´ to the opposite saddle. The views are great from there, valleys, dolines, the north peaks. Walk on the wide ridge for a while, and then climb down Kastro's large north slope for another 45´, heading for a faraway meadow on your left (the higher one). You meet the E4 path there which comes from the Niatos plateau and Askifou, though nothing indicates that you are actually on a path. The goat track is unclear, disappearing from time to time in small meadows. The signs are long gone. They were sparse anyway (iron poles with yellow rhombi on them). Keep on the goat track heading northwest at the foot of the lower summits (a long mountain range) on solid ground and stones, among phrygana and sparse vegetation.

Cross a shallow gully and climb west to a distinctive col between two low summits. It will take you half an hour to reach this spot. Ahead, to the West (on your left), you see the long Kakovoli mountain range (2,214 m) and on your right the Sorou Grias peak (2,331 m). Below you, are the numerous dolines and the peculiar ground relief which resembles a lunar landscape.

Descend gradually to the right for 20´ towards a saddle between dolines. From here on, the climb is tiring and long, heading west to a col at an elevation of 2,000 m. You will move among dolines, steep rocks, screes and stones. 45´– 50´ later, you reach the col and continue right, traversing the slope a bit to the North, where you find an E4 sign. Follow the narrow ridge to the Southwest, remaining at the same height, and then ascend on a steep stony slope moving west to a narrow col between two peaks. Traverse to a second col passing among broken rocks 200 m further away, and then descend on scree and stones having the Agio Pnevma peak (2,254 m) on your right and the Sorou Grias peak (2,331 m) on your left.

Here you meet the route from Agio Pnevma to Sorou Grias, Mesa Sorou Grias, Svourihti and Katsiveli. Continue descending gradually to a wide valley, an opening actually formed between the long Svourihti ridge on the left and Agio Pnevma and Ornio (2,153 m) on the right. The route goes from short steep sections with eroded rocks and dolines to flat valleys with low vegetation relieving your tired feet. The descent heads west-northwest on different goat tracks, sheep pens, E4 signs and finally next to a spring in the lowest valleys. Then you turn southwest, with the Anthropolitho summit (2,096 m) on your right and Svourihti (2,337 m) on your left. The path is obvious and easy now, climbing the Svourihti slope until it reaches Katsiveli's hut (or Takis Houliopoulos' hut) at a height of 1,970 m and lying on a col between Svourihti and Anonymi (2,125 m). It will take you an hour to get here from the spring.

28. IMBROS GORGE

DIFFICULTY	📈	■ ☐ ☐ ☐
DURATION	🕐	2 h 30', 7 km
ELEVATION CHANGE	📊	a) Komitades – cistern: 1 h, 150 m ascent b) Cistern – Imbros: 1 h 30', 500 m ascent
TERRAIN	⛰	Clear path which moves along the gorge's bed, with a lot of pebbles. Wear a good pair of boots.
SIGNPOSTING	🔼	No need for signs.
WHEN TO GO	📅	Any time of the year, except when it rains.
WATER	🌊	Take water from Komitades.
SHADE	🌳	Most of the hike is in shade, so it can be done even in the summertime.
POPULARITY	👥	A lot of people in the summer.
WHERE TO SLEEP WHERE TO EAT	🛏🍴	There are a lot of tavernas at Komitades and some rooms to let. Imbros has three tavernas.
ACCESS	📐	There are two daily bus services from Chania to Komitades, but a lot more from Imbros pass by, because it lies on the road connecting Chania to Sfakia.
SIGHTS	🏛	Agios Georgios' Byzantine chapel built in 1314 A.D. and painted by Ioannis Pagomenos.
DRAWBACKS	✖	Crowds of people in the summertime.

Imbros Gorge is the gorge that can be seen below, when you take the road to Sfakia. It is a very attractive gorge (the narrowest in Crete) but, being shorter and easier than the Samaria Gorge, it attracts a lot of people, especially during the summer. Because of this, Sfakia City Council decided to impose entrance fees. As well as its narrow walls, the needle peaks which stand high on its steep slopes are really impressive.

Our suggestion is the same as the one we suggested for the Samaria Gorge; climb the gorge instead of descending it. The reasons are first to move in the opposite direction to the crowds of people and second to be in higher and cooler ground when the heat of the day is unbearable. After the last tavernas at Komitades, climb the bed of the wide gully to the East. For 20´ you walk on pebbles which may tire you. Afterwards you come to the old path and everything is easier. After a while you'll see an impressive gate, and you cannot avoid a pain in your neck as you admire the gorge's high slopes. An hour later you come to a cistern where the shepherds bring their animals to drink water. The rocks seem to be cut by a gigantic axe that fell and tore them in the middle. At the gorge's narrowest section, you can touch both walls if you spread your arms.

The walls open up again slowly, and you reach the north gate's toll booth, 10´ from Imbros village.

The small Imbros (or Nimbros) village used to be a summer village and has just a few inhabitants. There used to be a path here, but now it is a gravel road which ascends west to Kali Lakki and from there to Anopoli (see route 18).

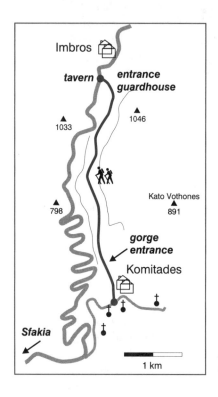

Rusks

One of the staples of the Cretan diet, and in fact one of the most nutritious and healthy foods, is the rusk. There are many types of rusk in Crete, barley rusks, wheat rusks, mixed rusks, rolls, dakos and many more. They are very popular.

Their nutritional value and the preparation process have been well understood since ancient times, when they used to call them "twice baked bread" (dipyritos artos: dis = twice, pyr = fire, and artos = bread). They were eaten in Roman and Byzantine times, mainly because they can be kept for a long time and they weigh very little. Poor people ate them, because they were cheaper. After the German occupation and the prosperity that followed, people forgot all about them, but the trend nowadays for healthier food has put rusks high up on the shopping list again.

Preparing rusks is easy. First you bake the dough as you would bake bread (cut into slices), and then the slices are re-baked at a slow temperature (80°–100°C) until they take on the right colour. It seems simple enough, but it requires skill. The well-made rusk must be baked properly, neither too hard nor too soft; when dipped in liquid it must get wet and soften easily, without crumbling, and must retain its taste etc. Different flours are used, mainly wheat and barley (flour from milling the whole barley is very popular). Other essential ingredients are salt, olive oil, spices (oregano, thyme and aniseed), wine or raki, and sugar. Rusks that are made for festivals and funerals or to accompany beverages are sweet (with sugar and spices).

Their shape can be either rectangular (dakos, small rectangular slices) or rolls (kouloura, a big roll with a small hole in the centre or cut across the middle horizontally, with the upper part called kafkalo, the skull). There are many recipes for eating rusks, but the most popular one is dakos koukouvagia, that is, barley rusk, half wet with olive oil, oregano, trimmed tomato, white cheese (feta or myzithra) and sometimes with olives on top. It is a healthy, nourishing and light food.

Lefka Ori Region

29. ASKIFOU – AGATHES

DIFFICULTY	📈	■ ■ ■ □
DURATION	🕐	4 h 30', one way
ELEVATION CHANGE	📊	a) Kares – Goni: 30', 90 m descent b) Goni – gravel road: 1 h 15', 320 m ascent c) Gravel road – sheep pen: 45', 180 m ascent d) Sheep pen – peak: 1 h 40', 350 m ascent
TERRAIN	⛰	At the beginning you walk on the road, then on goat tracks and finally on stony chalk ground.
SIGNPOSTING	🔼	No.
WHEN TO GO	📅	March–June, September–November.
WATER	〰	Take water from Askifou.
SHADE	🌴	Don't expect much by way of shade.
POPULARITY	👥	You'll meet practically no one, apart from some shepherds.
WHERE TO SLEEP WHERE TO EAT	🍴	There are some rooms-to-let and a very nice new hotel at Askifou, "Leukoritis", with detached stone-built houses. A few tavernas and simple food at Askifou.
ACCESS	📶	Take the bus to Sfakia from Chania and get off at Askifou.
DRAWBACKS	❌	It is difficult to find the starting point, because they have fenced everything around.

The hike to Agathes is not particularly difficult, but you must have good navigation skills as there is no path. You must improvise and wander on the lunar landscape, until you find your way. Agathes summit (1,511 m) is Lefka Ori's highest eastern peak, and the ascents can be made from Askifou, Kallikrati and Asi Gonia.

Stand in the middle of the small triangular square at Kares and look ahead to the plateau. You will see a lot of peaks. None of these is Agathes, though it lies in this direction, but is further away beyond them. If you look closer at the left edge of the plateau to the North, you'll see a gully heading to the peaks, like a natural exit to the mountains. This gully is your first target.

Descend to the last houses, pass behind the school and reach a road. Turn a bit right and then left to the fertile valley. After a while, you come to the new tar road and, in half an hour, to the half-ruined village of Goni, built on a low hill in the middle of the valley. You want to pass along Goni's northern side heading straight to the gully, but fences prevent it. But you can try this. At the entrance to the village, take the gravel road going left, almost north, towards the hill with the Turkish castles on the top. 400 m further

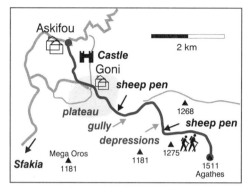

you'll see a gate to your right and something like a corridor running between the fences. The corridor ends, and you must pass through the field to the other side, where there is an exit, another gate. Pass behind the fences and walk to the right, parallel with them. The dense vegetation can be a nuisance, but as a lot a goats and sheep pass by here, it will be relatively clear. 20′–25′ later you reach the lower part of the gully. If you find a better way to get here, please let us know.

To start with, climb the left side of the gully, passing by an old sheep pen, and then walk almost on the bed. This path used to connect the Askifou plateau with Asi Gonia. A large part of the path is now a gravel road.

You must now move southwest towards the ridge. Try to climb as gradually as possible. Leave the road and climb up to the gully ahead of you as diagonally as you can to the slope on the right, until you gain 200 m in elevation. 30′–40′ later you reach a plateau with some trees, mainly wild apple and maple, and goat tracks.

Turn south and climb gradually for half an hour, passing among dolines. The area is dotted with them. You'll reach a large sheep pen built in a depression. Behind you, you can see the Askyfou plateau. High above, to the Southeast, you will see a distinctive peak with broken stone slabs on the top and further right a conical summit, like a dome.

Pass the sheep pen and climb towards these peaks. Follow the ridge for 30′ to an old sheep pen. From here, you only have to follow the ridge and 60′–70′ later you'll cover the 250 m height difference to the summit. If the weather is clear, you will enjoy one of the best views to Lefka Ori and Psiloritis.

Caper, The Edible Flower

Caper spreads across the barren rocks, sleeps on ruined walls, and blooms among the monotonous summer colours without demanding a single raindrop. It is a thorny plant which grows everywhere, but mainly on rocky and uncultivated terrain. Theofrastos, the ancient Athenian botanist, mentions caper six times in his books. The Cretan monk Agapios in one of his 15th Century writings suggests that caper "...should be eaten with vinegar, oil and raisins. If it is salted, put it in water first and then eat it, before you eat anything else". In the same paragraph the writer refers to the healing properties of caper which are extremely interesting "...it cures spleen, kills the worms, cures haemorrhoids, increases the quantity of the sperm, cures the liver, helps the urinary system, and eases rheumatic pain..."

When the traveller F.W. Sieber visited Crete in 1817, he recorded a kind of caper which was totally unknown to other Europeans; "what pleased me extremely was a branch of capparis egyptiaca which has neither leaves nor flowers. I understood that this was caper by its trunk, while by the two golden curved thorns I deduced that it belongs to the Egyptian kind".

What is actually used to add taste and scent in sauces and delicacies is not its fruit, which is not edible, but its calyx from the flower before it opens. The caper gathering period is between May and July. The small calyxes are gathered when they are still green and the size of a bean and must be put for 10 days in water, which should be changed often. When calyxes taste sweet, a strong solution of vinegar and salt is added, and the prepared caper is then stored, well covered in a glass vase. They are ready after 10 days. This kind of preparation is common in all Mediterranean countries, as well as the use of caper as a spice added to tomato salads in summer or even to cabbage salads.

30. ASKIFOU – ASFENDOU GORGE

DIFFICULTY	■ ■ □ □
DURATION	4 h 30'
ELEVATION CHANGE	12 km a) Kares – Goni: 30', 90 m descent b) Goni – col: 1h, 260 m ascent c) Col – Asfendou: 1 h 10', 200 m descent d) Asfendou – Agios Nektarios: 1 h 45', 630 m descent
TERRAIN	At the beginning you walk on the road, then on a semi-ruined path on chalk ground, partly stony, but easy.
SIGNPOSTING	From Goni to Asfendou sparse red signs and piles of stones.
WHEN TO GO	March–June, September–November.
WATER	Take water from Askyfou. There is a well before the col, but the water is of doubtful quality, and also a covered cistern inside the gorge.
SHADE	There is shade inside the gorge early in the morning and after-noon.
POPULARITY	You'll meet practically no one, apart from some shepherds.
WHERE TO SLEEP WHERE TO EAT	There are some rooms-to-let and a very nice new hotel at Asky-fou, "Leukoritis", with detached stone-built houses. There are also a lot of rooms at Fragokastello. A few tavernas and simple food at Askifou, more at Fragokastello.
ACCESS	Take the bus to Sfakia from Chania and get off at Askyfou.
SIGHTS	The castle on the top of Plana hill is Turkish, built in 1868, by Omar Pasha. There is also an interesting World War II private col-lection, owned by Mr Hatzidakis at Kares.
DRAWBACKS	It is difficult to find the starting point, because there are fences all around.

This is an easy but long hike moving on forgotten paths, which used to connect sum-mer settlements and fields with the seaside winter villages. A small basin is formed between the Kastro (2,218 m), Trypali (1,493m) and Agathes (1,511 m) peaks. This is the Askyfou plateau, where some small settlements are built amphitheatrically. The first houses belong to Kares. The entire bunch of settlements is called Askyfou and lies on the only road from Chania to Sfakia.

In this fertile basin, people cultivate grapes and vegetables. Apart from the good wine, the area is famous for its warriors. The whole area was the centre of many bat-tles before and during the World War II.

Descending to the last houses of Kares, you reach a gravel road going southeast below the hill with the ruined castles on the top, entering the small fertile valley. You walk for half an hour, until you reach Goni. This seemingly abandoned scenic settlement sits in the middle of the plateau, which is fertile and produces good quality potatoes and strong wine. Continue on the gravel road that heads southeast from the village and seems like it is heading for a valley.

The fertile valley ends after a while, between the Kampi and Mega Oros mountains. You keep on walking on the road for 1.7 km after Goni (35'). You will see the old cobbled path on the left side of a right-hand bend in the road. Follow it for 100 m, then walk on the road again. This is the last point with a view to the impressive Tavri and Kastro peaks.

The road forks, and you turn left. At the end of the sheep pen fence, go left inside the gully's bed, finding the path again and leaving the road for good.

10' later, you will reach a path branch. Follow the little red arrow pointing left. Soon afterwards, you find yourself at some small abandoned fields, full of daffodils in spring. There is a well there, nowadays used only for the animals. Climb a bit more up to the walk's highest point, 1 hour's walk from Goni. Your view extends through the Asfendou Gorge to the sea below.

For 15' you walk on a good cobbled path, until a sheep pen with a cistern gathering rain water. The ugly road meets with the path again. They criss-cross their routes for a while, until you finally take the road. Pass another sheep pen and in a while you are on the tar road.

Enter Asfendou village, at an elevation of 750 m, after a 2 and a half hour walk. Only a few of the houses are inhabited (only in the summertime). This mountain village took its name from flowers like daffodils growing on short, leafy trees, and was always a summer village. The inhabitants used to leave the village in the winter for their seaside fields, where life was a lot easier. After Daskaloyannis' rebellion, the Ottomans burned the village to the ground.

When you reach the main street in this village, continue straight on for a while. The road turns left after 60–70 m towards Kallikratis, but you must continue straight on. At the end of the road, you'll find a path among the ruins on your left. Pass a small gate and descend to the fields on the riverbed. You will see a lot of orchids here from April to early May.

Walk on the riverbed and soon you will be on the old path. The gorge's walls are getting closer now. The scenery is imposing and beautiful. The cobbled path is well preserved and 1.5 m wide. Who knows how many people and for how long they worked to build this amazing piece of work. The chalky walls make incredible formations. The air is full of the scents of thyme and sage.

The path is winding and descends the steep slope, among sages and oleanders, on the western side of the gorge. 40´ later, you reach an old cistern. The path, ruined now, moves from left to right, sometimes inside the bed until the gorge opens up.

Maybe there used to be an older path as well, because you will spot glimpses of it, but you'll not lose your way. When it opens up, you should be on the east side

of the gorge, where you find a fence. There is a gate on the bed. Climb down to the west side, towards an olive grove. Continue straight on, and in 15´ time, you will be in the village of Agios Nektarios.

If you want to climb the gorge, walk up the road that starts from the church. 4´–5´ later, before an electricity pylon, turn left on the gravel road above the gully's bed. Be careful – don't go inside the gully here. You will see a cistern and a sheep pen at the end on your right. Bypass it, keep straight on to the olive trees, and you will find the old path. The ascent to Asfendou takes 2 h 15´.

Drosoulites

At the end of May, early in the morning, very strange shadows appear in the sky above Fragokastello, human shadows. Ghostly warriors, dressed in black, holding their heavy, shiny arms, and standing in line, ready to fight. In the first row is Hatzimihalis Dalianis, behind him the horsemen, and further behind the foot soldiers. They all wait for a second chance to win a battle that was lost before it was joined.

The story has it that a couple of rebels stood against thousands of Turkish soldiers under Moustafa Pasha's command. The chieftain from Epirus, Dalianis, didn't like hiding up in the mountains and preferred to fight the Turks on the open plateau in front of Fragokastello. He had so many victories to his credit that he didn't like the shoot-and-run tactics of guerrillas. Cretan chieftains tried in vain to persuade him against this course of action.

He lined up his 600 soldiers from Epirus in front of the castle and waited for the Turks. When they arrived, a brutal hand-to-hand battle began. One of the first to be killed in this battle was Dalianis himself, who was beheaded the minute he was recognized. For seven days in a row, the Turks tried to get into the castle where the Greeks had taken refuge.

Rebels from Sfakia attacked the Turks from the surrounding mountains, and so Moustafa Pasha found himself in a very difficult position. He therefore told the defenders that they were free to leave the castle with their arms and guns. It was the 23rd of May 1828. Every year, on that very same day, Dalianis' army comes out again and they wander about, like shadows in the sky.

There is no scientific explanation for this peculiar phenomenon, even today. Some say that they may be reflections of Libyan soldiers from the Sahara. Whatever the truth may be, it is good to let our imagination fly. Let's not tell Dalianis' army that the war is over.

31. KALLIKRATIS' GORGE

DIFFICULTY	■ ■ ☐ ☐
DURATION	2 h 45' or 3 h 20' from Asfendou
ELEVATION CHANGE	a) Asfendou – Kallikratis: 1 h 40', 10 m up, 20 m down b) Kallikratis – trailhead 50', 80 m down c) Trailhead – Patsianos: 1 h 50', 550 m down
TERRAIN	You walk a bit on a gravel road, and on an almost ruined path with chalky terrain. It is stony in some places due to the screes on the slopes.
SIGNPOSTING	Sparse E4 signs.
WHEN TO GO	March–June, September–November.
WATER	Take water beforehand.
SHADE	Inside the gorge there is shade during the morning and afternoon.
POPULARITY	Some walkers cross it, but there are days when you will see no one.
WHERE TO SLEEP WHERE TO EAT	There is a good guesthouse at Patsianos. Lots of rooms-to-let at Fragokastello, though they could be a lot better, considering the large number of tourists in the area. The first cafe in Kallikratis offers good, home-made food.
ACCESS	With your own car from Asfendou or Asi Gonia, or by bus from Fragokastello.
SIGHTS	Fragokastello Castle, maybe the best preserved Venetian castle in Crete, built in 1371.
DRAWBACKS	There is no bus service to Kallikratis.

A relatively small gorge, which used to connect the mountainous pasture lands with the lowland villages. It is a very pleasant walk, offering great views and rare flowers that grow in these gorges. The Kallikratis' Gorge together with the Asfendou Gorge can be a full day's excursion. Start early in the morning, when it is still cool, and climb from Agios Nektarios to Asfendou, and from there head on to Kallikratis. Take your time to wander around the abandoned villages and, early in the afternoon, descend to Patsianos.

Until recently, if you found yourself at Asfendou or Kallikratis, you had the feeling that time had stopped many decades ago. With the recent construction of the tar road though, this feeling of isolation is lost. Nevertheless, life is now easier for the people who live there. Wandering on these rough paths is a unique experience.

If you climb from the Asfendou Gorge, turn right going northwest as soon as you reach the main road. Follow the tar road for 1 h 30´ until you reach Kallikratis. Before entering the village look south to the low part of the basin. You will see a small country chapel built on top of the hill. Make a picture of it in your mind, because it marks the start of the road that will take you into the gorge.

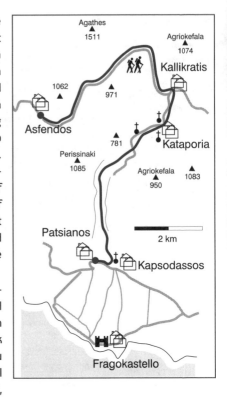

The village seems deserted, but there are still two or three cafes which offer food if needed. Walk to the church where you will see the ornate bell tower and then descend, towards Asi-Gonia, leaving the village behind. 400 m later, turn right. At the next junction, turn right again towards the small chapel on the hill. It will take you half an hour to get there.

From there, follow the gravel road to the right with the riverbed on this side, which is getting deeper as you move along. 45´ later, the road climbs to the left and the stream is quite deep now. There, on the left side of the gully, the path starts. A bit further on, the path is partly destroyed because of the rubble discarded during the road construction. This is progress...

The gorge is getting narrower and deeper. The slopes hang above the path, like they want to protect the walker from the harsh Cretan sun. Beautiful little plants grow in the middle of the cracks of the chalky walls. Depending on the season, you may see unique bell flowers and the dittany, a plant used to make a very healthy beverage.

Sfakia Cooking

A lot is written nowadays about the Cretan diet and its link to good health and longevity. The basis of Cretan diet is olive oil and a variety of vegetables. But is that always the case? The answer is no, at least not for everyone.

Shepherds spend their lives up in the mountains, where it is difficult not only to find but also to preserve vegetables. So the only solution is to consume meat. The imaginative Cretans found many ways to cook tough goat meat with excellent and tasty results. The basic ingredients of their success, as one shepherd cook, Roussos Tzatzimakis from Agia Roumeli, once told me, is virgin olive oil and half-wild goat meat. Half-wild goats (fouriarikes) are domestic goats that are not kept in a pen, but left to roam, so their owner must hunt them!

Meat with yoghurt

Put a ceramic vessel, which must close firmly, onto the cooker. Heat the olive oil and sauté 1 kg of meat (half-wild goat). Then add 1 kg yoghurt and let it boil for about 2 hours. The only spice you should add is coarse salt. Serving should be done 2 to 2. 5 hours later.

Tsigariasto

Cut the goat meat into pieces and put them in a pan with enough olive oil and salt. Put the pan on the cooker and let it simmer slowly for almost an hour. Before the end, bring the temperature up to sauté the meat. If the animal is old and its meat hard, it will take more than an hour and will need some water with the oil.

In the middle of the route, the path passes to the right-hand side of the gully. The old cobbled path is clear and partly cemented (a quick way of restoring paths, used in the 60s). The gorge opens up. Descend a large scree and you see a road on your left. Cross the gully one more time among huge rocks, which have fallen from the slopes and come to the road. You have walked 1 h 40´ now from the start of the trail.

Go down to the village following the road and in 15´ you reach the village's cemetery and the first houses. When you pass the village, you can take one of the numerous roads that lead to Fragokastello's sandy beach. It is worth visiting a good beach to the East called Orthi Ammos.

NORTHERN CHANIA – AKROTIRI REGION

Chania, one of the most attractive cities in Greece, is built on the northern shore of western Crete. It is the home town of Eleftherios Venizelos, a charismatic politician of the 1900s, and carries on its back the evidence of previous centuries. Landmarks of the long history of the city are the Venetian harbour, the castle, the lighthouse, the mosques, the churches, the dockyards and the archaeological findings from Ancient Kydonia. The city was inhabited from the Early Neolithic Age. There was no way for these first people building their houses here to know what would follow. The settlement developed into the very significant Minoan city of Kydonia, the main western city in the kingdom.

Kydonia's residents were not at all peaceful, like the other Minoans, and they were always in dispute with neighbouring cities. Their fighting skills proved very useful in 74 B.C. when Mark Antony tried to invade Crete. The Cretans became aware of the danger in time and dispatched the Roman navy to the bottom of the sea.

The city became independent and enjoyed an economic boom, producing its own coins. During the early years of the Byzantine era, Kydonia was a cathedral city and flourished until 624 A.D. But that year, the new superpower of the area, the Arabs, who were looking for new, rich and weak areas to conquer, came to the city and ruined it, as in fact they did to the whole of Crete. In 961 A.D. when Nikiforos Fokas* got rid of the Arabs, the city was rebuilt and fortified again.

At the dawn of the 13th Century, the new naval power, the Venetians, conquered the city and fortified it even better, but to no effect. In 1645, Ibrahim Pasha gathered 60,000 soldiers and decided to go to Crete. The cunning Pasha sent a message to the Venetians, telling them not to worry, since his actual target was Malta. However, his captains had their orders to head to Kissamos instead of Malta. The next day, they attacked the small castle on Theodorous Island, outside Chania. The defenders had no option other than to blow up the castle.

After a long chain of rebellions, the Ottomans finally left Chania in 1897, and the autonomous Cretan Confederacy was founded. The city was damaged once more during the World War II, when a large part of the old city was bombed during one of the biggest aerial invasions, enabling Nazi parachutists to conquer the island.

This is a brief history of the city. A stroll among the city's narrow streets will tell you a lot more. Most of the old buildings are still in use. Some have become museums, others hotels and restaurants, while others are still houses, adding to the long history of the place.

It is worth visiting the covered public market with its 70 shops. Some of them were converted into tourist shops, even though they were actually food stores. Enjoy a coffee in Splatzia, take a look at the shops in Skrintlof Street and don't forget to pay a visit to the Archaeological and Maritime Museum. Walk to the lighthouse and see the old dockyards. A replica of an old Minoan ship was built in one of them.

At the edge of the town, on Profitis Ilias hill, are the graves of Eleftherios Venizelos and his family. The hill is next to the road that goes to the airport and offers one of the best views over the town. Near there, at the cove of the peninsula called Akrotiri, is the most famous military base in the Mediterranean. Souda is considered one of the most strategic harbour sites, and NATO has a base there. The commercial and passenger harbours are also there.

A few kilometers north of the harbour is the airport. There is nothing particularly special to see on this route and, if we consider the expansion of different businesses towards the airport, the whole picture is rather ugly. Nevertheless, a small diversion to the northern area of Akrotiri is worth the drive. Two very important monasteries lie there. Tzagarolon Agia Triada, one of the most beautiful Cretan monasteries and the nearby Gouverneto Monastery with its magnificent architecture. At the bed of the nearby impressive gorge are the ruins of the Katholiko Monastery, which is the oldest monastery in Crete. These monasteries used to produce the famous Cretan honey of sage and wild pomegranate. Some short but very interesting walks can be taken here.

*See appendix page 159.

32. GOUVERNETO MONASTERY – KATHOLIKO MONASTERY

DIFFICULTY	■ □ □ □
DURATION	2 h 30' return trip
ELEVATION CHANGE	a) Agia Triada – Gouverneto: 1 h, 180 m ascent b) Gouverneto Monastery – Katholiko Monastery: 40´, 170 m descent c) Katholiko Monastery – sea: 30´, 100 m descent
TERRAIN	Well defined trail to Katholiko Monastery, then an easy walk in the gorge bed until you reach the sea.
SIGNPOSTING	None, but none is needed.
WHEN TO GO	All year round, except during heavy rainfall.
WATER	In the cave of Arkoudospilio there is a leaking water tank.
SHADE	Almost no shade whatsoever.
POPULARITY	It is quite popular, due to its proximity to the city of Chania.
WHERE TO SLEEP WHERE TO EAT	In the area around the city of Chania.
ACCESS	Two buses daily to Agia Triada.
SIGHTS	The monastery of Agia Triada Tzagarolon (small entrance fee), built before the 13th Century and rebuilt in its current form in the 17th Century. The Gouverneto Monastery, possibly built in the 11th Century. The ruins of the Katholiko Monastery, one of the first monasteries in Crete, built in the 6th or 7th Century A.D. The cave of Arkoudospilio and St. John Xenos' cave. The Katholiko Monastery festival takes place on October the 7th, and gathers a large crowd of worshippers.
DRAWBACKS	Some days the trail can be crowded and so noisy. Lack of information about the Katholiko Monastery.

A short distance from the city of Chania, in an area where only military and communication antennas seem to grow, there is a small oasis. Near the airport, one finds the impressive monastery of Agia Triada Tzagarolon, and, moving on just a bit further, a second, equally impressive monastery, the Gouverneto. This is the beginning of a clear trail that leads down a small but spectacular gorge. In its depths, lie the ruins of the Katholiko Monastery, looking just as if they were there since the beginning of time. They are truly a part of the landscape.

If you take the bus and travel to Agia Triada, the Monastery is well worth a visit. You will certainly be impressed by the cypress tree road. The Ottomans called it Chekvili Monastir, that's "cypress monastery" in Turkish. Then you will be surprised by the Monastery walls that turn it into a real castle. As soon as you go through the front gate, your attention will be taken by the ornate church front and the sign on the upper tier that reads B Γ Υ Θ Τ Π. If you are curious to find out what it means, it is an acronym of the Greek words: Βάθος Γνώσεως Ύψιστος Θεός Τρισυπόστατος Παντοκράτωρ. These words translate as "At the Depth of Knowledge (lies) the Trinity of Almighty God". Note the two old trees which are orange, lemon, and tangerine trees, all in one!

To reach Gouverneto, walk out of the Agia Triada Monastery gate and turn right on the road. You will walk through a beautiful small gorge and reach Gouverneto in about an hour.

Take a closer look at the Venetian sculptures at the church entrance. You will also be impressed by the walls and the fortifications. One has to imagine the situation one thousand years ago, when the fastest communications were achieved with the help of pigeons, and the best roads were wide enough for two mules walking side-by-side. At that time, when pirates wanted to attack in order to make a living, things did not look good for the monks at the Katholiko Monastery. When the attacks on them became unbearable, the founders of the seaside monastery climbed up here and built "The Lady of the Angels", the other name of the Gouverneto Monastery.

North of the Monastery, on the right bank of the gully, a beautiful trail starts. For a short distance, it is stone-paved. In 15´ you will see some ruins and, a little more to the right, you will see a cave with a small chapel cooling in the cave's thick shade in the middle of this waterless, rugged landscape. The chapel is in the name of "Panagia Arkoudiotissa", the "Virgin

Mary of the Bear". Inside the cave, a cistern collects the water that drops from the roof's stalactites.

From here continue on a northeastern course. As you walk down-hill, your eyes will be filled by the magnificent view to the Cretan Sea, which is beyond Cape Melehas. But now you must also watch the path carefully, as it becomes steeper. In a little while, it turns towards the gorge and, in about 20´ from the first cave, you will find another, low-er but much longer, after you walk down the steps that are carved into the steep slope.

This cave was the hermitage of Saint John Xenos ("the stranger" as he was known). It is 135 m deep and covers a total area of 1,500 m². A bit downhill you will find the church of St. John, hewn in the rock

The Arkoudospilio Legend

This is a small cave, the middle of which is dominated by a bear-shaped stalactite over a stone-built basin that col-lected precious water for the local people. These people built a cistern to collect the little water that flows from the stalactites.

Once upon a time, a bear that lived in these parts found out about it and started going there every day to drink the water. When the villagers whose turn it was to collect the water saw the empty cistern, they got angry, but said nothing. When the same thing happened again, they reacted against the other villagers. But the other villagers, accused of taking the water when it was not their turn, swore that they were innocent of such charges.

But who then had drunk the water? Nobody knew, so the villag-ers decided to stake a look-out. After a while, the bear appeared and stepped on the stone in front of the cistern, ready to drink the water. The villagers stood there, unable to do anything against the beast. They were in a terrible position, not knowing what to do. When the animal bent its head to drink the water, somebody screamed in despair "Virgin Mary, help us", and the bear was imme-diately turned to stone. To commemorate the miracle, the villagers built a chapel in the cave in honour of "Virgin Mary of the Bear". This chapel's festival takes place on the 2nd of February each year.

(V.Haronitis, "Crete of the Legends")

as well. According to some scholars, this must have been the first monastery built in Crete. It was probably destroyed in raids by Saracen pirates. Around it, you can see small hermitages, but the most impressive building is a huge 50 m long and 15 m wide bridge, used both as courtyard and warehouse.

The bridge is built on the small but wild Avlaki Gorge. The trail winds down steeply from the side of the bridge into the gorge, and, following the stony bed, you will reach the sea in about half an hour.

In a natural niche on the rocky coast, you can still see the remains of a slipway, and also the remains of a sandstone quarry. The scene is so alive; one could imagine that the workers are on their lunch break. Enjoy your lunch and a small rest and return the way you came.

33. GOUVERNETO MONASTERY – STAVROS

DIFFICULTY	■ ■ □ □
DURATION	3 h 15'
ELEVATION CHANGE	a) Gouverneto Monastery – Katholiko Monastery: 40', 170 m descent b) Katholiko Monastery – col: 1 h 10', 50 m descent – 280 m ascent c) Col – end of trail: 1 h 10', 250 m descent d) Gravel road: 20´– 25'
TERRAIN	You walk on a well defined trail until the Katholiko Monastery, then on the stone gorge bed, on goat tracks and on a trail among phrygana.
SIGNPOSTING	A few scattered signs.
WHEN TO GO	March–May, October–November.
WATER	A leaking water tank inside Arkoudospilio.
SHADE	There is almost no shade whatsoever.
POPULARITY	You will meet other people on the part leading to Katholiko Monastery.
WHERE TO SLEEP WHERE TO EAT	In the area around the city of Chania. Many rooms-to-let and tavernas in Stavros.
ACCESS	There is a bus from Chania to Stavros and Agia Triada.

SIGHTS 🏛	The Gouverneto Monastery, possibly built in the 11th Century. The ruins of the Katholiko Monastery, one of the first monasteries in Crete, built in the 6th or 7th Century A.D. The cave of Arcoudospilio and St. John Xenos' cave. The Katholiko Monastery festival takes place on October 7th, and attracts a large crowd of worshippers.
DRAWBACKS ❌	The lack of signposting.

This is a demanding hike on a medium-difficulty terrain, and there is almost no signposting whatsoever (sometimes there is no trail at all). The landscape is arid and almost completely the same the whole way. The gorge underneath Katholiko is really wild and impressive, but can be impassable when it rains.

See route description 32 for the start of the walk.

Underneath Katholiko Monastery bridge, you find the small but wild gorge called Avlaki. From the end of the bridge, climb up into the gorge (a bit steep) and continue uphill to the West. Sometimes a bit of scrambling is required to get past the obstacles you find in your way inside the gorge. It's like a game in a huge natural playground.

20´ on, you will see another gorge on your right connecting with the one you are in. Turn right and follow its bed. The gorge becomes a gully. Luckily, the locust trees and holm oaks cover the gully offering a good shade. You will see a lot of stone walling, reminding you of the fields that were once there. There is an occasional red mark indicating the trail which generally moves to the Northwest.

At some point, the gully is really shallow, and the trail moves on small plateaus which end at an unfinished church (2003). Follow what seems like a trail southwest, but be careful not to continue climbing where the trail seems to go, but turn a bit to the South 5´ later, heading to a col which connects two summits. If you walk straight on, you will see a huge cross standing in the abandoned fields. If you see that, you are on the wrong path and you should go back.

From the col, climb down to the right side of the gully and 20´ later you will be in the middle of an open valley with a well, an old stone pond and two lean trees. Follow the right side of the gully among phrygana and low holm oaks. Piles of stones are scattered from time to time, indicating the right direction. Another well and some ruins are further away. A bit above these, lies the Ai Giorgis church and the ruins of an old monastery.

You are heading south now, but you soon turn west, as the gorge narrows and changes direction. Pass through this section carefully, sometimes walking on the goat track, some-times on the gully's

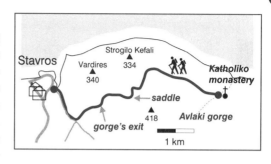

bank. Before the end, at the point where the gorge opens up, you must cross it and move to the right side under the rocks. 30´ from the last well, you come to a fence. Behind the fence, 100 m further, there is a gravel road. Follow this road and after a while, you will see Stavros village in front of you.

Look again to your right and ask "does this remind me of something?" Probably not because the place has altered completely, but if you saw the film "Zorba the Greek" you would certainly remember the scene with the self-made cable car which crashed dishonourably. Remember the beach where they danced? Believe it or not, these scenes were shot here. You walk for 20´ on the road and you get to Stavros just before the last houses.

34. DIKTAMO (DITTANY) GORGE

DIFFICULTY	■ ■ □ □
DURATION	3 h
ELEVATION CHANGE	200 m descent a) Entry to the village – gorge entry: 20', 100 m descent b) Gorge entry – gorge exit: 2 h, 100 m descent c) Gorge exit – road: 30´–40´
TERRAIN	There is no trail. You walk inside the bed and on the road at the beginning and at the end of the hike.
SIGNPOSTING	Good with red markings.
WHEN TO GO	Ideal summer trekking, because you will get wet.
WATER	Take water from the public fountains in the villages at the start and end of the hike.
SHADE	Dense shade (apart from the last section).

Northern Chania - Akrotiri Region

POPULARITY	👥	Probably you will meet no one.
ACCESS	🚌	There is a daily bus from Chania to Kambi or take a taxi.
SIGHTS	🏛	This is a small but rather wild and steep gorge with typical Cretan landscape.
DRAWBACKS	❌	The fences at the beginning and the walk on the road.

This is one of the most attractive and mildest hikes inside a gorge. Green scenery with great variety of trees and plants. The gorge's bed is flat and tranquility reigns the place. Some easy scrambling (for fun), ideal for hot summer days.

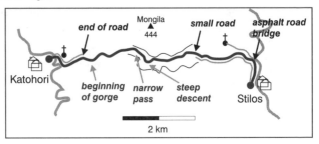

The hike starts from the entrance to the village. At the first right-hand bend before the coffee shop, follow a descending cemented road to the left. Further back you will see the gorge, and 10′ after you pass some ruined houses, you will be at the village square. There are 2–3 cafes and tavernas, a public fountain and some oak trees. A sign on the left indicates the way to the gorge. Follow the road for 10′, until it reaches the shallow riverbed among olive and oak trees, oleanders and many more plants.

Pass the fence to the right (through the gate) and you are inside the bed. At this point, the bed is flat and there are fields all around, full of orange and olive trees. You walk inside the bed following red marks. You walk on stones, pebbles and sand avoiding or crossing the shallow water, which runs at the start of the gully. In summer and autumn the gully has little or no water at all, so crossing is easy. During other seasons, or after a heavy rain, the water level can be high, making some crossings difficult. You may need to get in the water up to your knees or even to your hips. Shade is dense and refreshing during your walk next to oak trees, cedars, high oleanders. 40′–45′ later, the gorge

The 12 Young Masters

An historical event that happened years ago and sounds like a fairy tale, complete with armoured knights and spears, took place on the island of Crete sometime at the end of 12th Century. But let's take first things first!

The Saracens, a nomadic tribe of northwestern Arabian origins, were notorious for incursions, looting and piracy. When they occupied Crete and settled there in 824 A.D., they had a new base, and therefore could expand the areas they could raid. The occupation lasted until 961 A.D. when the island was liberated by the Byzantine General, Nikiforos Fokas.

Officials in Constantinople had had very serious reasons to be concerned by Saracen presence, taking into account that they could no longer collect taxes and felt like they were losing the island. So they decided to send Nikiforos Fokas to liberate Crete and organize it through lawmaking. However, during his relatively short stay there, he didn't succeed in solving the island's problems.

But let us continue our story...

Some years later, we don't know exactly when, maybe during the reign of Alexios Komninos, it was decided to solve the problem once and for all. So they sent the son of the Emperor, Isaac Komninos, accompanied by 12 young noblemen, to improve the island's spiritual and social life, as well as to bring the rebellious Cretans into line, forcing them to pay their due taxes.

Konstantin, a senior delegate (he was a grand duke), was given the job of deciding how best to distribute the cultivated ground and pastures between the 12 young noblemen and the large group of retainers in their court.

This story has been transformed into a fairy tale with armoured knights, golden garments and proud horses. Place names, coats of arms and family names are the silent witnesses to these 12 young noblemen and their stay on the island.

narrows. The walls are now vertical, full of plants with a rock-face 30—40 m high, offering shade. Rocks in the bed are more numerous and bigger, forcing you to do some easy scrambling. At some points, apart from the oleanders, huge trees grow inside the bed, adding to the wildness and beauty of the landscape.

After a while, the gorge opens up again, and walking is easy until you come to the next rocky and narrow part. Here are some rock descents, a few meters high. You can choose your own way, but the signs lead you through the easiest path. When the water level is higher, this part is difficult and demands some experience. It can also be impassable with high water. At the beginning of summer though, the water is not a problem. On the contrary, it is cool and refreshing.

The gorge opens up again and the last 30´ are easy and on flat ground. At the end, the gully becomes totally flat with some stones and pebbles, and a water pipe in it. You will see more olive trees around and signs of human civilization (such as rubbish, small houses, quarried slopes etc.). Leave the bed behind, turning to the right, and follow a narrow track for 15´—20´ moving parallel to the gully. Go left at the first branch crossing the gully and then right, climbing to the bridge and the paved road. Follow the road to the right, and 15´ later you will be in Stylos village.

35. LYKOTINARIA – KEFALAS

DIFFICULTY	📈	■ ■ ☐ ☐
DURATION	🕐	3 h 30'
ELEVATION CHANGE	📊	350 m ascent – descent a) Argyropouri – Lykotinaria: 1h, 180 m ascent b) Lykotinaria – Kefalas: 45', 70 m ascent c) Kefalas – Souri: 45', 100 m descent, 100 m ascent d) Souri – Argyromouri: 1h, 200 m descent
TERRAIN	🔺	A narrow well defined trail. A large part of the walk is on gravel roads (with no traffic) and a small part on paved road.
SIGNPOSTING	🔼	The first section is good with visible markings. The rest has no markings.
WHEN TO GO	📅	All year round.
WATER	〰️	Take water from the public fountains in the villages at the start and end of the walk.
SHADE	🌳	No shade (apart from the section Kefalas – Souri).
POPULARITY	👥	You will meet some people from Argyromouri to Lykotinaria.
WHERE TO SLEEP WHERE TO EAT	🍴	In Georgioupolis and the surrounding area.
ACCESS	➡️	A lot a buses go from Chania or Rethymnon to Georgioupolis (one every 30'). From there, take a taxi to Argyromouri or walk there.
SIGHTS	🏛️	The scenic little villages, especially Kefalas with its old mansions and attractive architecture. The view from Kefalas and Lykotinaria Square.
DRAWBACKS	❌	Lack of shade, walking on the road and the rough trail after Sellia.

This hike is in Vamos County, at the northeastern part of the Chania Prefecture, offering great views to the northern summits of Lefka Ori. The whole area is green, thanks to plentiful water supplies coming from the mountains. The largest of these rivers, Almyros, flows to the sea at Georgioupolis, creating unusually beautiful scenery at its mouth.

The walk starts from Argyromouri's tavernas. Go right after a left-hand bend in the road where you will see a sign indicating "to Lykotinaria". The view from here is really beautiful with the green Georgioupolis plain below, the sea further back and Lefka Ori on the opposite side.

During the first 5´ you walk on a narrow climbing street. On the right, by the last houses in the village, is the trailhead with the same sign "to Lykotinaria". The trail soon becomes a goat track climbing the slope in front of you with zigzags among sage, thyme and other aromatic plants. The air is full of their scent. Even though the goat track is narrow and winding, it is easy to spot and well marked. You will see rocks and holm oaks here and there, adding to the variety, as the horizon expands behind you.

Aromatic Plants

We call aromatic plants all those that contain aromatic substances in one or most of their parts, i.e. in their flowers, their roots, their body, their shoots etc. These substances are combinations of essential oils that give the plants their characteristic scents and taste. Intense scents are due to volatile oils which evaporate quickly.

Aromatic plants are found mainly in dry and warm countries with intense sunshine, like Mediterranean countries, including of course Crete. The most common plants and those that usually cover all the rocky slopes, the valleys and the gullies are thyme, sage, oregano, wild mint, dittany, chamomile, fennel, myrtle and laurel.

The harvest takes place each spring, at the end of the season, when the plants have gathered all their aromatic juices. They are first dried under the sun and then stored in cool and dry places. They are still a lot of people in the villages that gather aromatic plants for their personal use or for sale. For the past few years some of them, like oregano, spearmint, basil and dittany, are cultivated, but their scent is not of the same quality as when they grow in the wild. Most of them are used in order to add scent and flavour to the local dishes (oregano, thyme, basil, fennel, spearmint, rosemary, wild celery) and give them their distinctive taste. Others are used as herbal teas (sage, dittany, mint, spearmint), in cosmetics or even as remedies. A lot of books have been written, scientific or not, about the pharmaceutical use of these plants. In some of them, one can find the usual exaggerations about the miraculous use of plants which are believed to cure every disease.

45´ later the trail ends on a gravel road. Continue left following the road. Pass by a house, climbing gradually and then descend to a small plateau dotted with little villages. 10´ on, a narrow road goes off to the right and descends among cultivated fields and olive groves to Lykotinaria. You reach the village 5´ later. This is a typical mountain village with many houses and few people. Most of them live in Chania City and visit the village. Many houses are ruined. The road ends at the square, offering

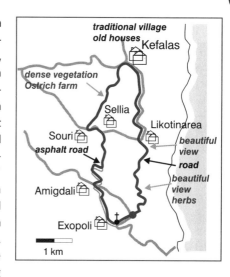

beautiful views to the sea which lies 300 m below and to Almyros Bay. Further back you see Rethymnon City.

If you take the road to the left, it leads to the main road and to the village's shops. Continue right towards Kefalas. Unfortunately the small gravel roads/trails are fenced (a fence every 50–100 m) and often fade out among phrygana and thorny bushes. So don't try to find old abandoned trails to Kefalas; just follow the road for half an hour (2.5–3 km), when you will reach the large attractive village of Kefalas. There are a lot of good, big, stylish houses of typical Cretan architecture. Some have been converted to guesthouses or shops. The village has great views, very good infrastructure (a few traditional-style tavernas offering local dishes with vista, and some cafes) and churches built in a neoclassical 19th Century style. Wander around the village and have a coffee or a meal in one of its restaurants. Over the last few years, foreigners (mostly English) bought old houses and land and live here permanently, as well as some Greeks who returned to their village, giving the place a new lease of life.

Leave the village behind you, and follow the road to Xyrosterni and Vamos. Immediately after the first right bend, take the road to the left. Pass by some newly built country houses on your right and continue descending. On the right you will find the old cobbled trail which soon turns into a road heading straight, passing in front of the last house. The road is flat now and runs among olive groves and other trees offering welcome shade. 25′–30′ later, you come to an ostrich farm lost in the lush vegetation. Some birds wander around a fenced area, always curious about any stranger who walks by.

The road continues to the right, and after a while you see red marks and the well marked trail, which climbs gradually among dense shadowy vegetation and some ruined houses towards Souri (20′). On the main road, turn left and, 400 m further, you will find yourself in Sellia village. After the first houses, a narrow street to the right leads you to a big country house. On the wall to the left, you see sparse red marks leading you to the trail.

It is narrow at the beginning, but easy to walk. Soon after and for the next 20′–25′ the vegetation is dense and the terrain is rough. You walk among holm oaks and thorny bushes always following the marks. You descend the slope, until you reach the paved road coming from Sellia and heading to Amygdali. Your wandering in the Cretan jungle now comes to an end (wear long trousers and shirts). Follow the bends in the road until the main road below, where you turn left and continue to Argyromouri (3 km, 30′ from the end of the trail).

36. ALIKAMBOS – KOURNAS LAKE

DIFFICULTY	■ ■ ■ □
DURATION	4 h
ELEVATION CHANGE	a) Alikambos – Metohi Klima: 1 h 30', 180 m up b) Metohi Klima – gravel road: 2 h, 410 m down c) Gravel road – road to Kournas; 30', 70 m down
TERRAIN	At the beginning you walk on a boring paved road, and then you walk where there is no trail among the dense vegetation, until you reach the lake. Wear trekking shoes, long trousers and shirts.
SIGNPOSTING	Almost none.
WHEN TO GO	March–June, September–November.
WATER	Take water from Alikambos.
SHADE	For most part of the walk there is no shade. The only shady part is inside the gorge. Start early in the morning.
POPULARITY	Even though Kournas Lake is very popular, you are highly un-likely to meet anyone on the walk, apart from a shepherd.
WHERE TO SLEEP WHERE TO EAT	In Georgioupolis and the surrounding area. For food, go to the taverna in Kournas to avoid the crowds that dine around the lake.
ACCESS	Take the bus to Alikianos from Chania (the one that goes through Vrysses). The buses that go to Sfakia can leave you at the junction if you ask, and from there you walk to the village (15').
SIGHTS	Visit Panagia's church painted by Ioannis Pagomenos in the 14th Century. The small Kournas Lake with the blue, cool waters and the small cave.
DRAWBACKS	The boring part at the beginning and the trail full of thorny bushes.

A surprising walk which is demanding, despite not gaining much elevation. You will walk on many different terrains and you will need good navigational skills. You will often be trying to find your way through a lot of goat tracks. As soon as you are inside the gorge, before the exit to the lake, you will wonder whether this part belongs to the same route you were on before.

Alikambos was flattened by the Venetians as punishment because of its disobedient inhabitants who belonged to Konti family, one of the 12 royal Byzantine families. They had participated in the Kantanoleon rebellion in 1527 and Ieronymos Kornaros thought it right to burn down the village and threaten its residents with death, if they tried to return there.

Little is left of this large and great village. Panagia's church and its hospitable people are the most significant things in the village nowadays. To the East a road begins, paved at the beginning, turning into a gravel road 1 km further on. After 200 m, you reach a junction where you go to the right. The road to the left leads to the antennas. Almost immediately, the road makes a tight turn to the right. At the apex of the turn, you will find a track which climbs up, too wide to be a trail, but too rough to be a road.

If you follow it, you will soon come across the old trail on the right behind the fences and among thorny burnets and brooms. You can go back to the road after 500 m or continue to the Southeast and find it again after 40′ near a new sheep pen. This sheep pen is a bit below the main road, which is visible from there. If you don't feel like trying to find your way among the many fences and holly trees, then you'd better follow the road which takes you to the same spot after 4 km.

Before you reach the sheep pens, you will notice a metallic tank on the second group of buildings, 1 km after the first sheep pen. What is really impressive apart from the size of this sheep pen is its technological equipment! After 10′ walking you will reach a flat area on a small col where there is a junction and an oak tree. On your left, at a height of 700 m, is Dafnokorfi, 200 m above you. Follow the right-hand road (South) and, 200 m on, you will be at Klima, an old monastery dependency that was seasonally cultivated, but is almost totally abandoned today. A commemorative sign informs you that here, during the 1st Assembly of Free Crete on 3rd September 1895, Manousos Koundouros read his famous "Note" to the delegates.

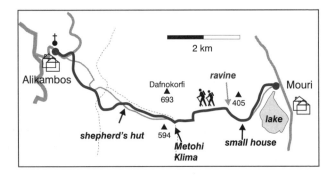

Things are getting tough now. There is actually no trail, the signposting is so sparse that it is practically nonexistent, and the furzes have taken every possible inch of the ground. In the springtime though, you will smell magnificent scents, as the yellow flowers of the thorny brooms combine beautifully with the mauve flowers of the sage. You must wear long trousers and shirts to pass through these. In front of the ruined houses lies a field, fenced all round, with a cistern in the middle of it. Opposite the ruins, at the back of the field, climb some more and you will come to the edge of a steep slope with great views to the Northeast. From here the route descends all the way.

Right below you, among the hills, there is a small abandoned field which ends in the gully. Descend carefully without a trail to the field, which is fenced. You will need 20´ for this descent and you will perhaps see the odd blue or red mark, but don't expect to find more. Cross the field and climb down, on the right side of the gully following the bank. Don't go into its bed.

At some point you will notice, to the North on the opposite slope, a visible trail which climbs up. Walk towards this trail passing by the left bank, which has an eastern orientation. It will take you about an hour to get here from Klima, walking slowly due to the dense vegetation. Climb upwards on the wide goat track for a while and then you will see a blue mark and an indistinct trail that traverses east moving downhill. 10´ later, you will be on a distinctive scree, and the trail disappears again. Look towards the gully and you will see a large holly tree. Walk below this tree and get into the gorge.

The dense vegetation is a problem at the beginning, but as you walk on, things become easier and more pleasant. The trees and the overhanging slopes offer good shade. The vegetation inside the gully is completely different from what you have seen up to now. Half an hour after the point you entered the gorge, you will see a lake among the dense foliage and a small house comes into sight 100 m away on your right. Follow the cement road and climb down to the west bank of the lake. The shores are encircled by willows and chastetrees, which make it impossible to get to the lake for a refreshing swim.

Continue to the left for 20´ and you will come to the paved road. If you want to walk to Georgioupolis, turn left and continue for 45´. For the tavernas, turn right and follow the signs. The first taverna is only 5´ away.

NORTHERN RETHYMNON REGION

The Rethymnon Prefecture can be described as the least inhabited or perhaps as having the most cattle rearing or even the one with the fastest growth in tourism. Rethymnon City is evolving into a modern city with the advantages and disadvantages that such evolution brings. Nevertheless, the old town is picturesque, beautiful and lively. Probably it always used to be like this, from the time that it was called Rithymna. Rethymnon, continuously regenerating, was built again and again on this really ancient city. It was always small and noble, as shown by the mosaics which have been discovered through the years.

But it was not until the invasion of the Venetians that the city really took its proper place. Since they were proper seamen, they understood that this was the right place to build a safe harbour for the boats that travelled between Chania and Handakas, a difficult journey at the time. A harbour meant new jobs, new jobs meant more people, and so the small village became an active city. The prosperity was so great that, up to 1583, 213 noble Cretans lived here. But then, unfortunately, a period of misfortune prevailed. The city became a target for pirates, and especially for the famous Barbarossa and the less famous but equally disastrous Ulutch. The final blow was a devastating flood which destroyed the city completely.

The Venetians decided to strengthen the city's fortifications. This project cost 51,454 ducats and 7,000 days of forced labour (no payment, of course). As a result, the city acquired a great fort on the hill that today is known as Fortezza. Nevertheless, all these efforts were fruitless. The Turks managed to invade the city after just 22 days, on 3rd November 1646.

From this time on, the city decayed. All the noblemen, all the traders and all the intellectuals fled. When Pashley visited the city in 1834, he saw only 80 poverty-stricken Cretan families. It was fortunate that the Turks didn't really feel like working, so they left all the Venetian buildings unharmed and used them for their own purposes.

Rethymnon is a relatively quiet town, even in the summertime. You can use it as a base for all the nearby tours and expeditions. Some of the best walks are in the Amari area with its beautiful green villages, the slopes of Psiloritis and the very cool Argiroupoli (avoid Sundays).

The only real problem for the walker are the countless kilometers of wire fences erected by farmers to protect their land from sheep and goats and by the cattle breeders to keep their stock under control.

It still makes us wonder "why has a place where so many noblemen and intellectuals lived never managed in modern times to show its real beauty?" On the contrary, they have built ugly and tasteless rooms-to-let, not to mention the problems with refuse. The most amazing thing, though, is that all the people I've ever met here are kind, well-meaning and open-hearted. How can anyone blame them?

37. VEDERES GORGE (GERANI GORGE)

DIFFICULTY	📈	■ ■ □ □
DURATION	🕐	3 h, 6 km long
ELEVATION CHANGE	📊	a) Gerani beach – path leading to Gerani: 45', 30 m up b) Path leading to Gerani – gorge exit: 1 h 40', 135 m up c) Gorge exit – Gonia: 40', 60 m up
TERRAIN	🏔	At the start there is a path. After that, it is walking and easy scrambling over rocks in the riverbed.
SIGNPOSTING	🚩	Some red signs at the beginning that disappear afterwards.
WHEN TO GO	📅	April–November, unless it rains.
WATER	💧	You must carry water.
SHADE	🌳	A lot of shade even at high noon during summer.
POPULARITY	👥	You will be by yourselves.
WHERE TO SLEEP WHERE TO EAT	🍴	Only in Rethymnon city and suburbs.
ACCESS	🚌	Frequent bus services from Rethymnon. Get off at Gerani Cave and head to the beach.
DRAWBACKS	⊗	Even though the gorge is very beautiful, unfortunately it is full of rubbish, shameful for us Greeks. Additionally, the signposting is not completed.

Six kilometers west of Rethymnon City, you will find Gerani Village. There are two reasons to visit this place and two other reasons not to. The first two are the caves and the gorge. The caves are small, but Neolithic findings were discovered in these caves, as well as significant fossils. The gorge is also small, but with rich vegetation and at-

tractive chalky formations. The drawbacks are that both the caves and the gorge are abandoned and full of rubbish. We give you the description of the walk in the hope that maybe someday the situation will improve.

Take any bus that travels west of Rethymnon. Get off the bus 6 km later, as soon as you pass a large bridge and a sign pointing to Gerani. Walk down to the little bay. What the local people thought would be the best improvement they could possibly make here is a fast food outlet by the beach! There is a small cave, 100 m west from here, while another is a further 100 m south. Dwarf elephant fossils as well as fossils from other mammals, dating back to the Pleistocene era, were found in the first, really small cave. The second one has stalactite décor and, during a trial excavation, findings from the Neolithic era were discovered. The archaeological authority decided to install an iron gate to protect the findings, but some "nobles" broke it down and destroyed most of the stalactites. The funny thing is that on the main road there is a brown sign, normally used to indicate monuments, saying "Gerani Cave"!

Anyway, time to head for the gorge. Follow the gully under the bridge. After a while, you will find a pretty wooden tablet, informing you that this is the Vederes Gorge, and on the rocks just above your heads there is a small church. Keep on walking through the rich vegetation. 20′ from the beginning, you will come across a gravel road that crosses the gorge. Cross it and keep on the right side (West) of the gorge. You walk for 1.5 km in the gully and on your right you will see another wooden sign informing you that the path climbing west, leads to Gerani village. 50 m up is another good sign indicating that on the left there is an exit to Vederes, but if you continue in the gorge, you can go to Frageskiana and Metohia. "Very good work!" is perhaps what you might think seeing all that signage. Don't jump to conclusions though, because this is the last sign you will see. The money from the European Community was not enough …

Keep on the left of the gully, which is full of laurels, oleanders, locust trees, withes, willows and plane trees, until the path disappears completely. Go into the riverbed. Pass the wire fences (there are technical difficulties on this walk to keep you alert — you have to keep trying to find the best route between rocks and rubbish!).

If the quantity of rubbish indicates the culture of a community, then this community is undoubtedly "super-civilised"! The condition here is shameful for all of us. It is not only a matter of environmental conscience, but also of respecting others.

The chalky rocks create a lot of good passages, and on more than one occasion you will need to use your hands to pass over them. In about 15´ you will come to what the locals call a "rechti", a 5 m high vertical rock (when there is enough water, it forms a waterfall). If you cannot climb it, go back about 100 m and climb the left slope (the east one), using something that looks like a path, and as soon as you have passed the waterfall, climb down again to the riverbed. This is the only difficult part of this route.

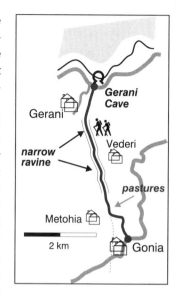

Walk for another 20´ between the rocks and the tree branches, until you find wire fences once again. You can easily pass through them. Climb up following the left side and after 5´ the gorge ends. Now you will walk through small abandoned fields, carefully set out next to the gully. 15´ more and you will see a vertical wire fence and a path with blue signs. This path heads west and goes to Metohia.

There is no gully anymore, and the abandoned fields are full of sheep. Only wire fences grow here. Walk with in a south-southeast direction and in 40´ you will be in Gonia village. Now you have two options. You can go back to Rethymnon or you can go to Valsamonero village and follow Route 38 to Armeni.

38. VALSAMONERO – ARMENI (BONRIPARI CASTLE)

DIFFICULTY	📈	■ ■ ■ □
DURATION	🕐	4 h
ELEVATION CHANGE	📊	450 m descent and 350 m ascent a) Valsamonero – castle: 45′, 100 m ascent b) Castle – Kastellos: 1 h 45′, 250 m descent, 150 m ascent c) Kastellos – Armeni cemetry: 1 h 30′, 100 m ascent, 200 m descent
TERRAIN	🗻	You walk on minor gravel roads. A small part of the hike is on a path, another part is on rocky terrain and wild plants.
SIGNPOSTING	🚩	None.
WHEN TO GO	📅	Avoid hot days.
WATER	〰	Water in villages and coffee shops.
SHADE	🌿	A little shade, only before and after Kastellos village.
POPULARITY	👥	No one, but you may meet some people between Valsamonero and Castle.
ACCESS	🚗	Only by taxi or your own vehicle.
SIGHTS	🏛	The ruined Venetian Bonripari castle and the Armeni Minoan cemetery. Typical Cretan landscape full of olive trees, vineyards and the wild desert vegetation after Kastellos.
DRAWBACKS	✖	The lack of shade and the rough terrain in a section of the Bonripari – Kastellos route.

A calm and easy walk, mainly on gravel roads, moving in typical Cretan/ Mediterranean landscapes far from the tourist-infested areas. It combines beautiful views, solitude, history (a ruined castle) and rural economy (olive groves, gardens, sheep pens), with enough variety but no particular high spots.

The starting point is Ano Valsamonero's pretty little square. Walk for 15′ on the paved road until you reach Monopari village, actually just a few houses and sheep pens. The road descends left and, 20 m before a big white house, you leave the tar road and follow a gravel road to the left. Almost immediately, the gravel road divides in two. Continue left on the road that climbs smoothly with a good view to the olive groves and the gullies to the right. In front of you, you will see the hill where the ruins of the castle are. 20 minutes on, you reach a fence (yes, there is a gate which opens easily) and a few minutes later you are at an open area under the castle. Leave the road and climb the path to

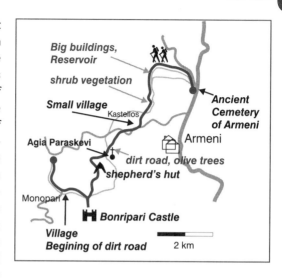

the right, which stretches among the locust trees of Bonripari Castle.

The Venetians built this castle in the 13th Century in order to control the inner part of Rethymnon Prefecture and use it as a refuge, in case of enemy or pirate attack. Even if it was a strategically vital site, it wasn't much use during peace time. It was never inhabited by local farmers or peasants and was gradually abandoned. The hill on which it is built is steep (especially to the East and the South) and the peak is flat. There are extensive ruins of walls, houses and other buildings. Unfortunately, most of them are just piles of rocks and only at the western and northern sides are there some sections of the outer walls in good condition.

After a stroll in the castle admiring the view from every corner, the steep slopes and the strategic site of the castle, walk down the same path to the road and continue north. 15′ on and you arrive at a sheep pen (beware of the dogs) and climb for a while on a goat track going right. Pass through a fence and you will be on an abandoned gravel road with tall grass and bushes, making your walk hard. Leave it after 300 m or so, and climb down the easy slope (although there is tall grass as well as tree branches) to a small gully with olive trees. 30′ later, you reach a small road next to this gully. Follow it, still descending and pass a fence (using the gate) and climb up to the opposite road among olive groves and fields, seeing in front of you the houses of Kastellos.

You can take a shortcut, if you follow the path to the right, which leads you straight to the village and the tar road. The first houses belong to the first settlement, while the main village is 1 km further. Fill up with water from the local spring in the middle of the village (on your left-hand side on the main road) and keep to the left in the narrow street going uphill to the old school, an attractive, stylish building, which nowadays houses a family. The path heads left of the school, out of the village (among olive trees, locusts and cedars – some shade at last) going a bit uphill until it reaches a huge flat area, a plateau, where it turns northbound among bushes and brushwood (mainly prickly brooms, 1.5 m high). Keep the large cistern to your right.

After a while, you will find a second one (40´ from Kastellos). The road continues right, passes through a clear, flat building site (probably a cheese dairy) and then turns left. Leave the road and continue right for 10´–15´ among brushwood on flat terrain without any particular difficulty until you come to a narrow road. Follow that to the left passing 2–3 vineyards. Some minutes later, leave it and walk to the right by a flat area among thorny burnets and brushwood. In 10´ you will find a windy road which descends. Walk on it until you reach a junction, 100 m below. Turn right on to the ascending road, which brings you to Somata village. For the next 20´ you walk on the tar road, which crosses the village and continues south to the ancient Minoan cemetery of Armeni. The site is fenced (usual visiting times) and it has some remarkable graves and found artifacts. Join the main road to Rethymnon.

39. PRASSIES – VRYSSINAS PEAK – ARMENI

DIFFICULTY	■ ■ ■ □
DURATION	4 h 45', 13.5 km
ELEVATION CHANGE	500 m ascent, 500 m descent a) Gravel road – sheep pen: 30', 50 m ascent b) Sheep pen – Seli: 45', 100 m ascent c) Seli – Vryssinas peak: 1 h 45', 350 m ascent d) Vryssinas peak – sheep pen: 40', 160 m descent e) Sheep pen – gravel road to Armeni: 1 h 15', 340 m descent
TERRAIN	Tar and gravel road, path and no path! Gradual inclines.
SIGNPOSTING	Some E4 signs. A lot are missing, and most of the rest are destroyed.
WHEN TO GO	All year round; spring is better.
WATER	Fill up with water before starting, because water is available only in Seli village.
SHADE	Almost no shade.
POPULARITY	Only a few walkers choose this route.
WHERE TO SLEEP WHERE TO EAT	In Rethymnon City.
ACCESS	Take the bus from Rethymnon to Amari. Get off 1 km after Prassies at a small church and some buildings. There are a lot of bus services for Armeni.
SIGHTS	An incredible pile of rocks west of the peak and the beautiful view to Rethymnon. At the end of the walk there is the significant ancient Minoan cemetery of Armeni.
DRAWBACKS	A lot of fences and lack of signposting.

Since the Minoan era, the island's residents have considered certain peaks as highly significant. They attracted them in a particular way. On certain of these peaks, they built some of their shrines, offering presents to their gods in order to thank or appease them. If you look at this low mountain from Rethymnon, you will see one of these sacred peaks. But don't look for the shrine; you will see only a bunch of antennas. Times change...

Prassies stands 14 km from Rethymnon and is a lovely, quiet village with some very attractive old houses. 1 km after the village, you will see the small church of Agia Fotini at the left of the road, while on the right you will see a house on which the name of the owner, Papadosifos is written in huge letters. 100 m before that, there is a junction with two roads going uphill.

Follow the road to the West. As you proceed, you will see the ruins of a small Turkish castle on the nearby hill, which used to serve as a look-out post for the rebels. Actually, you walk on the E4 path, but it is difficult to recognize it, because some locals didn't like the infrequent signs and thought it a good idea to destroy them all. 10′ later, you will reach the first junction, where you must turn left. The beautiful rural landscape with its smooth hills and Mediterranean vegetation is amazing, especially in spring. Walking in blossomed fields feels good and carefree.

At the next junction on your right (and a bit lower), you'll see a sheep pen. At the slope, in the front, you'll see a range of rocks. Go past the sheep pen and continue on the road which ends after a while. Climb without a specific path to the base of the rocks. When you reach there, you'll see the old path that goes south.

In 10′ or so, you'll reach the edge of the gully which separates you from Mirthios. The village lies on the opposite col. Follow the stone-built road to the right, parallel to the gully and the fences, and climb until you reach the gravel road, above which is a very large olive tree.

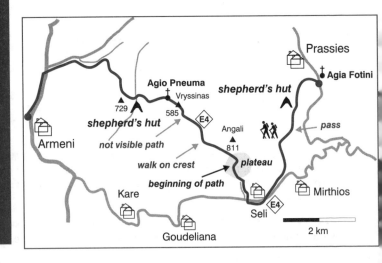

Peak Sanctuaries and Sacred Caves

A custom that has its roots in ancient times and that people in Crete still practise is to celebrate ritual festivals on the mountain peaks.

Since the first Minoan era, the island's residents have found various reasons to climb up the mountains and pay their respects to a goddess or god. Believers scaled steep slopes and plateaus to gather at these peak shrines, usually built just underneath the summits, to celebrate, and to offer presents to the god that was worshipped there. These customs still survive today, and believers still make, offerings which can be seen on the icons inside churches.

Carrying a big animal up there wasn't very easy, so they offered animals effigies, mainly of bulls, oxen or birds to replace the blood sacrifice. These presents wouldn't be complete without flowers and fruit!

The peak sanctuaries had a precinct and an altar. These two elements were the prerequisite for a place to be called a shrine. The precinct specified the sacred area, and the altar the point of the sacrifice or offering, hence the god's presence.

One of the main characteristics of these sanctuaries was the use of the natural terrain for offerings. So, niches in the rock were filled with oblations, usually copper or terracotta statues.

It is a fact, valid from prehistoric times right up to today, that climbing a mountain is strongly connected with human enlightenment and man's desire to get closer to the divine. It is known that there used to be peak shrines at Vryssina in Rethymnon, at Karfi in Lassithi and at Petsofa in Sitia.

But man doesn't only climb up, he also climbs down and inwards, towards the earth's centre, expressing his struggle to conquer the underworld's secrets and understand this unknown space. So, as well as the peak shrines, there were sacred caves also used as sanctuaries, especially those that had stalagmites and stalactites.

Let's not forget that the father of all gods, Zeus, was born in a cave up on the mountain, more specifically in Diktis' cave!

Walk on the gravel road. On your left there are some small vine-yards. In 10´ to 15´ you'll reach the tar road and 10´ later, you'll be in Seli.

At the other exit of the village, there is a small church and a cement road going uphill. Follow this road until it ends. It will take you about an hour, but when you get to the top, you'll see a panorama of mountains. To the Southeast are Kedros and Kastro, to the East Psiloritis and to the Southwest the other Lefka Ori peaks. The climb is not so hard now and after a while you'll reach a plateau.

At the end of the gravel road you'll see fences many kilometers long, and a small church on the west side. It's really difficult to get there, because you have to cross all those fences. The best option is to follow a path which starts just where the road ends. One feels a bit uneasy walking among all those wire fences, even though the route is beautiful.

This path brings you to a plateau that used to have fields, but now hosts a few sheep and goats. Approximately northwest, lies a mountainside and a few peaks. Far right to the North is the peak. There is practically no path here. You have an open view though, and the slope is not steep. Walk straight northwesterly and follow the ridge. Before reaching the church on the peak, where the ridge is only two steps wide, you'll see rock crevices just like the ones in which the Minoans left their offerings. You'll need about an hour from the end of the gravel road to reach the peak and the newer shrine, the Agio Pnevma church. Walk down the steep path to the gravel road and follow it for about 20´, with holm oaks and fields around you. Turn right at the junction and continue for 10´. You are now at a bend in the road, where straight ahead you can see the landscape that lies below and an ugly building to your left. You'll find the E4 signposting again, but not for long.

Walk below the sheep pen, heading north, and follow the gully. In 15´, having crossed the fences twice, you'll come to another gravel road, where you turn left. The peak west of you is full of antennas, those modern peak shrines. Follow the road that passes below them. 10´ later, the road turns right (North) making a circle around the mountain. In front and below you there is a small pine forest and some light industry. Keep walking straight (West) downhill in a steep channel next to electricity poles. You'll lose height easily, and in 15´

you will reach a gravel road. Turn left here. At the beginning, traverse south but very soon you'll climb down to a cement road that leads you to the tar road in about 10´. There is another E4 signpost here! In about a kilometer, this road gets to the main road connecting Rethymnon to Armeni, and, right at the junction, a late Minoan cemetery. It is worth a visit.

40. PRASSIANO GORGE

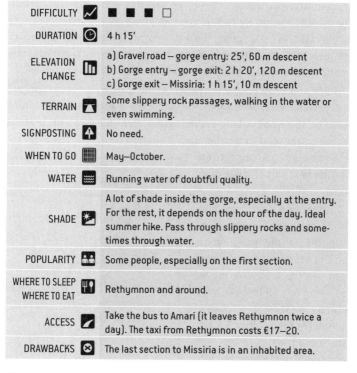

DIFFICULTY		■ ■ ■ □
DURATION		4 h 15'
ELEVATION CHANGE		a) Gravel road – gorge entry: 25', 60 m descent b) Gorge entry – gorge exit: 2 h 20', 120 m descent c) Gorge exit – Missiria: 1 h 15', 10 m descent
TERRAIN		Some slippery rock passages, walking in the water or even swimming.
SIGNPOSTING		No need.
WHEN TO GO		May–October.
WATER		Running water of doubtful quality.
SHADE		A lot of shade inside the gorge, especially at the entry. For the rest, it depends on the hour of the day. Ideal summer hike. Pass through slippery rocks and sometimes through water.
POPULARITY		Some people, especially on the first section.
WHERE TO SLEEP WHERE TO EAT		Rethymnon and around.
ACCESS		Take the bus to Amari (it leaves Rethymnon twice a day). The taxi from Rethymnon costs €17–20.
DRAWBACKS		The last section to Missiria is in an inhabited area.

Close to Rethymnon, one can find some of the best hikes, like Prassianio Gorge, a relatively easy walk through smooth rocks and often through water, depending on the season. The plane trees and the oleander flowers add to the spectacular scenery. You'll probably see eagles and birds of prey flying above you through the steep slopes. Together with Patsiano Gorge, it is one of the loveliest walks, and you can do both in the same day.

Take the first bus to Amari. After Prassies village, ask the driver to leave you at the junction to Mirthios. Walk the tar road for 5´ and, when you reach a very distinctive right bend, turn left onto the gravel road that goes down to the gully. Pass a cottage and keep walking on the gravel road. Open the fence gate, and in 20´ time you will be by the river.

Cross the river and continue along the right bank. You could walk in the river bed; you'll get wet anyhow.

20´ later, you will be in the gorge, with its walls coming really close. You should always try to find your way through the water pools and white rocks. In early spring, the water might be higher and fording is a lot more difficult. At the end of May though, the water level drops dramatically and most of the time there is no water during the summer.

One and a half hour after you enter the narrow part of the gorge, it will become wider once again. The landscape is a bit monotonous now, even tiring. A good option, assuming you have your own vehicle at the gorge entrance, is to turn back the same way you came, to enjoy the best part of it one more time.

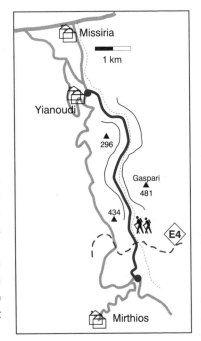

Otherwise, you must continue walking for about 45 minutes to the gully, going up the gravel road as soon as you see the first olive groves on your left. This ugly road, always west of the stream, continues for another 1.5 km. There are piles of refuse here and there, destroying the otherwise beautiful landscape. A sign of our times...

An attractive arch bridge lies at the end of the road. You have two more kilometers to Missiria, near the tourist resort

Tsikoudia

When the first raindrops fall to earth and the first cold days arrive, in every Cretan village you will see steam floating out of a raki copper distiller. Drop by drop "tsikoudia" (raki) is being distilled; it is Crete's elixir, a tradition followed from the beginning of time right up until today.

Anyone who happens to be in Crete will receive at least one invitation to drink tsikoudia, which is the local drink closely associated with Cretan hospitality. The really lucky ones, though, are those who participate in the process of raki production ("kazanemata", in Greek). It is also highly unlikely they will drink just the one glass of tsikoudia!

In order to produce tsikoudia, grape pulp must be distilled. Grape pulp is what remains after the pressing of the grapes when wine is made. The pulp, usually from making white wine, should be left to ferment. So, when the grapes are pressed and the must is produced, the pulp is closed in small airtight vessels for a whole month, and the unfermented sugars turn into alcohol.

The fermented pulp is then put into specially designed copper distillers and, with the help of a fire that burns underneath them, two things are achieved: alcohol is liquefied and floats away with the water vapour. The vapour is then cooled down, with the use of running water, and warm tsikoudia flows out of the copper distiller's nozzle. Simultaneously, potatoes or different kinds of meat are slowly baked in the hot charcoals; a tasty snack for everybody. If the company is comprised of a bunch of enthusiasts, a feast follows.

Even though it is not legal to produce your own alcohol, vine growers can pay for a licence allowing them to produce and sell alcohol locally. This way, they can supplement their income. When the time comes, those who have this special licence renew it for a time. During this period, all the locals who have grape pulp take it to the village "distiller" to produce their own raki, paying a fee which is either money or a few litres of the tsikoudia.

Tsikoudia is a product of pure distillation (compared to drinks that are produced by extract or pulp that is distilled for a second time with the addition of herbs). It is considered a drink that you can take without fear of a bad hangover, and in Crete they believe it can cure everything!

of Platania. 150 m left of the bridge is the bus station to Rethymnon.

If you want to do both gorges in one day, go early in the morning to Patsos, go through the gorge and, after coming out near the dam, walk for one and a half hours on the tar road or hitchhike until the point where the gravel road descends to the gully.

41. PATSIANO GORGE

DIFFICULTY 📈	■ ■ ☐ ☐	
DURATION 🕐	3 h (with return)	
ELEVATION CHANGE 📊	a) Patsos – starting point: 20´, 130 m descent b) Starting point – gorge exit: 40', 100 m descent	
TERRAIN	Proper path at the beginning. Then swimming, and passages over steep and slippery rocks.	
SIGNPOSTING	No need.	
WHEN TO GO	June–October.	
WATER	From the village or the tavern at the gorge entrance.	
SHADE	A lot of shade inside the gorge. Ideal summer hike.	
POPULARITY	More popular recently, but most visitors stop at the end of the path.	
WHERE TO SLEEP WHERE TO EAT	Only in Rethymnon and surrounds.	
ACCESS	Take the bus from Rethymnon to Patsos early in the morning. Otherwise take a taxi (about €25).	
DRAWBACKS	When the construction of the irrigation channel is complete, the landscape will change dramatically.	

The Amari area is not well known by tourists, even though there are a lot of interesting places for everyone who enjoys nature. One of the most impressive places is the narrow Patsiano or Tsirita Gorge, even though it is difficult to reach. It is spectacular and unique, cool and refreshing, an unexpected oasis. When full of water, its crossing is very difficult for the average walker, and one needs special equipment. In summertime though, it is a very pleasant and refreshing hike. Take care when you walk over smooth and slippery rocks.

The moment one arrives at Patsos, one immediately notices two cafes and a refreshing public spring with plenty of water. The village, as well as the whole area, is really green.

A narrow street descends between the houses, exactly opposite the cafes. It turns left 20 m beyond. Keep on walking, until you see an old house with a distinctive outer arc. Turn right at that spot and follow the descending path. In the right season, you can eat some wild plums, but don't overdo it! Turn right at every junction you meet, until you come to a gravel road running vertically from your route. At the opposite side, you'll see a fenced sheep pen. Go left, descending on the road among small fenced fields. At the next junction, turn left again and at the next one go right, still descending. The gorge lies in front of you. Keep walking on the road, past a stream, and climb for a while until you reach the tar road. It will take you 25´ for this first 1.2 kms. 3´ later, the road ends right in front of a taverna, which serves those who visit the small church of Agios Antonis and hikers who have already learned about the gorge.

The defined path begins at the right side of the huge parking area and leads to the church. On Agios Antonis' name day a very good festival is organized every year by the believers who gather here. The place was sacred long before the Christians and Agios Antonis (Saint Antony) of course. Craneos Hermes was worshiped here until the 4th Century A.D., Craneos coming from the word krini (spring), pronounced krana in the Doric dialect.

Leave this area and follow the right-hand path where you will find two signs saying "north exit". Nothing though informs you that the path ends after 20´, and you have to walk on slippery rocks. Use your hands and get wet.

While descending, you will see another sign saying "Fournare Cave". The path goes to a cave 300 m north.

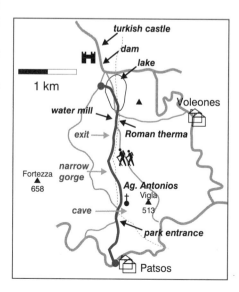

You cross a wooden bridge, which swings above the huge rocks and then the path suddenly disappears. Go to the left behind a huge rock and right across the bridge. You will see a kind of ladder which will help you to climb down the difficult passages. You will get wet up to the thighs. If you don't want to get wetter when you reach a bigger pool, follow the path which climbs up the rocks to the left.

Things get better after that. Unfortunately, the gorge is not very long and after an hour walking the riverbed opens up, and you find yourself in a stream under large plane trees. After a while, there is a cement cistern and a pump house, collecting the water that flows from there. Climb up to the gravel road or return to Patsos reversing your trip.

42. PRASSIES – ARKADI MONASTERY

DIFFICULTY	■ ■ ■ □
DURATION	5 h
ELEVATION CHANGE	300 m descent, 500 m ascent
TERRAIN	A small section on a path (goat track). Route variety, tar road, gravel road, walking on slopes.
SIGNPOSTING	Some E4 signs.
WHEN TO GO	All year round. Avoid the hot days in the summer.
WATER	At Prassies and Arkadi.
SHADE	Only in few places.
POPULARITY	No one until Arkadi.
WHERE TO SLEEP WHERE TO EAT	In Georgioupolis and the surrounding area. For food, go to the taverna in Kournas to avoid the crowds that dine around the lake.
ACCESS	With the bus from Rethymnon (4 services daily in summer) or by taxi.
SIGHTS	Arkadi's historical monastery.
DRAWBACKS	Walking on a tar road, lack of shade (for most of the walk).

The starting point is on the main road right outside the village. Walk for 400–500 m on this road, until you see a big country church on your left with some other buildings around it (dairy houses, sheep pens) bearing the name Papadossifos. Immediately on the left a rough gravel road begins. It is not suitable for cars, with high grass and big potholes. 10´ later it ends. On your right, a small goat track begins among brushwood, following the ridge which descends gradually to the gully and the road. The descent continues for about 20´, steep at some points but always clear. On your left, the ridge becomes an abyss above the gully, which becomes a gorge. Avoid this by keeping to the right.

When you come to the road, continue left for 5´–10´. Then descend among the trees to the gully. There is some water there, as well as E4 signs. The gully narrows abruptly forming the Prassiano Gorge (another good walk). Cross it and continue to the right following a goat track, climbing up in parallel with the flat pebbly gully, among brushwood and bushes. You turn slowly eastwards climbing the slope (no E4 signs here) heading to the right.

Continue the ascent for about another 45´, following different, hard goat tracks which often disappear. Cross a smooth gully and climb to a ridge before reaching a narrow rural road. Walk on this road for 20´ going south, until you reach a good gravel road. Follow this road for another 20´ and at a big junction continue left (North), until you come to a spring in the rocks. This spring has running water, even during the summer.

Some minutes more, and you come to a crossroads on the col with E4 signs again. Follow the narrow road to the right leading you to a sheep pen

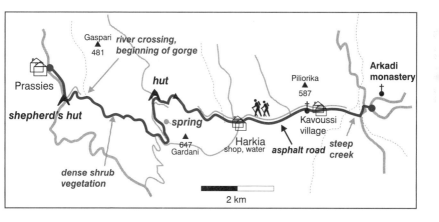

(no dogs here, thank goodness). Open the fence gate and keep on for 10´ until the end of the road. Climb up the slope on your left, and walk for 100 to 200 m on a rugged road. At the end, you see some red signs going up the wide, smooth ridge in an easterly direction. Descend the smooth slope in front of you on its right-hand side, until you find a road. Continue to the right, climbing slightly, and in 20´ you are in Harkia, a very pretty village in a very beautiful area. On your left you see the square, the church and a cafe (probably the only one, where you can cool down and buy some water).

From Harkia you have two options; follow the tar road to the right for 2 kms or follow the E4 path (no signs), going along a smooth gravel road on the right of the church to the gully bellow you. Then, climb up another gravel road to the right, until it reaches the tar road that goes from Harkia to Kavousi (30´ in total). Walk on the tar road for 15´. Don't try to follow any of the gravel roads because all of them end after a while, without connection to paths. Kavousi is almost deserted. Only a few shepherds and their families live here. Keep on the tar road to the right.

You might want to take some shortcuts, but any attempt to follow other narrow roads or paths ends in dense vegetation (holm oaks, brushwood and lentisks). If you keep walking for about an hour you'll come to Arkadi. Otherwise, in 30´, you can cross the fence to your left and follow a parallel gravel road for some minutes. Turn left towards a field, continue straight and climb down (a bit steep) to the gully (small gorge). Cross through dense vegetation and ascend steeply to the road on the other side, next to the Arkadi Monastery and its parking area.

Arkadi

Arkadi was at first just another monastery, but nowadays is considered a symbol of the fight for freedom in Crete.

It is built like a fortress, up on a green plateau overlooking the sea. Everything from the monks' cells, the stables, the warehouses, the guesthouses and the hospital to the dining room are built around the yard, with the church built in the middle. This is considered the main church as there are usually more within a monastery's confines.

The structure of the monks' cells is like that found in catholic monasteries. Cells are built around an arcade overlooking an inner yard.

The monastery church consists of two large spaces, the north aisle devoted to Jesus' transfiguration and the south to Saints Constantine and Helen.

The monastery's foundation is somewhat of a legend. They say that it was built by the Byzantine Emperor Arkadios in the 5th Century A.D. or, as others claim, from a monk named Arkadios.

Travellers who visited through the years give us a clear picture of the monastery:

1700, Tournefort: Arkadi is the most attractive and richest monastery of Crete, with 300 monks and more than 200 barrels of amazing wine!

1817, Sieber: there are only 20 monks left here, and most of the cells have been turned into barns. They still produce amazing wine.

A basic element of the spiritual enrichment of the area is the fact that the monastery was the place where many Hellenic manuscripts were copied, at least until 1645, when the whole place was burned down during the Ottoman invasion.

15,000 Turkish soldiers besieged the monastery. Inside, 325 men and 964 women and children were hidden. The battle was unequal and doomed from the start. When they were unable to resist any longer, a powder keg was lit by the rebel fighter Jiamboudakis. It was the night of the 9th November 1866, and the air was filled with smoke, fire and the cremated body parts of women and children. As many of the Turks outside were also killed, it was a sacrifice for freedom.

43. ARKADI MONASTERY – ELEFTHERNA

DIFFICULTY	■ □ □ □
DURATION	2 h
ELEVATION CHANGE	80 m ascent, 200 m descent a) Arkadi – E4 sign: 30´, 20 m up b) E4 sign – church: 30´, 20 m up, 100 m down c) Church – village centre: 1 h, 100 m down
TERRAIN	A small section on a path (goat track), then varying terrain, including tracks, tar road, gravel road, and walking on slopes.
SIGNPOSTING	No, except for two E4 signs (E4 follows the tar road from Arkadi to Eleftherna).
WHEN TO GO	All year round.
WATER	You'll find water at Arkadi and the cafes at Eleftherna.
SHADE	Only a little shade at the middle section.
POPULARITY	No one, apart from the tar road.
ACCESS	With the bus from Rethymnon (4 services daily in summer) or by taxi
SIGHTS	Arkadi's historical monastery, the ancient cemetery in Eleftherna, and the ruins of the Minoan city. There isn't much landscape variety. The vegetation is typical (brushwood, bushes, cedar trees and typical farming). The view is unobstructed.
DRAWBACKS	Walking on the tar road, lack of shade (for most of the walk).

An easy walk that connects the legendary Arkadi Monastery with Eleftherna where many important archaeological sites are located.

The route starting point is the Arkadi Historical Monastery. In the beginning, it follows the tar road to Eleftherna–Margarites. The E4 path is going the same way, unfortunately on the tar road, which you might want to avoid. When you see the E4 sign on your right at the beginning of a gravel road going upwards, obstructed by a fence (fortunately there is a gate), turn right and immediately left.

Carry on straight, traversing the slope. The terrain here is rocky and full of brushwood (heathers, thyme and thorny burnet). From time to time you'll see a bush, or some bigger rocks.

The view on your left stretches as far as the sea through typical Cretan landscape; hills, smooth valleys, villages, olive groves, fields and roads. Walk on the slope for almost 20´, until the path meets an unpaver road. Go right slightly descending and you will see a small gorge in front of you. Descend to

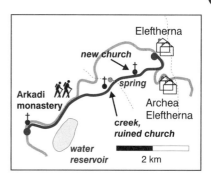

the gully following the gravel road. Go past the dilapidated church and an old spring just 100 m further. Cross the gully and climb to the left on a goat track which when reaching the top (50–60 m ascent) becomes a gravel road. Cross the gully and climb to the left on a goat track which, when reaching the top (50–60 m ascent), becomes a gravel road. Pass the fence door and follow the road among cultivated fields.

15´ later, you come to a new small church and a bigger road. Turn left facing the village's houses. Descend to the tar road and the first houses, and continue left for almost 500 m, until you come to the centre of the village. Tavernas and cafes are waiting for you there.

Olive Tree

It is not by accident that the olive tree is a sacred and blessed tree in Christianity, as it was in ancient Greek religion. The wise goddess Athena had a contest with Poseidon over the dominion of Athens, and in order to win, she made a gift of the olive tree to the Athenians.

Olive trees have been cultivated almost since the first days of western civilization. Archaeological findings indicate that olives have been cultivated in Crete and Syria since 2,500 B.C. Its cultivation spread from these areas throughout Greece, Rome and the whole Mediterranean.

Even today, this evergreen tree with its silver green leaves covers most of Crete's land. According to a 2001 census, there are 1,800,000 olive trees there. Over recent years, because olive production is subsidized by the EC, every free patch on the island is covered by olive trees. Unfortunately, olive trees were very often planted in places where vines had previously been growing, thus destroying old Cretan grape varieties.

In Crete, to make olive oil, they cultivate the variety of olive trees that produce small fruits. As well as being the main Cretan export commodity, olive oil is the basis of Cretan cuisine. Indeed, it is probably due to the use of olive oil that Cretans have the lowest death rates from coronary disease. One of the pioneers of nutritional studies, the American Ancel Keys, compared the diets of different nationalities and showed that the average Cretan consumes 95 gr. of olive oil and 35 gr. of meat per day, while the average American consumes 33 gr. of olive oil and 273 gr. of meat per day!

44. ELEFTHERNA GORGE

DIFFICULTY	〽	■ ☐ ☐ ☐
DURATION	🕐	2 h
ELEVATION CHANGE	📊	a) Village centre (cafes) – Ancient Eleftherna: 20´, 50 m descent b) Ancient Eleftherna – north bridge: 50´, 50 m descent c) North bridge – Alfa (or Alexander's inn): 30´ and 50´, 100 m ascent, 100 m descent
TERRAIN	🔺	Smooth, easy-going, in some parts narrow. Part of the route is on a gravel road. The last part is on a paved road.
SIGNPOSTING	🔼	E4 signs until Eleftherna, none afterwards.
WHEN TO GO	📅	All year round (not if it rains).
WATER	〰	Water only in villages.
SHADE	🌲	Enough shade. Almost all the walk inside the gorge is in shadow.
POPULARITY	👥	No one, apart from the peasants going to their olive groves.
ACCESS	🚌	By bus from Rethymnon (1–2 services daily) or by taxi.
SIGHTS	🏛	The Ancient Eleftherna cemetery and the ruins of the Minoan city, the old watermills inside the gorge (ruined) and the old stone-built wells next to the riverbed with their pumps.
DRAWBACKS	⊗	The dense vegetation in some parts and the last part, where you walk on a paved road.

This is an easy, beautiful walk among dense (sometimes exuberant) vegetation. You'll walk through olive trees, fruit bearing trees and wild plants. This hike brings back memories of the past with ruins in old architectural styles (stone bridges, mills and wells, terraced areas), all drowned in dense vegetation next to the water, some-thing altogether unusual in Crete.

The starting point is the village centre, where the cafes and the shops are. Follow the road to Margarites and Ancient Eleftherna. When out of the village, turn left and immediately afterwards, next to a sign and a bench, you will see the beginning of a good, reconstructed and signposted path, which descends to the archaeological site. In 15´ you come to a road next to the gully. The path to the right continues to Ancient Eleftherna. A part of the ancient settlement can be seen on the hill across the bank.

Continue left on the road. When the road begins to ascend turning left, you will see a path on the right, moving parallel to the gully. Follow this among dense vegetation, olive trees, fruit trees and a lot of bushes. This place used to be, and still is, cultivated in terraces with stone walls supporting the flattened fertile soil. Although the area between the gully and the steep cliffs is relatively small, the abundance of water helped to create a small oasis of vegetables and fruit bearing trees. Nowadays you will not find a lot of them because olive tree cultivation dominates here as well. From time to time, you see abandoned wells (take care because most of them are half covered by dense vegetation) with large pumps rusting on the top.

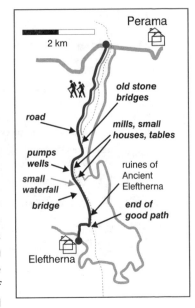

After half an hour of easy and shaded walking, you reach a small stone bridge connecting the two shores. Continue on the left bank. After a while you'll see a small cascade that has running water, even at the beginning of the summer.

Some minutes more, and you are at a small, old, stone, uninhabited building (it used to be a cottage or a storehouse). Its site is ideal for a small break. It is interesting to examine the old rusted pump that lies on a well below you, trying to figure out how it worked. It indicates the abundance of water that used to flow in the gully here (does it still flow?).

Continue on the path under the shade of the fruit trees and on grassy terraced fields. 10´ to 15´ later, you arrive at a small stone bridge with a gravel road on its left. Follow this ascending road for 10´ and it will bring you to a paved road. Continue right after passing a quarry (with a storage house full of flat stones) and in 10´ you are in Alfa village. Buses from here are scarce, so you'd better keep on for 2 kms, until you reach Hani Alexandrou and the main road from Perama to Rethymnon.

Domenikos Theotokopoulos, The Greek (El Greco)

El Greco was born in 1541 in the village of Fodele. The son of a wealthy, orthodox family, he was raised and grew up in Handakas (Herakleon) on Crete, in an era when the artistic and spiritual life of the island was flourishing.

Painters during this period were exploring new approaches and methods, combining Byzantine and Venetian traditions and influences from Constantinople and Venice. Domenikos took his own first steps in that direction as a young man and, at the age of 25, he acquired the title of "grand maestro". He was probably a pupil of the famous painter Theofanis Sterlitzas Bathas, some of whose work can be seen in the monasteries of Athos and the monasteries of Meteora.

Some years later, he travelled to Venice, where he studied art and was trained in colour techniques in Titian's workshop. But he wanted to learn more. He didn't hesitate to say that, even though Michelangelo was a very nice person, he didn't actually know how to paint. He also said that if he had painted the Sistine Chapel himself, the human forms would be humbler and of the same artistic value.

His restless spirit found refuge in Spain, where he migrated and spent most of his life painting religious and secular themes. His uniqueness can be seen in the tortuously elongated figures and their ghostly pigmentation. No one could imitate his style, and he is considered so individual that he belongs to no conventional school.

Toledo was his refuge and the place where he created his mature work. Dopa Jeronima de las Cuevas was his life-long companion and gave him a son, Jorje Manuel. In 1614 he died there, beaten by a long-suffered disease, leaving behind more than 200 paintings.

SOUTHERN RETHYMNON REGION

Probably the best Cretan beaches can be found in the Rethymnon Prefecture. Some years ago, they were quiet and isolated, but, over the past few years, as the tourist market presses more and more for new, undiscovered destinations, more visitors arrive every season. Thank goodness everything is still under control, with the exception of Preveli beach. We cannot justify keeping it to ourselves, because beauty belongs to everyone. How many palm tree beaches with a river running to the sea can be found in Europe?

You can always visit these places off-season, and the chances are that you are going to be by yourselves. It is not only Preveli which is worth visiting in the southern part of Rethymnon. Beautiful little villages like Rodakino, Alones, Gerakari, Meronas and many more add to the landscape's tranquility without being tourist traps. And there is a second beach next to the one with the palm trees and the river.

Kryoneritis, Asideroto and Kedros, the highest mountains in southern Rethymnon, create a magical atmosphere and even though there is no higher plant in the area than the chamomile, it has a peculiar beauty and tremendous views. Easy and difficult gorges cut across the land. Rodakino Gorge is considered one of the most difficult gorges in Crete, and Preveli Gorge one of the finest.

45. ALONES – KRYONERITIS

DIFFICULTY	📈	■ ■ ■ □
DURATION	🕐	4 h 30', 8.5 km (with return)
ELEVATION CHANGE	📊	a) Alones – Mousouria col: 2 h, 650 m up b) Mousouria – spring: 30', 50 m up c) Spring – Kryoneritis peak: 30', 210 m up
TERRAIN	🏔	The path is on chalk rock, confusing at times, where you just follow a general direction.
SIGNPOSTING	🚩	E4 signs, but in some parts it is better not to follow the signs.
WHEN TO GO	📅	April–June, September–October.
WATER	〰	There is a spring underneath the church near the peak.
SHADE	☀	There is almost no shade on this walk.
POPULARITY	👥	Not many people walk here.
WHERE TO SLEEP WHERE TO EAT	🍴	The area is not touristy, so there is no such infrastructure in the villages around. You can pitch your tent freely anywhere. There are no tavernas in the area. Carry the necessary food supplies with you.
ACCESS	🚌	There is a daily bus to Alones from Rethymnon.
SIGHTS	🏛	A fantastic view from the peak.
DRAWBACKS	❌	It gets very hot during the summer.

This walk is not particularly demanding, leading you to a peak with panoramic views. A great advantage is that near the peak there is a spring with cold running water all year round. The name of the peak derives from this spring. It is really amazing to find water at this altitude, considering that there is no higher mountain around. Another advantage of this walk is its solitude.

If the small cafe is open, stay here for a while and enjoy the quiet atmosphere of the village, which exists far away from anything that has to do with tourists. Don't attempt to explain to the hospitable residents why you want to walk up to the mountain top, when you could go there by car. Smile at them and say that you are mountaineers. They are not really going to understand what you mean, but who cares?

Look towards the mountain to see the indicators that will help you find the way. A bit above the village, on the left side of a sheep pen, there is a gully with some green trees. Further up to the left of the big gully, a part of the slope is whiter than the rest of the ground. At the point where the gully ends and the steep rocks begin, underneath the peak, lies the spring (you cannot see it from where you stand).

Behind the old school, nowadays the cafe, climb a bit on a cement road. After 20 m, the road becomes a trail. Pass the fence and the fields, and head for the first trees of the gully. Continue, always on the left of the gully, and try to go to the white area. In 40´ you will come to a gravel road. On the opposite side, you will see a rock wall. Pass by with the rock wall on the right (there is a shrine there), and then turn to the left (Southeast). Continue uphill, and in 10´–15´ you'll reach a basin immediately below the white rocks. A stream seems to flow down this basin. Turn left from this stream, heading south, as you would if you wanted to move away from the peak. The sparse vegetation disappears, and now you walk on eroded and bare chalky stones. You must climb for half an hour to reach the ridge you see in front of you. You walk towards the peak and change direction going west now. As you climb you'll see small plateaus.

When you reach a plateau where the trail descends steeply and in the background you see a gorge that ends in Rodakino village, you are at a point that is called Mousouria. Go back for 20 m, look to the North at the slope and you will see an E4 sign or a pile of stones. Climb steeply heading northwest, later without a real trail, and you will come across a gravel road (15´–20´). More specifically, you will find yourselves on a bend in the road.

If you want to go to the spring, follow the road to the right. In less than 10´, you'll reach an ugly red-roofed building and next to it there is a small church (Agio Pnevma) with an oversized cross next to it. Refreshing water flows among the rocks below the road.

If you want to climb right up to the peak, there are two options. Behind the ugly building, there is a scree. Climb up this scree, turning right after 20 m and through the steep, narrow gully you see in front of you. After 30´ of tiring ascent, the incline becomes normal again, and you are only a few meters south of the peak. The second choice is to go back to the bend in the gravel road where you were before, and continue northwest behind the steep rocks which hang above the dreadful building. The incline is more gradual here, but it takes almost the same time to reach the summit.

It is preferable to come down using this route. As you descend from the peak, the E4 signs start to point to a steep descent. Instead of following them, turn a bit to the right and continue southwards. In 20′ you'll come to the road's bend and, 10′–15′ later, you are at Mousouria. From there it will take you 30′ to get back to Alones. Alternatively, you can continue and walk to Rodakino or Finikas (Route 46).

Sketch-map for 45 and 46 routes.

46. RODAKINO – KRYONERITIS

DIFFICULTY	📈	■ ■ □ □
DURATION	🕐	4 h 30'
ELEVATION CHANGE	📊	a) Rodakino – end of gravel road: 2 h, 630 m up b) End of gravel road – Mousouria: 170 m up c) Mousouria – Kryoneritis peak: 45', 210 m up
TERRAIN	🏔	A large section at the beginning is a gravel road. It then continues on a rough trail with unsteady chalky terrain (no trail inside the gorge).
SIGNPOSTING	🔺	E4 signposting (no signs inside the gorge).
WHEN TO GO	📅	April–June, September–October.
WATER	〰	There is a spring under the church before reaching the peak. Another one is at the beginning of Finikas gully.
SHADE	🌳	There is almost no shade.
POPULARITY	👥	You will probably meet no one.
WHERE TO SLEEP WHERE TO EAT	🍴	There are enough guesthouses on Korakas beach below Rodakino and on Souda beach under Sella. You will find tavernas there too.
ACCESS	🚗	There are two daily buses from Chania to Rodakino.
SIGHTS	🏛	The view from the peak is fantastic as well as Souda beach with its palm tree forest.
DRAWBACKS	❎	The ugly gravel road.

This route can be combined with the route Alones–Kryoneritis or taken as a separate climb from Kato Rodakino. You can return either on the same route or through Finikas Gorge, for those who love adventure. It is generally an easy route, but crossing the gorge demands some easy scrambling.

Though the name of the walk is Rodakino–Kryoneritis, the description is from Kryoneritis to Rodakino, in order to combine it with Route 45, from Alones to Rodakino.

Starting from Rodakino is easy. Follow the ascending narrow street at Rodakino's eastern exit. This street leads you to a trail among olive trees. You will walk for almost half an hour, until you come to a gravel road. Follow the road, because the fences will make your way on the trail difficult. 1 h 45´ from Rodakino, climb to the North, reaching a distinctive ridge where the road passes a bit below it heading west. Remember this col, because from here you will descend, if you want to go towards Finikas.

After a while the road turns left. Follow the road, until it turns right and heads for the fallen rocks, which seem like a quarry. If you look closer above the cliff, you will see a series of peaks and cols. The second col from the right is Mousouria.

Basically you climb heading north, constantly crossing the gravel road which winds around the steep slope. 30′–35′ on, you reach the last bend in the road. From there, the road runs almost straight on to the West. You must try to find a big rock with the number 98 written on it with red paint (for no known reason whatsoever). The imperceptible trail climbs inside the gully left of this rock. It moves a bit to the right and then left again, underneath the steep slope. Traverse for a while going uphill. Continue straight on until you find yourselves at Mousouria, 40′ from rock 98. Follow Route 45 to climb to the peak.

DESCENT

When you come down from the peak and you are at Mousouria, the steep cliff and the unobstructed view to Crete's southern seashore will stop you in your tracks. At the point where the cliff starts, you will see a yellow E4 sign. Climb down to the left, and then mostly to the right, until you reach the base of this steep slope. Walk towards the bend in the road you see below.

20′ later you will reach the road. From there, continue straight on for another 20′ to the South, crossing the zigzags of the road until they end, and the road moves almost southeast. In a few minutes you pass by the distinctive ridge, where the road heads south towards Rodakino. If you follow the road, in less than 1 h 30′ you will be in Kato Rodakino.

VARIATION

If you feel like doing something more extreme, then you can descend through Finikas Gorge. It is not a difficult crossing, but sometimes you need to scramble a bit in order to climb down to the rocky riverbed.

It is very easy to find the gorge entrance. As you descend crossing the road which winds round the slope, you will see a green patch in the barren landscape left of the road behind a low hill. The gorge starts among the steep rocks and disappears near the mountain ridge.

Climb up to the distinctive ridge leaving the road, and then descend —no trail here— until you will see a small plane tree forest. Finikas gully starts here. In 15′ you reach the trees, and you should take a break under their shade. At the left side of the gully, 30 m up, there is a spring.

Follow the road which moves parallel to the gully. 10′ later, the road crosses to the left, while the stream goes to the right and disappears among the broken chalky slopes. Pass the low fence and let the gorge lead you. When you reach a point which seems impassable, search on the right-hand side of the gully and you will find a narrow trail.

This entertaining experience will take something between 1 h and 1 h 30′. The gorge ends on the road between Sellia and Rodakino at a distinctive cut in the rocks, 5 kms from Kato Rodakino. Find the gate to the fence and get to the road. The gorge then continues for another 1 h 30′, until it reaches the quiet and almost tropical Souda beach dotted with the Cretan palm trees. We don't recommend this though, because the vegetation is very dense and has closed off all paths, making progress very tiring.

47. ANO MEROS – KEDROS

DIFFICULTY 📈	■ ■ ■ □
DURATION 🕐	3 h ascent and 1,200 m elevation gain
ELEVATION CHANGE 📊	a) Village – Kaloidenas Monastery: 30′, 140 m ascent b) Small chapel – col: 1 h 30′, 600 m ascent c) Col – peak: 1 h, 450 m ascent
TERRAIN 🗻	You walk on the road and on goat tracks without a trail. The upper part is very stony with dense vegetation.
SIGNPOSTING 🔼	No.
WHEN TO GO 🗓	March–November (avoid the hot days of the summer).
WATER 〰	Take water from the cafes in the village or from the springs (the first one is at the chapel and the second a bit further up).
SHADE 🖼	There is no shade, unless you stay below the rocks.
POPULARITY 👥	You will meet no one apart from some shepherds.

ACCESS	There are 3 buses per week from Rethymnon to Kedros or 1–2 daily bus services from Rethymnon to Amari. Take a taxi from there.
SIGHTS	Visit the small renovated chapel at Kaloidena. Enjoy the impressive view to the Libyan Sea, Psiloritis and the valleys, from the summit.
DRAWBACKS	The lack of shade and the rough terrain for most of the time.

A quick (a bit tiring though) mountaineering hike without a trail. You walk on goat tracks on a rough, barren and rocky terrain offering great views to Psiloritis, Lefka Ori, the sea and Cretan plateaus.

The walk starts 500 m outside the village towards Hordaki village. You will see a road on your right and a sign indicating "to Kaloidena Monastery". Follow the road for 20′–25′ to the West. Pay no attention to any junction, and you will arrive at a chapel with a spring. Continue on the uphill road for 30′, following its bends, until you reach a sheep pen and a fence (with a gate!), which blocks the road. Open the gate and keep on walking on the road for 10′–15′ until it ends. From here on there is no path nor markings, only goat tracks and rough terrain. You are heading west (and a bit southwest). After a while, you see some huge vertical rocks in front of you with a spring on their right (probably without water in the summer) and the goat track continues to the right.

The landscape is typically Cretan, rocky, full of sage, thyme and spiny shrubs. The view now expands, and you can see more villages with Psiloritis and the Amari valley at your back. 30′ after the spring, you come to a ridge looking west towards Gourgouthi and Gerakari villages. Continue in the same direction, turning a bit southwest and climb on steeper slopes for almost 40′, until you reach a wide flat area with a slight incline. The high peaks are now in front of you (Kedros is basically a long narrow mountain with a smooth ridge which ascends from the East to the West and with steep slopes West/Southwest).

The highest peak is the western one (the one on the right). Continue slightly

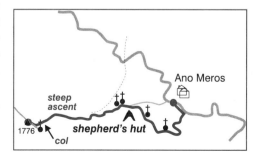

uphill for 10´–15´ to the col on the ridge. From there, you will enjoy the view to the other side of the mountain and to the southern seaside. Turn west/northwest from the col, climbing a steep slope for 20´–25´ until you come to the peak (1,777 m). There is the usual cement column there and an amazing view. The Lybian Sea, Paximadia Islands and Messara Valley are on one side and the Aegean Sea, Psiloritis and the northern Rethymnon provinces on the other. Far back to the West you can see Lefka Ori.

48. GERAKARI – KEDROS

DIFFICULTY	■ ■ ☐ ☐
DURATION	3 h and 1,050 m ascent
ELEVATION CHANGE	a) Gerakari – spring: 1 h 30', 500 m ascent b) Spring – plateau: 30', 200 m ascent c) Plateau – peak: 1 h, 350 m ascent
TERRAIN	You walk on a trail and goat tracks, but the biggest part is without trails. Low vegetation and lots of stones.
SIGNPOSTING	Good E4 signposting.
WHEN TO GO	March–November (avoid the hot days of the summer).
WATER	Take water from the village and from the spring at the end of the road.
SHADE	There is no shade, unless you stay below the rocks.
POPULARITY	You will meet no one apart from some shepherds.
ACCESS	There are 3 buses per week from Rethymnon to Kedros or 1–2 daily bus services from Rethymnon to Amari. Take a taxi from there.
SIGHTS	Visit the really attractive village of Gerakari and enjoy the typical mountainous Cretan landscape and the marvellous views from the peak.
DRAWBACKS	The lack of shade (in the summer), walking on the road at the beginning and the rough terrain further up.

This is an alternative (and easier) ascent to Kedros and it starts from a pretty village with great views to Psiloritis, Lefka Ori, the sea and the steep mountain slopes.

The climb starts from the village and its lovely central square. Follow the paved road to the right towards Spili. In about 1 km a good gravel road goes off to the left, climbing southwards. Follow this road, and 15´ later you come to a large sheep pen. Continue uphill for 15´, and after some bends you will see on your left an E4 signposted trailhead (yellow rhombuses). The metallic E4 signs start from the village and come up to this point, but they are

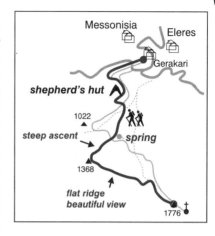

sparse and need attention. You can do this part of the route with a car, avoiding a 4 kms walk on the road, a recommended option in the summer and a necessity, if you are planning to return the same way.

Follow the trail for 45´ (it is actually a goat track with enough E4 signs) climbing the slope among phrygana, bushes and large stones, so try not to lose your way. You cross a bad (rough to impassable for vehicles in spring) dirt track twice until, at 1,200 m altitude, you come to a junction and a spring with drinkable water (perhaps dry in the summer). Take the road on the left and 5´ later you see on your right the trail (E4 signposted) climbing on a steep ridge. You walk across this ridge gaining height as you walk on a rough stony terrain full of phrygana. The signs (dense and visible) lead you southwest on the steep mountain slope, with a magnificent view north to Psiloritis, Lefka Ori, the Aegean Sea and the Amari villages.

The uphill and trail-less traverse continues, until you reach a plateau after 1,400 m (half an hour later). Follow the signs to the left (South). You will ascend steeply and scramble in 2 or 3 points, but 10´ later you will be on a wide flat ridge heading southeast, which you will follow for 20´, climbing gradually, until you reach the foot of the peak. The last part of the ascent is steep (with the west side having enough rock walls and steep gullies). You will not need to climb though, and 30´ later, you will be on the wide peak looking down to the Libyan Sea, the southern seaside, Paximadia islands, Gavdos, and Messara valley, Lefka Ori to the West, the Aegean Sea, Rethymnon and its villages to the North, Psiloritis with its impressive massif to the East. The whole picture will reward you for these three tiring hours of ascent.

Southern Rethymnon Region

Cattle Stealing

Rustling is a widespread practice. It is an everyday topic for local TV channels and newspapers, where it is put across as an epidemic. The truth is not that terrible.

It is an old custom in some of the mountainous villages in Psiloritis, where stealing animals was common practice. It was an act that showed not only the thief's skills, but also a spirit of insubordination towards the authorities. The roots of the practice are found in the era of the Ottoman rule, when rebels from the highlands or lawless locals (mainly from the villages of Psiloritis) raided neighbouring villages to steal cattle and other livestock, which they butchered for food or kept for calving. The practice continued after the liberation of Crete as well, but it is now disappearing slowly.

These days rustling happens only in certain places and, as rumour goes, the culprits are organized groups from villages in Psiloritis, while their targets are animals grazing in pastures anywhere between Chania and Sitia. The use of modern technology (cars, guns, mobile phones, binoculars) allows them to commit the crime easily and to get away quickly. They spot the cattle, the sheep pen or the stable days in advance, and they keep watch to see how well it is guarded and where the weak points are. They then decide on their plan of action and strike at night, opening the sheep pen or the stable and leading the animals to a waiting truck. They convey them to a nearby slaughter house, or even to one far away, where they butcher them and hand the meat to collaborative butchers and merchants, with fake certificates of course.

Very often the operation has a bad ending, as the owner of the cattle, alone or with other armed guards, is lurking inside the sheep pen and a shoot-out follows, forcing the invaders to retreat. The police and their special forces are frequently involved in chasing the thieves, in an effort to eradicate the phenomenon. They set up road blocks and organize snap inspections at small slaughter houses and in suspicious sheep pens.

49. KOTSIFOS GORGE

DIFFICULTY	■ ■ ☐ ☐
DURATION	2 h 30'
ELEVATION CHANGE	280 m ascent a) Plakias – entrance: 20', 30 m ascent b) Entrance – old water mill: 50', 100 m ascent c) Old mill – springs: 50', 100 m ascent d) Springs – bridge: 40', 50 m ascent
TERRAIN	There is no trail. You walk in the gorge's bed.
SIGNPOSTING	No.
WHEN TO GO	All year round.
WATER	Take water from Plakias; you will find nothing in between.
SHADE	The entire route is in shade. Only at high noon are there some sunny parts.
POPULARITY	You will meet no one.
WHERE TO SLEEP WHERE TO EAT	There are a lot of hotels, guesthouses, rooms-to-let and restaurants in Plakias.
ACCESS	There are a lot of buses daily going to Plakias, especially during the summer.
SIGHTS	You will see a ruined mill and the river's springs. It is an unusual walk for Crete because it is shady, full of water and the gorge is narrow. On the other hand, don't expect great views and landscape variety.
DRAWBACKS	Lack of landscape variety, your shoes and clothes might get wet and to return you have to walk on a paved road.

It is a small, easy gorge with water even in the summer. The hike is in the shade with easy scrambles on small rocks. It combines adventure with joy, with some worth seeing places for variety.

The walk starts from the bridge above the river's mouth, which lies next to the bus terminal in the tourist-trap village of Plakias. Follow a narrow street, recently paved, which runs next to the Youth Hostel on the right of the gully and then winds up climbing gradually among olive trees and some fruit trees. You see some houses here and there, and, 15'−20' later, you will see a gravel road on your left, which ends in an olive grove next to the riverbed. Pass through some bushes and enter the flat stone bed which is never dry.

Southern Rethymnon Region

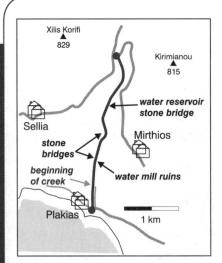

It's very pleasant from this point. The route climbs gradually and you walk under the shade of high reeds and other plants (you will need to walk through them from time to time). After a little while you come to little rocks which you can climb easily, rocks that add a dose of adventure to your hike.

In 45′–60′ you reach an old stone bridge. The trail is on the right, leading to a ruined water mill with an unusual and very high drop (10 m at least) through a vertical stone-built canal. A propeller and the transmission mechanism used to be at the bottom. Take a look at the other parts of the mill (millstones, melting pots etc.) and then get again in the stream which is becoming deeper (but passable). The gorge's walls are getting closer, and the vegetation denser. The rocks are bigger now, and you need to climb above them. The water is knee-high, sometimes even higher. When you pass under another bridge and climb above the last and even bigger rocks, you reach a cement base and a water tank with soil and stones around.

You continue for 2′–3′ uphill stepping on the cemented bed until you come to the spring (unfortunately, it is covered and the water flows through an iron pipe to the water tank and from there to the village). At this point, the gorge is deep, steep and dark. Right ahead, you see a rock wall some meters high, obstructing your walk up. Return to the water tank and you will see a goat track climbing up on the right. Follow it for some minutes, and then climb again down to the riverbed, which is now dry and full of large stones with wide open walls.

You walk on this bed for 40′–45′. The view opens up in front of you, the vegetation disappears and, as you climb, you can see more and more refuse. At the end, you come to a bridge and the main road from Sellia to Mirthios. Climb up to the right, and that's the end of this walk.

50. PREVELI GORGE

DIFFICULTY	■ ■ ☐ ☐
DURATION	2 h
ELEVATION CHANGE	120 m descent, 100 m ascent a) Bridge – first rocks: 30', 20 m descent b) First rocks – trailhead: 40', 90 m descent c) Trailhead – beach: 20', 10 m descent d) Beach – parking area: 20', 100 m ascent
TERRAIN	You walk without a trail inside the riverbed at the beginning. The third part is passable, clear but narrow, among palm trees. The fourth part is easy and wide (with steps). There are some parts that require easy scrambling in the middle of the hike. You must wear trekking shoes (they will get wet). Flip flops are not recommended.
SIGNPOSTING	None.
WHEN TO GO	April–October (not if it rains).
WATER	Take water from the shop at the beginning of the walk. Avoid drinking water from the river.
SHADE	The hike is mostly shady, as it moves under trees and rocks. The gorge's walls offer shade in the morning and later in the afternoon.
POPULARITY	It depends. You will meet some people in spring and autumn, more in the summer, but never too many.
ACCESS	There are several daily buses from Rethymnon (in summer 3–4).
SIGHTS	Visit the old Preveli Monastery (Ai Yannis) at the beginning of the walk (it has been abandoned for 100 years now) and the stone-built Venetian bridge. The last part is in a unique palm tree forest of amazing beauty, one of the last remaining in Crete.

This is a trip in a truly African landscape with palm trees, warm waters and steep slopes ending on one of the most beautiful beaches you've ever seen (try to ignore the many people that flock here). A walk with landscape variety, and ideal for photography.

The walk starts from the road which crosses the river next to the old Venetian bridge, before the abandoned Preveli Monastery, 30 kms from Rethymnon. Get into the shallow river (try not to frighten the ducks that swim here) and continue for 30´ in the water, among dense vegetation, oleanders and other plants which offer valuable shade. Unfortunately, walking on the bank beside the riverbed is impossible due to the lack of a trail, dense greenery and the many fences placed across it.

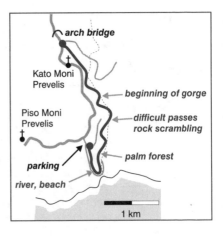

This part of the hike is easy and the gully is wide. Soon it gets narrower and you reach a point where there are some steep rocks ahead which you must climb down on the right-hand side. The gully, for the next 30′–40′, is steep with its bed full of rocks and stones, while the water is up to your hips. At some points, you must actually climb down, but there are proper holds all around. This part is very impressive and interesting, with high vertical walls, huge rocks with peculiar formations and dense vegetation on the banks. Gradually the bed becomes flatter, the rocks smaller, pebbled little beaches appear, and palm trees are spreading to form a copse. Leave the bed, go to the right bank and you will see a small trail in the forest leading you to small terraces (these used to be places designed for tents, but camping is now forbidden).

The landscape is truly African, and you see the beautiful Preveli beach divided by the river. Unfortunately, the beach is crowded. There are also two small shops here offering drinks and food. Take a break, enjoy a swim and then take the trail on the right, which leads to the parking area after 20′ of walking on dozens of steps. As you climb, admire once again the palm tree forest, the beach and the river, and further away Gavdos and Paximadia islands.

Preveli Monastery

This monastery is dedicated to St John the Divine and has a stunning view over the Libyan Sea. It lies 170 m above sea level. The site on which it was constructed, possibly in the 16th Century during the Venetian occupation, is really amazing, as is the case with many similar buildings all around Greece. There is only one inscription to indicate when it was built. The date 1701 is on the fountain.

It is said that it was founded by a landlord named Prevelis from Ardaktos, who dedicated it to the existing small chapel. There were also six monks with the same name and from the same place, giving the monastery its name.

It seems that the monastery grew wealthy in a very short time, thanks to those devotees who left their fortunes there to save their wealth from the Turks and, at the same time, to save their souls. So the monastery came to own a very large area from the Libyan to the Cretan Sea. This fortune was the key in helping to educate the locals, founding the first Greek Academy in 1831.

It played a very active part during the War of Liberation from 1770 (Daskalogiannis' rebellion) to 1866, offering refuge to rebels on the run. One year later, it was burned to the ground by Reshit Pasha, thus proving that wealth and privilege cannot always solve problems!

Once more, during World War II, it offered a helping hand to the Allies' submarines, and it was consequently demolished by the Nazi invaders in retaliation. The most recent story comes from those days. It is said that the miraculous Holy Cross of the monastery prevented the enemy's aeroplanes from taking off from Maleme to fly to Germany.

Talking About Reptiles and Amphibians

When wandering in the countryside, walking amongst phryga-na and dry stone walls, it is almost certain that you'll hear a slithering noise in the dead branches. Don't worry; it isn't some kind of poisonous snake, since there are no poisonous snakes in Crete, strange as it sounds. Of all the different kinds of snakes that live on the island, only one has poison and this is in its back teeth, making it totally harmless.

The Whipsnake which lives everywhere in Crete as well as the Ottoman Viper have no poison and are totally harmless. They usually eat lizards, mice and sometimes snails. The Ocellated Skink, a grey brown lizard is one of the 11 species of the island's reptiles. Even though some Cretans consider it very dangerous, it is a harmless creature. The largest lizard in Crete is the Green Lizard and the smallest the Gecko, which eats mosquitoes and moths.

Another very attractive little creature, a remnant from the era of dinosaurs, is the turtle. In Crete there are no tortoises at all! There are only turtles that live in lakes and rivers and feed themselves on tadpoles and worms.

So, have no fear if you want to enjoy a midday nap on the ground, underneath the shade of a holly tree. The only thing that might disturb your peace is the buzzing sound of flies ...

51. KOURTALIOTIKO GORGE

DIFFICULTY	■ ■ ■ □
DURATION	2 h
ELEVATION CHANGE	a) Road – small chapel; 50', 80 m descent b) Small chapel – dam; 20', 30 m descent c) Dam – bridge: 1 h, 100 m descent
TERRAIN	You walk without a trail on the riverbed or on the slope, where you must have good sense of balance and hiking experience on screes and stones. Don't be afraid of getting wet.
SIGNPOSTING	None.
WHEN TO GO	March–October (not if it rains).
WATER	There is a spring in the riverbed 30' from the start, at the point where the river flows out of the rock.
SHADE	The shade depends on the hour of the day. The vertical walls offer full shade early in the morning and late in the afternoon, but none at noon.
POPULARITY	This gorge is seldom walked by people, so you will probably meet no one apart from some people at the chapel above the cascade and at the end of the walk at the old bridge.
ACCESS	With your own vehicle or by bus going from Rethymnon to Plakias or Preveli (4–5 daily services in summer). Get off 2 kms after Koxare village.
SIGHTS	Visit the small chapels (by a cave next to the road and at the opposite side above the waterfall), the old stone bridge and the abandoned Preveli Monastery. A walk which offers landscape variety and natural beauty.

This is a walk inside an impressive small gorge offering variety in landscape and vegetation. The "civilised world" is getting closer and closer (the road from Rethymnon to Preveli passes inside the gorge 100 m above you, but you don't even notice it). You are in another world at the bottom of the gorge. The small river that runs along its bed, the small chapels built inside the caves or above the waterfall, the easy access and the connection with other walks add to its beauty and to the feeling of adventure.

Two kms after Koxare village, at the point where the gorge narrows, leave the road leading to Preveli and pass carefully above a low wall and descend the slope to the riverbed. You now walk inside the bed. For 30' you step on small and larger stones on the dry bed, until you reach a point where the water springs out from the left bank. From here on, the bed and the right bank become very steep. For that reason you must traverse up-hill on the left slope following narrow, rough goat tracks. When you pass a steep passage you see below to your right the small chapel and a cement bridge. Climb down carefully. It is a bit steep and the various plants make it more difficult.

Take a break and admire the gorge below, as you stand on the small bridge. You will hear the sound of the falling water and,

from the balcony outside the small chapel, you will have a better view of the cascade. Keep on climbing the steps on your left, until you come to even more steps on your left which lead to a small dam with iron gates. Climb down to the bed (better from the left side).

For the next 10′ the trek is difficult as you move among huge rocks. Later, things get better and the rocks become smaller. Follow along the gorge bed walking in the water (knee height but sometimes up to your hips) and after a while you will walk by a sheep pen full of sheep, goats and dogs (tame ones!). You may meet the shepherds as well.

The gully is getting narrower now. There is vegetation here and there, which makes your journey more difficult. Some larger rocks are scattered around. Soon the gully widens again at the end of the gorge. A small plain lies in front of you, full of olives and other trees, the vegetation is denser and you can see the old arched stone bridge. The road is higher up behind the bridge, leading to a small shop and the old Preveli Monastery on the right. Rest a while and you can continue if you like to the sea, passing through Preveli Gorge (Route 50).

Palm Trees

Palm trees come from Africa and Asia, and from there they spread around the world. Cretan palm trees are self-sown and were thought unique. They belong to the Phoenix Theophrasti family (or in simple terms the "Cretan palm tree"), but, as recently proved, they are not in fact unique; a small number of the same tree was found in the Middle East, Iran and Egypt. The first scientist who referred to the Cretan palm tree and described it in full detail was the botanist Theophrastus (3rd Century B.C.), and that is why the species bears his name.

It is common belief that the palm tree came to Crete from Egypt, during the third millennium B.C., as an exchange of goods between the two populations. The climate was favourable for its growth and it was grown in many Cretan cities, as it can be seen from murals and pot remains. In some cities they used its leaves, after special preparation, as a paper for writing, like papyrus. Laws, poems and calculations were written on them, but unfortunately nothing remains today. From Crete the tree spread to a few other Greek islands (Cyclades, Dodecanese), but not to many.

The Cretan palm tree is a bit smaller than the Date Palm. It grows up to 10 m high and lives up to 100 years. It blossoms after four years, but its fruit is not edible like that of Date Palms. The trees are divided into male and female, unlike other trees where male and female flowers exist on the same tree. Water is essential for their growth, and that is why water is always somewhere nearby, in springs, gullies or underground streams. As the ancient Greeks used to say, it should have its roots in the water and its head in the sun. It can also withstand salty water and for that reason it grows well near the sea (e.g. next to the river mouth).

In Crete, one can find the largest forest of its kind, the palm tree forest in Vai in northeastern Crete, with almost 1,000 trees. There are also smaller clusters around the island, at Preveli beach, at Almyros near Agios Nikolaos, at Almyros near Heraclion, at Georgioupolis, at Arvi, and in many other places, as well as in parks and hotel gardens.

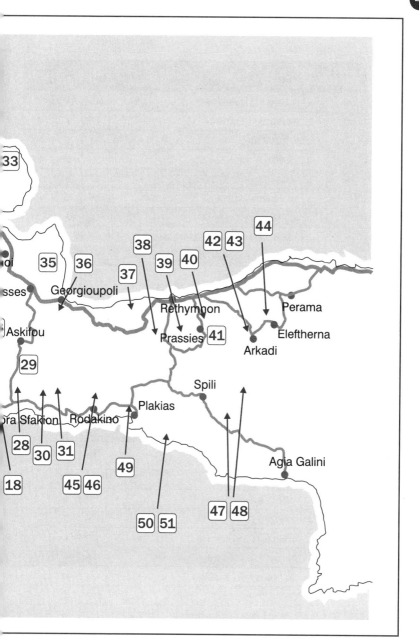

SUMMARY TABLE OF ROUTES

REGION		ROUTE	PAGE	DIFFICULTY	HOURS
WESTERN CHANIA	1	GRAMVOUSSA PENINSULA	44	A	2
	2	FALASSARNA – PLATANOS	47	A	2
	3	TSIHLIANI GORGE – POLYRINIA – SYRIKARI	49	B	3½
	4	RODOPOS PENINSULA	52	B	4½
	5	ELAFONISSI – PALAIOHORA	55	B	3¾
	6	PALAIOHORA – SOUGIA	58	B	5¼
LEFKA ORI (WHITE MOUNTAINS)	7	AGIA IRINI GORGE	64	B	3½
	8	KOUSTOGERAKO – OMALOS (THROUGH GINGILOS)	67	D	6½
	9	KOUSTOGERAKO – OMALOS	72	C	6
	10	SOUGIA – AGIA ROUMELI	75	D	9
	11	SAMARIA GORGE	79	B	5½
	12	AGIOS YANNIS – AGIA ROUMELI	84	B	3½
	13	LOUTRO – FINIKAS – AGIA ROUMELI	87	B	5
	14	ARADENA GORGE	89	C	2½
	15	LOUTRO – LIVANIANA – ARADENA	93	B	3
	16	ANOPOLI – LOUTRO	97	A	1½
	17	HORA SFAKION – LOUTRO	99	A	2
	18	ASKIFOU – ANOPOLI	100	D	9
	19	ANOPOLI – PACHNES	104	D	6
	20	ANOPOLI – HORA SFAKION	108	B	2
	21	ILIGAS GORGE	110	C	3½
	22	GINGILOS ASCENT	113	C	3
	23a	OMALOS – KALLERGIS' HUT	116	A	1¼
	23b	KALLERGIS' HUT – KATSIVELI	119	D	6¾
	23c	KATSIVELI – PACHNES	122	C	3¼
	24	LAKKI – POTAMI (VRYSSI GORGE)	124	D	9

A			easy
B			
C			
D			very tough

ELEVATION CHANGE		TRAIL LINKS	APPENDICES
UP (m)	DOWN (m)		
150	150		GRAMVOUSSA PENINSULA
250			
250	250		THE TRAGEDY OF A CRETAN WEDDING
500	500		BATTLE OF CRETE (OPERATION MERKUR)
60	60	6	TRAGIC ELAFONISSI
400	400	5−8,9,10	ANCIENT LISSOS
	460		DITTANY OR ERONTAS
1,200	470	6−11, 22, 23a	THE COFFEE SHOP (KAFENEIO)
740	150	6−11, 22, 23a	THE CRETAN LYRE
1,050	1,050	6, 8, 9−11, 12	
1,220			CHAMOIS ("KRI-KRI")
	750	10, 11− 25	
250	250	10, 11− 14, 15, 16, 17	
	550	12− 13, 15, 16, 17	VENDETTAS / CICADAS, THE SUMMER TROUBADOURS
680	160	12−13, 15, 16, 17	THE "SAINT GENERAL" / "THE COCKFIGHT"
50	650	12, 25, 18, 19, 20−14, 15, 17	
200	200	14, 15, 16−20	
850	950	12, 25, 19, 20− 27, 29, 30	SETTLEMENTS (METOHIA)
1,850		2, 25, 18, 20−23C	THE SHINIEST GEM
50	650	2, 25, 18, 19−17, 21	
700	100	17, 18, 20	GUN POSSESION
860	100	8, 9, 11, 23a	DANCES
370		8, 9, 11, 22−23b	KOKALAS (LAMMERGEIER)
1,180	450	23a−23c, 25, 27	
690	40	23b−19	
1,650	450	23b−25	

Summary Table of Routes

REGION		ROUTE	PAGE	DIFFICULTY	HOURS
LEFKA ORI (WHITE MOUNTAINS)	25	POTAMI – AI YANNIS	127	D	6½
	26	KASTRO ASCENT FROM ASKIFOU	132	D	8
	27	KASTRO – KATSIVELI	135	D	7
	28	IMBROS GORGE	137	A	2½
	29	ASKIFOU – AGATHES	140	C	4½
	30	ASKIFOU – ASFENDOU GORGE	143	B	4½
	31	KALLIKRATIS' GORGE	147	B	2¾
NORTERN CHANIA - AKROTIRI	32	GOUVERNETO MONASTERY – KATHOLIKO MONASTERY	152	A	2½
	33	GOUVERNETO MONASTERY – STAVROS	155	B	3¼
	34	DIKTAMO (DITTANY) GORGE	157	B	3
	35	LYKOTINARA – KEFALAS	161	B	3½
	36	ALIKAMBOS – KOURNAS LAKE	165	C	4
NORTHERN RETHYMNON	37	VEDERES GORGE (GERANI GORGE)	169	B	3
	38	VALSAMONERO – ARMENI (BONRIPARI CASTLE)	172	C	4
	39	PRASSIES – VRYSSINAS PEAK – ARMENI	175	C	4¾
	40	PRASSIANO GORGE	179	C	4¼
	41	PATSIANO GORGE	182	B	3
	42	PRASSIES – ARKADI MONASTERY	184	C	5
	43	ARKADI MONASTERY – ELEFTHERNA	188	A	2
	44	ELEFTHERNA GORGE	191	A	2
SOUTHERN RETHYMNON	45	ALONES – KRYONERITIS	195	C	4½
	46	RODAKINO – KRIONERITIS	198	B	4½
	47	ANO MEROS – KEDROS	200	C	3
	48	GERAKARI – KEDROS	202	B	3
	49	KOTSIFOS GORGE	205	B	2½
	50	PREVELI GORGE	207	B	2
	51	KOURTALIOTIKO GORGE	211	C	2

A   easy
B
C
D   very tough

ELEVATION CHANGE		TRAIL LINKS	APPENDICES
UP (m)	DOWN (m)		
350	1,350	12, 23b, 24	RIZITIKA SONGS / LAMB HAIRCUT (KOURA)
1,450		29, 30	
850	1,100	23, 25	
650		26, 29, 30	RUSKS
850	100	27, 28, 30, 31	CAPER, THE EDIBLE FLOWER
260	920	27, 28, 29, 31	DROSOULITES
	650	29, 3	SFAKIA COOKING
180	270	33	THE ARKOUDOSPILIO LEGEND
280	470	32	
	200		THE 12 YOUNG MASTERS
350	350		AROMATIC PLANTS
180	480		
230		38	
350	450	37–39	
500	500	38–40, 42	PEAK SANCTUARIES AND SACRED CAVES
	190	39, 42	TSIKOUDIA
	230		
500	300	39, 40, 43	ARKADI
80	200	41, 44	OLIVE TREE
100	200	43	DOMENIKOS THEOTOKOPOULOS, THE GREEK (EL GRECO)
900		46	
1,010		45	
1,200		48	
1,150		47	CATTLE STEALING
280			
100	120	51	PREVELI MONASTERY / TALKING ABOUT REPTILES AND AMPHIBIANS
	210	50	PALM TREES

USEFUL PHONE NUMBERS AND ADDRESSES

Useful Phone Numbers and Addresses

Phone codes:	Greece	(+) 30
	Chania	28210
	Rethymnon	28310

- Police Station
  - Chania — 28210 71111, 51111
  - Rethymnon — 28310 22333
  - Tourist Police, Chania — 28210 24477
  - Tourist Police, Rethymnon — 28310 28156
  - Sfakia — 28250 91205
  - Palaiochora — 28230 41111
  - Spelie — 28320 22026
  - Sougia — 28230 51241
- Port Authority
  - Chania — 28210 98888
  - Sfakia — 28250 91292
  - Palaiochora — 28230 41214
  - Rethymnon — 28310 28971
- CHANIA KTEL (bus services) — 28210 93306
  www.bus-service-crete-ktel.com
- RETHYMNON KTEL (bus services) — 28310 222120
- Olympic Airlines — 28210 57701
  www.olympicairlines.com
- AEGEAN AIRLINES — 8011120000
  www.aegeanair.com
- Chania Airport — 28210 63264
- ANEK Lines (ferries) — 28210 27500
  S. Venizelou SQ, 731 34 Chania
  www.anek.gr

- CHANIA EOS (mountaineering club) — 28210 44647
  Str. Ganakaki 90, 731 00
  www.eoshanion.gr
- RETHYMNON EOS (mountaineering club) — 28310 23666
  Moatsou, 701 00

• Chania General Hospital	28210 27231
• Rethymnon General Hospital	28310 27491
• Rural Medical Facilities	
— Agia Roumeli	28250 91151
— Sfakia	28250 91214
— Kanatnos	28230 22550
— Fourfouras	28330 41215
— Zoniana	28340 61298
• Archaeological Museum	28210 90334
• Chania EOT (tourist organization)	28210 92943
• London EOT	020 7495 9300
4 Conduit Str., W1S 2DJ London	
• German EOT	069 236561
N. Mainzer Str. 22, D-6000 Frankfurt	
• British Consulate	2810 224019
Papalexandou 16 Heraklion	
• German Consulate	28210 57944
Daskalogianni 64	

KEY TO MAPS

●——●	route	✝	church or monastery
▬▬▬	main asphalt road	⋀	shepherd's hut
———	asphalt road		
———	gravel road	●	spring
··········	riverbed	⊢⊣	castle
		⊓	archaeological site
🏠	village		
⌂	refuge	Ω	cave
⌂	hut		
□	sheep pen	▲ 2133	mountain peak

BIBLIOGRAPHY

- CRETE Volume II, Stergios Spanakis. Sfakianakis Publishing, Heraclion, 1964.
- UNEXPLORED CRETE, Stephanos Psimenos. ROAD Press, Athens, 1996.
- TRADITIONAL CRETE, Antonis Stivaktakis. Smyrniotakis Press, Athens, 1988.
- TRAVELS IN CRETE, Joseph Hatzidakis. Syros, 1881, re-published by Karavia Press.
- SFAKIA TRAVELOGUE, Giorgos Manousakis. Kedros Press, 1980.
- A SURVEY OF CRETE, Zacharias Praktikidis. Crete, 1818. Re-published by T.E.E., 1983.
- RECONNAISSANCE OF THE ISLAND OF CRETE, P. Bonneval, M. Dumas 1781. Mitos Press, Rethymnon, 2000.
- SFAKIANS IN THE CRETAN WAR, Paris Kelaidis. Karavi and Toxo Press, Athens, 1992.
- CRETAN GEOLOGY GUIDE, Haralambos Fasoulas. Cretan Natural History Museum, Heraclion, 2001.
- WILDFLOWERS OF CRETE, Giorgos Sfikas. Efstathiades Press.
- FLOWERS OF CRETE, Giannoukos – Iatridis, Athens, 1988.
- FLORA OF THE CRETAN AREA, N. Turland, L. Chilton, J. Press. HMSO, London, 1993.
- FLOWERS OF GREECE & BALKANS, Oleg Polunin. Oxford University Press, re-published, 1997.
- THE EUROPEAN E4 MOUNTAIN TRAIL, Giorgis Petrakis, Heraclion.
- CRETE THE WHITE MOUNTAINS, Loraine Wilson. Cicerone Press, Cumbria, 2000.
- CRETE WEST, G. Hirner, J. Murbock. Rother, Munich, 2000.

Photo Album

Gramvoussa island.

Wading at Elafonissi.

The old path near Ai Yannis.

Steep section between Ahlada and Gingilos.

Old church at Lissos bay, built from ancient remnants.

Agia Roumeli as seen from west.

The Byzantine church of Apostle Paul.

Anchusa, an endemic plant of White Mountains.

Just after Tripiti bay towards Agia Roumeli.

The serpentine trail leading to Aradena Gorge.

The famous Dittany plant.

Traditional weaving.

Loutro bay.

The old cobbled path from Anopoli to Hora Sfakion.

Ascend to Pahnes, White Mountains summit.

Into Vryssi Gorge.

The twin colored peak, Modhaki.

The trail ascending to Gingilos col.

Lunar landscape at White Mountains.

Finikas bay.

The old monastery of Katholiko.

From Sougia to Agia Roumeli.